A JOURNEY THROUGH

Balance
Pedal
Breathe

CLAIRE UNIS, MD

ISBN: 978-1-957723-10-5 (hard cover)
978-1-957723-09-9 (soft cover)

Edited by: Monika Dziamka and Amy Ashby

Published by Warren Publishing
Charlotte, NC
www.warrenpublishing.net
Printed in the United States

Dedicated to those who are called to practice medicine,
and to the patients whose stories we carry.

Table of Contents

PREFACE: A Calling...3

CHAPTER ONE: Into the Chrysalis 7

CHAPTER TWO: Momentum.. 17

CHAPTER THREE: Balance, Pedal, Breathe 31

CHAPTER FOUR: Babe in the Wards............................. 47

CHAPTER FIVE: "Poof: The Psychiatrist"..................... 83

CHAPTER SIX: Gestation 105

CHAPTER SEVEN: Winter's Promise............................129

CHAPTER EIGHT: Touch 155

CHAPTER NINE: Lifeblood.. 177

CHAPTER TEN: Bounds of Care.................................. 193.

CHAPTER ELEVEN: Wonderland 213

CHAPTER TWELVE: Adolescence................................239

CHAPTER THIRTEEN: Unsure Footing........................ 251

CHAPTER FOURTEEN: Lost Glasses............................ 275

EPILOGUE: A World on Fire....................................... 291

GLOSSARY 294

ACKNOWLEDGMENTS 296

PUBLICATION CREDITS..299

ENDNOTES 300

BIBLIOGRAPHY 302

The Invitation

It doesn't interest me what you do for a living. I want to know what you ache for, and if you dare to dream of meeting your heart's longing.

It doesn't interest me how old you are. I want to know if you will risk looking like a fool for love, for your dream, for the adventure of being alive.

It doesn't interest me what planets are squaring your moon. I want to know if you have touched the center of your own sorrow, if you have been opened by life's betrayals or have become shriveled and closed from fear of further pain.

I want to know if you can sit with pain, mine or your own, without moving to hide it or fade it or fix it.

I want to know if you can be with joy, mine or your own, if you can dance with wildness and let the ecstasy fill you to the tips of your fingers and toes without cautioning us to be careful, to be realistic, to remember the limitations of being human.

It doesn't interest me if the story you are telling me is true. I want to know if you can disappoint another to be true to yourself; if you can bear the accusation of betrayal and not betray your own soul; if you can be faithless and therefore trustworthy.

I want to know if you can see Beauty, even when it's not pretty, every day, and if you can source your own life from its presence.

I want to know if you can live with failure, yours and mine, and still stand on the edge of the lake and shout to the silver of the full moon, "Yes!"

It doesn't interest me to know where you live or how much money you have. I want to know if you can get up, after the night of grief and despair, weary and bruised to the bone and do what needs to be done to feed the children.

It doesn't interest me who you know or how you came to be here. I want to know if you will stand in the center of the fire with me and not shrink back.

It doesn't interest me where or what or with whom you have studied. I want to know what sustains you, from the inside, when all else falls away.

I want to know if you can be alone with yourself and if you truly like the company you keep in the empty moments.

—Oriah "Mountain Dreamer" House[1]

Preface

A CALLING

L ike so many of his papers, my eight-year-old son's assignment was crumpled into a half-origami crane, carelessly compressed at the bottom of his backpack. "All About ME!" it announced in playful letters across the top. I unfolded it curiously and smirked at his sloppy handwriting as I scanned the page, noting favorite foods (mac 'n' cheese) and sports (soccer). My eyes caught on a word just as I was about to see what else was in his backpack, and I unfolded the page again. The word "doctor" floated clearly above the last line, next to the prompt "When I grow up I want to be …" And I cringed.

It's not easy to articulate the reason I don't want him to feel called to medicine, as I did from a very young age. My parents will tell you I was born with the desire to take care of every animal and person I met. Even as a child, I wanted to do something that mattered to others. This book is a testament to the many lovely, uniquely magnificent experiences I was privy to as a physician-in-training. I cannot say I regret becoming a doctor; I am grateful every day for the opportunity to help my patients.

But what a painful road.

Over 60 percent of doctors in the United States experience frequent symptoms of burnout.[2,3,4] The commercialization of medicine—by which I mean the intrusion of insurance companies and corporations dictating how many patients we see, how much time we can spend with them, and even what we are allowed to prescribe—has broken the hearts of America's physicians. My medical training prepared me to provide thoughtful, well-informed care. Post-residency, the landscape changed completely. Efficiency and likability are prized in our current system, often to the detriment of thorough and medically appropriate care. The requirement that primary care doctors, with their 15,000 hours of post-graduate training, spend time filling out forms and writing letters justifying their decisions, instead of focusing on caring for patients, is but one example of the devaluation of our education.

There has been a huge shift in doctor-patient relationships as well. Some patients arrive to their visits well-informed, having already researched their symptoms and learned useful information. Others come armed with skepticism, and I have little hope of reaching them. As I write this prologue, in the midst of the COVID-19 pandemic, 24 percent of people in the United States plan to refuse vaccination, many of them for reasons that are more political than medical.[5] Being compelled to explain how the vaccines work, with less and less time to do it well, leaves me feeling like I am failing.

Love will break your heart into a million shining shards, and my love for the practice of medicine is no exception. I never know what a day will hold. I show up. I offer my best self to every patient. Sometimes I am greeted by the assumption that I am an instrument of the very corporate medical industry that is squeezing me, or of a nefarious government plot. In the next visit I might be overwhelmed by kindness I have hardly earned. During the COVID-19 pandemic, I have had friends drop contact completely, as though I personally bore responsibility for the mask mandates they disagreed with.

Following the science is not always convenient. In truth, doing what is right can be incredibly difficult. As was modeled for me over and over in my medical training, putting the health of others before our own desires is the only respectable option for doctors—but when it means friendships and relationships suffer, medicine can be a lonely occupation.

As I made my way through medical school, I often wondered whether it would be possible to show people what that education was like. Does the key to better doctor-patient understanding lie in sharing how we learn what we do? What if patients understood the spiritual journey required?

Knowing myself, there is no doubt I would do it all over again. Optimist that I am, and stubborn as I was, I would indeed sign myself up for a medical life. It's hard to explain where a calling comes from, but I always believed I was meant to be a doctor.

That's not the same thing as encouraging my child to follow in my footsteps. I have been fortunate in choosing my specialty for fulfillment, not for money. I have been able to work part-time, to counterbalance emotionally exhausting days with time spent outside, with my children, or doing something else. Working full-time in medicine is simply not tenable for me, not the way it is structured now.

In these pages lies the story of a willful, would-be doctor who tried to hold on to the before-self, the not-doctor self, even as she could feel herself changing over the four years of medical education leading up to her degree. In my collection of memories are also the reasons why, if my son must follow this path, I will swallow my misgivings about this career. Though the road itself shudders with ruts and sinkholes, boulders and sand, practicing medicine means living a considered life. More than just the obligation to continue learning, to offer current medical knowledge and treatments, it means digging deep to offer grace. It means acting lovingly even when you feel hurt. It means noticing beauty even in the direst of circumstances, and offering perspective—that glimmering speck of hope—to make another human being's life better.

I smoothed out my son's school paper and put it in the pile of things to keep.

Chapter One

INTO THE CHRYSALIS

The shape of the human body is unmistakable, even when draped in nondescript white plastic, even if the lights are on and the room hums with nonchalance. We entered a whole room of death, bodies laid out on individual stainless-steel tables in rows of three, extending down an eerily quiet, long hall where the only noise was the buzz of fluorescent lighting. Beneath each sheet lay answers to questions I had not yet fully formed, mysteries wrapped in sinew, shrouded by flesh, concealed by skin.

In any other circumstance I might have paused to absorb the grandeur of the view from there: an expansive wall of windows along the entire length of the hall faced north, where Golden Gate Park gave way to the Easter-egg-colored Victorian buildings of the Richmond district, and the trees of the Presidio appeared through the fog that swirled around the towers of Golden Gate Bridge.

I did not notice.

We tiptoed into that first day in anatomy lab with the careful steps of supplicants approaching an altar, afraid to lift our eyes for too long, scuffing our feet as we wended our ways around and between the numbered corpses with what we hoped was appropriate reverence. Gathering around the bodies, we murmured greetings to one another in hushed voices like mourners paying our respects at a funeral, honoring the deceased with silence.

Our assignment was brief: to uncover our assigned cadavers. To get acquainted with the incontrovertible deadness of the person we would be cutting open. All I knew about the woman on the table was her age (seventy-eight) and cause of death (heart attack). My classmates and I barely spoke as we followed instructions and pulled back the sheet gingerly—as though our gentleness mattered to the woman we would be dissecting.

Her head and hands were wrapped in gauze and clear plastic bags for better preservation. What we saw before us was the rest: moist, pale skin over her chest and abdomen, small breasts sagging to the sides, and her arms decorated with sun spots and scattered moles. Under my gloved hand, her skin felt rubbery from the formalin, making her seem more like a waxen replica than an actual human being. That thought eased our first introduction.

Too intimidated to uncover the rest of her, we replaced the sheet and had a business-like meeting about who would acquire the tools we needed. We approached our job with solemnity, painstakingly following the lab manual we kept at our station. I knew little about the other students in my lab group: a Latina athlete, an Iranian MD-PhD student, and a Chinese researcher. Though we would work together that entire first semester, our acquaintance started and ended with the discomfiture of our task: gradually stripping away layers of skin, fat, muscle, nerves, blood vessels, organs, bone.

We never named our cadaver, as some other groups did. Though we didn't discuss it, a name would have reminded us, I suspect, that she was not a laboratory specimen but a human—making our study not purely academic, but barbaric as well.

She was not the first dead person I had touched, but the first experience had hardly prepared me for the second one. Just before my first medical school interview, as a new volunteer with the Mono County Search and Rescue Team, I had hiked five miles to a campground to help remove the body of a man who had died in his sleep.

When I joined the team, I had envisioned searching for lost and injured hikers. I would push my hiking and navigational skills, I thought. I would use the first-aid training I had recently reviewed and help people get back to their homes and doctors. It would help me prepare for medical school.

I had not thought about death.

The call came around ten in the morning: "Meet at the trailhead for Laurel Canyon for a body recovery at Hilton Lake Four."

Morbid curiosity drove me to accept the assignment. Tossing the supplies I had by then learned to bring (tarp, flashlight, first aid kit, water purifying tablets, baggies, warm clothes) into a backpack along with some almonds, fruit, water, and an energy bar, I drove twenty minutes outside of Mammoth Lakes to the trailhead. The two search and rescue vans were already there.

I joined a cluster of seasoned outdoorsmen who fiddled with walkie-talkies and murmured in low tones. Nearby, the sheriff was briefing our leader, and the two men stood next to a short, sweaty, unshaven man in his early fifties wearing sagging jeans and a dirty shirt. He was the best friend of the deceased.

The heat hovered around us as we waited for instruction. Even the buzz of insects made the familiar sage-covered hillside look ominous, the way knowledge you wish you didn't have can make your vision more critical. Death was up there, past where the trail slithered out of sight.

Gradually, information filtered through the hushed voices. The man who had died was forty-three years old. He had a known heart condition, for which he took medication. He had been fine yesterday, when he and his best friend hiked in with another friend to set up camp, but he didn't wake up in the morning. At first, his two friends didn't want to disturb him. Finally, they went to rouse him; he wouldn't move, and his skin was cold.

We hiked in silence, dragging with us a one-wheeled gurney designed for rugged trails like this one. With six people, balancing the unloaded contraption still required some effort. The dead man's friend walked ahead of us, shoulders hunched forward, pausing while we negotiated turns and obstacles but otherwise plodding forward no more than three paces in front. As we made our way slowly up the trail, the man talked about his deceased friend. His voice sounded far away, as if he might be talking to himself. But every now and then he glanced over his shoulder, checking to make sure I was still there.

"Mark was so lively yesterday, I just couldn't stop taking pictures of him. I even said it was like my whole roll of film was going to be a tribute to Mark. ..." His voice trailed off.

I imagined the shock of having someone so alive disappear overnight. It seemed impossible, to be hiking up this hill with legs aching and lungs working, filled with inspiration and energy to get to the top, and then for all of that to drain away in a few hours of sleep.

We reached a ridge, and the group fanned out to take drinks of water and a rest. Mark's friend didn't budge from the trail; he just looked out over the canyon we had climbed out of.

"L-last night," the man stammered, "last night we were sittin' there, after dinner, you know, just lookin' at the stars. And he said, 'When I die, bury me here.'" His voice caught in his throat, and he looked down and away from me. "I-I dunno, maybe he knew something and was tryin' to tell us."

When the dusty trail finally leveled and dropped down to the chain of lakes, the going became easier. We arrived to find the other friend sitting in a chair, looking at the blue-green alpine lake. It was an extraordinary place to die, if you had a choice. Tall trees shaded their campsite. Mountaintops rimmed the view.

The men exchanged greetings. One of the two backpackers indicated Mark's tent, and our team leader drew us to the side to make a plan. Four of us would crawl in to get him out. I felt guiltily glad to be chosen. If I intended to become a doctor, I thought, I had to be able to face anything.

Now past noon, it was warm in the tent, and faintly malodorous. Mark was in his sleeping bag. It looked, for all the world, as though he might be sleeping. Snapping gloves on, one of our team leaders touched his neck to confirm he had no pulse.

"Take him in the bag?" one team member asked.

"Hang on, let me check him."

The gloved team member rolled him to the side in his sleeping bag and inspected the back of it. Someone explained to me later that people lose continence when they die. Taking him out of the sleeping bag might have been messy.

"Might as well."

We inched the black body bag up under his sleeping bag with businesslike sobriety. I focused on my hands and the bag and the task in front of us. Just before it zipped over his face, I took one last look. His hair was matted on his forehead, and his full mustache hid all but his smooth, relaxed cheeks and the thin line of his bottom lip. His eyes were closed. He had been asleep, perhaps unaware, when the moment came. He looked peaceful.

Loaded down, the gurney was unwieldy and heavy. It took nearly an hour to go about half a mile to the nearest place a helicopter could land. Once it touched down, we jammed him awkwardly into a carrying basket on the outside of the chopper. His knees wouldn't bend.

I watched the body being airlifted away, not a "him" but an "it" now, a thing in a heavy black bag that had to be removed from national forest land.

Our group spread out on the trip back. Half were ahead of me and half behind. I hiked alone for a while. But as the brilliant golds and oranges of the aspen trees grayed, and the sky darkened, I hurried to catch up to those in front, straining to hear their voices. I chided myself for my fear, but I didn't want to be alone just then. Mark had been alive and wondering at the beauty and mystery around him twenty-four hours before. And then he had suddenly slipped into inanimacy, taking his soul with him into the stillness of the never-ending night sky.

Facing my cadaver that first day in the anatomy lab, I wondered how vitality had left this woman's body. Would some part of her know our clumsy discomfort in the face of mortality? She was the first incontrovertible evidence that we, as doctors-to-be, were to be not only champions of life, but also stoic students of disease and death.

On the second day in anatomy lab, determined to participate, I wielded the scalpel long enough to cut through the elastic skin on our cadaver's chest and, as our manual instructed, draw a flap. There was almost no blood, except for some maroon-colored crust in a few small vessels. I put down the instrument and stood by, holding our cadaver's arm as though she might sense this gesture of apology and solace. Elias dissected back the skin and muscle from the rib cage, while Teresa held the anatomy book to direct him. Lily fussed with the instruments and stared. Tiny sinews seemed to stick everything together, resisting our exploration. We cut them away, pushed fingers along the bone to separate muscle, find our landmarks.

"We were like vultures," I wrote in my journal that night, "the way we fell onto our cadaver, eager to cut as instructed and find out what was under the surface of the skin... I will never think about the human body the same way again. Anatomy is going to change that perception forever."

My own fascination worried me. Until then, the human body as I thought of it was young, vibrant, athletic: my friends skinny dipping in the hot springs; a lover; a roommate. It was always healthy, and whole.

Even in death, Mark had been whole. I would not have dreamed of violating his peaceful stillness the way I had my cadaver's. Wasn't one's body an extension of the yearnings and soul that lay beneath?

The hardest moment of my first semester came the following week, after I bravely reached my hands into the cadaver's chest cavity and separated out one of her lungs. Peeling it up and out of the rib cage, I felt proud and amazed: there were the cross-sections of arteries and airways, and the smooth surfaces of the three lung lobes, just as the book showed me. Then, looking at the gaping hole in her chest, I burst into tears.

The stench of lab—formalin-soaked, dead humanity—is still pungent in my memory years later. I often stood at the wall of windows in the lab that faced Golden Gate Bridge and the Marin Headlands, daydreaming about getting on my bike and riding out over the ocean, breathing clean air. Whenever I could leave early, I would head straight for the park or the shoreline, someplace I could be free of the smell that clung to my hair, my skin, even the papers that I took home with me.

If my roommate and fellow medical student, Nicole, joined me on these outings, we could not help but talk about the dismembering we'd witnessed and participated in. The concept itself troubled me: I feared the demystification of the body. Drawn to studying medicine by the enigma of human capabilities and limitations, I feared that too much knowledge would dispel myths I cherished, laying pathetically bare the mechanics that made each person's physicality characteristic and unique. I could admire the anatomy—how, incredibly, every person developed a brachial plexus, muscles of the thigh, a liver and intestines, and even the tiny, blind appendix—but I refused to let go of the desire to put down my instruments and just appreciate what was there.

"Would you do it?" Nicole asked me one day as we walked in the park. "Would you donate your body so medical students could learn?"

I looked down at my legs stretching solidly in front of me one at a time, my arms swinging in time to the step of one heel and then the other, and I considered. I inhaled the green of the plants around me and the cool of evening approaching. What use would I have for this body when I was gone? What difference would it make, the miles I had walked and granite I had climbed, the accustomed thumping of my heart, and the days I had swallowed, gasping for air and whooping with relief at the top of a mountain or end of a ski day? What matter who had touched it or loved it, if it would bear children and show scars?

Yet, I couldn't say "yes."

We trudged onward, both of us absorbed in our own thoughts.

"Judaism doesn't allow it," she commented finally, "but I think otherwise I might. I mean, I'll be gone. It's just my body. Other people may as well learn from it."

I murmured my agreement half-heartedly. How could I explain what I felt with the certainty of knowing: that my soul could not survive without the body that housed it? That for all the intellect medical school might demand, I knew no passion disconnected from motion and activity. If my body were taken from me, my soul would surely crumple and refuse to leave. No, I would have to be cremated and scattered to the winds to find any sort of liberation.

I vowed then to hang on to my sentimentality as long as I could. How else to retain compassion in the face of unnamed and uncertain trials in the years to come? At the outset, four years seemed like an eternity. Change whispered to us from the foliage of the park and lingered at the end of the day like a promise and a curse, settling in with the glow of lamplight on our cheeks at night as we perused our textbooks. The language of medicine was still awkward on our tongues, but it worked its way into our mouths, changing people into patients, limbs into muscle groups, death into expiration—a debt repaid, inevitability past due.

Nicole and I often walked until sunset, squeezing the last glimmer of light from the sky as we left the park and turned our conversation from lofty humanism to plans for dinner. Sometimes, having struck out eagerly in a new direction, or followed a thin footpath where it dwindled into itchy shrubbery, we had no idea where we were when it came time to head home. We'd keep on walking and searching, checking the sky for nightfall and absorbing the unfamiliar surroundings. After dark, the bushes reached fingers out to grasp at our arms and shoulders. Haunts chuckled in the blackness and then scuttled back when a passing car tossed illumination in our direction.

Eventually, we'd find a familiar roll of the landscape and a trail we recognized. And then we would be home, the fresh air having almost lifted away the odors of lab and fears of inhumanity that started each trek with us. Our companionship protected each journey, smoothing the gradual process of becoming someone else while reminding us, step after determined step, of the idealism that brought us to this place.

Over time, walking in Golden Gate Park with Nicole became a ritual. We traveled various paths through the botanical gardens, always going a slightly different way than the time before. We remarked at the changing scenery around us—flowers blooming as the seasons turned, new plants showing up where we had noticed nothing before. I wondered, as we wound through shaded paths, whether I would come to know my way around the human body the way I learned landmarks in the park: the paved roads like major vessels, the footpaths like capillaries, and we like blood cells bumbling blindly through.

Physicians speak another language, and I will learn it, but I do not want to lose my mother tongue. Mine is a poetic language that creates truths where there are none, describing my heart's imaginings as though my mind does not exist. I yearn with my fingers, hate with my stomach (which, contrary to my anatomy book illustration, is centered just slightly below my navel), love with my lungs. My body is mine. Let no one teach me to believe it is just like anyone else's, nor that medicine can replace intuition.

(EXCERPT FROM MY JOURNAL, FALL OF FIRST YEAR)

Chapter Two

MOMENTUM

"Take a breath?" I asked, pressing the bell of my stethoscope awkwardly into the freckled skin above my classmate's breast, just below the scooped neckline of her shirt.

I heard the obvious *lubdub*-ing of her heart reverberating through her chest, but the flow of air through her lungs was harder to trace. Building and receding like ocean tides, not quite rhythmic, the ebb and flow of her breath moved like a background breeze, barely audible to my inexperienced ears.

Then we switched, and it was Melissa's turn to perch that timeless symbol of doctoring on my chest (*A little too hard*, I thought), and mine to take slow, deliberate breaths for her to hear.

In a schedule crammed with didactics, these opportunities to toy with the skills of practicing medicine appeared sporadically like a trail of breadcrumbs. We paired up with one another to fumble with otoscopes and ophthalmoscopes, to touch one another's necks looking for lymph nodes, and eventually even to press clammy fingers into one another's abdomens, pretending we could feel a liver edge or spleen if one offered itself up.

"Ow! Your fingernails are sharp!"

"Oh my gosh, try that again. I will hold still this time."

"How did you make that noise?"

"Wait, did you know you had a double—what's that thing called?—uvula?"

We chattered nervously, pretending it was normal to touch and peer at one another, forgetting for the moment the textbooks and exams that awaited our attention.

But we could not forget for long.

Our classes that first fall seemed benign at first. Our homework mostly involved reading and orienting ourselves to the structure of lectures, small group sessions, and labs. Other than anatomy lab, medical school promised to be little different from the four years of college that had come before. Or so I assumed.

The first test, in cellular biology, was a take-home, open-book exam in which we were to apply basic principles to more complex problems. Having been an English major in college, I wordsmithed answers I thought would suffice—and then left for the weekend. When I returned that Monday, feeling rather satisfied for having gotten away with a mini-vacation, I found the exam with a "Please see me in my office" note penned at the top. I felt like a hot brick had just slammed into my chest. I had never failed a test in my life.

Then I realized: if anyone were going to flunk out of medical school, it would be me. Instead of padding my resume with science research or preparing for medical school in any way academically, I had taken a year off after college to be a ski bum. Waitressing, teaching skiing, bagging peaks—none of it had prepared me for the kind of studying that was expected of me as a medical student. Hadn't I just returned to those same mountains, instead of spending time on the very assignment in my hand?

When I shuffled my way into the course instructor's office, I was unsure what to expect.

"Please close the door," she requested.

Everything was neutral: her tone of voice, her professional attire and short brown hair, the small office with full bookshelves and an industrial-looking desk. My heart kept trying to flee my body while I forced myself to shut the door, perch on the edge of a chair, and face her, feeling very much the penitent, and also very much out of my element. Just two days ago I had been hiking beside a chain of lakes in the Eastern Sierra, basking in the change of colors and reassuring myself that I was someone I could still recognize.

"I need you to clarify your response to the first question," she said, looking down at a packet of papers. I recognized my handwriting at the top right corner. "What is it you are saying here?"

My chest was too tight to draw in air. I swallowed, trying to recall the question.

Mercifully, she read my words back to me. And then, likely seeing the terror on my face, she handed me a photocopy of my exam so I could read the question.

"You said the cell membrane is permeable, but not what significance this has in the situation described," she prompted. "How does this affect the cell?"

I don't remember her actual words, or the phrasing of her question, just the evenness of her tone, and the evaluative way her blue eyes studied my face, maybe trying to determine the odds that I would make it through my first year.

I eventually squeaked out a satisfactory answer, and though I scrambled my way back to passing that exam, that horrible feeling of incompetence would linger. Flames of self-doubt would periodically threaten to devour me as we marched through a daunting course list those first two years. All around me, I believed, people were thriving on the challenges that kept me ever on alert for signs that I was on the verge of falling into the fire.

On my way home from that meeting, I found myself walking with a classmate whose reflexive kindness had impressed me from the moment we met during orientation.

"How *are* you? Somehow, I haven't even seen you in like a week!" she crooned affectionately.

I shrugged and pretended to study the uneven pavement to avoid her smiling, hazel-eyed gaze. "I'm okay," I feigned. "I guess I got a little behind on studying."

"Oh, me too!" she offered. "I was still waiting for my desk to arrive, and it's just not that comfortable to study on my futon, so then I just got distracted watching the debates last night and didn't even start until like eleven. ..."

All I heard was that she had been studying—and I had not. Worse, I had done all I could to avoid it. I bid her goodbye at Sixth Avenue and continued the next six blocks to my street, feeling the necessary loneliness of the hours of studying that lay before me. Certain as I felt of my intellectual inferiority, I did not feel worthy of her friendship.

Studying could be enjoyable, and often was once I gave into the obligation of it. Mastery of a topic—even short-lived—brought me a small snap of satisfaction. I had to reorganize the information, jotting notes from our syllabi into outlines of my own construction, and there—it wasn't gibberish after all! The right cafe could make all the difference: quiet but not empty, well-lit, with good-sized tables (square better than round), spicy teas or frothy hot chocolate, preferably undiscovered by classmates. I loved windows if it was daytime, so I would not lose touch with the progression of the day. At some point my mind would wander out to squint at the waning light, and I would have to follow, squeezing in a bike ride or walk in the park before dark, and then usually resuming my task either at my own desk or in the painfully well-lit library.

Soon I scheduled everything: purple and green and black appointments blocked off time in my calendar for meetings and workouts and studying. I started each day with a plan in mind: how much class; when to exercise and where I would do it; what time I would get home and plan for dinner; whom I needed to call; and how many hours of schoolwork I needed to put in. Often there were pieces I hadn't figured out—where to study, for example—and these were the spaces left for my cravings to fill at the time, a tiny corral in which to exercise my yearning for freedom. Once a week I planned a bike ride that would exhaust me, on Saturday morning, or a few hours before dark on Sunday. I needed something to draw my focus away from books, into the simple rhythm of breathing, moving forward and on and on.

I sent an electronic message out to the entire class during the first few weeks of school, asking whether anyone would be interested in mountain biking sometime, and no one responded right away. That silence only reinforced what I suspected: I was the only one who prized my time outdoors over my time in the library. The only one whose sanity relied on remembering who I had been before medical school.

That Friday, David called out to me from one of the back rows of seats as I arrived in lecture. "Hey, I'll go biking with you," he said casually. "Want to go this weekend?"

The first time we met to ride, on a typically foggy San Francisco morning, he was wearing regular cotton shorts, a T-shirt, and Teva sandals. There were no foot-cages or clips on his plastic bike pedals, and he had nowhere to put water or a spare tube. Beside him I felt overequipped, wearing bike shorts, layers for cool weather, and a hydration backpack. I carried an extra tube and a bike pump.

He smirked. "You're looking kind of hard-core," he commented as I tied a bandana over my head and snapped my helmet on. "I'm not that fast, dude."

"I'm not either," I chuckled, relieved that our ride would be low-key. "I just like biking."

"Need to bike" would be more accurate, I thought.

As we started through Golden Gate Park, I could feel a familiar sense of freedom and escape take over with each stroke of the pedals. Maybe it was the wind flapping against my arms, or just being surrounded by green. As we bounced off the curb and negotiated our way around tourists and cars, and then onto a less popular road, I felt the stress of being in medical school melt away behind me.

Our pace was well-matched from the get-go. Later, I would realize that our speed mostly had to do with David; if I went faster, he did, too, but if I let him lead, he slowed down till I caught up with him. We fell into a comfortable pace and held it, chatting along the way.

David had just graduated from college. He and his girlfriend had then looked for a place to live in San Francisco, finding a small apartment a few blocks away from the medical school. He had grown up here, so in a sense this was like moving back home for him. Still, true to his character, he preferred to let me choose our route. He rarely had a strong opinion about where to go—he was generally up for anything.

Over time we developed a pattern to our rides. Our usual loop took us west through Golden Gate Park, with its seasonal mud and blooms, out to the ocean; then north along the coast, winding through the wooded Lands End area, where the trail crumbled into the sea; then past the mansions of Sea Cliff; along the edge of the forested and hilly Presidio; and across Golden Gate Bridge to the exposed hillsides of the Marin Headlands. We talked when the hills were not too steep, otherwise giving in to the mesmerizing whoosh-whoosh-whoosh of tires on wet pavement.

David and I only talked at any length when we were on our bicycles. We gossiped about our friends, ridiculed ourselves, poked fun at the inanity of studying for exams. Often, we just biked in silence. David's laid-back attitude covered up a quiet sharpness and good-natured sense of humor, always at the ready along with a broad smile. Gradually I learned more about him. He thought he would be a radiologist, an internal medicine doctor, an emergency room physician, or an anesthesiologist. He traveled when he had vacation time: to Germany, to Fiji, to Australia, Japan, Honduras, Hawaii. He never gave up his free time or seemed to worry much about exams. In the four years I biked with him, his brother went off to college, his mother became very ill, David himself got engaged and then married. All the while he just seemed to take everything in stride, with little more than a slight change in the curve of his sardonic grin.

His companionship was reassuring that way. Certain classmates needed only mention what they were studying, and my insecurities would rise up and try to choke me. I balanced tenuously on the cusp of self-confidence my entire first two years of medical school. The knowledge that people's lives would be in my hands one day made my attempts at mastering test material feel like perpetually tiptoeing over hot coals. One day I was bound to get burned.

David was one of the only people who didn't inspire self-doubt in me. He never talked about what we were learning in class, or even studying at all. Our friendship managed to exist outside all of it.

As Boards approached at the end of second year, we still biked together. I made reference to my anxiety level once, and he looked surprised.

"Whatever, dude. Everyone passes. Your score doesn't even matter, unless you want to be a hard-core ENT doc." He grinned playfully. He knew I had no interest in being a surgeon.

We pedaled for a few moments in silence. I knew he was right.

"I'm playing golf tomorrow," he added helpfully.

When I was on my bike, I felt sure of myself in a way that never happened in class. I felt capable, even when I was gasping for breath; I knew that perseverance would pay off, that every uphill climb would end, that I knew how to handle sudden drops and quick swerves and even most of the rocks that might appear in the road. My biking skills seemed irrelevant to learning medicine, but if nothing else, they kept my self-esteem off the floor.

Only the opportunities to observe doctors at work nourished my idealism. Each student was matched up with a community physician, spending a few afternoons each month in a primary care office. There I witnessed mannerisms I would emulate, consciously or unconsciously, in the years to come. I tried out my physical exam skills with tremulous fingers, aware of both my lack of knowledge and the inexplicable privilege of being allowed to touch other living human beings in order to learn.

"See how none of the hairs are broken-off around the bald area? The scalp is completely smooth." Dr. Braun was gently parting the coarse gray hairs on the head of a Filipino man. "This is *alopecia areata*," he continued, and proceeded to give instructions to the patient. I had learned a few years of science, but no actual medicine. The words meant nothing to me.

"Can you feel that nodule in her neck when she swallows?"

"Did you hear the extra heart sound?"

"See the petechiae on the roof of her mouth?"

I did not learn what anything meant medically—nor was I expected to—but I observed a man whose time and energy spent with patients mattered. My future profession, if only I could learn all that lay ahead of me, promised to be meaningful.

Perhaps most inspiring of all was a class called "The Healer's Art." Funded by alumni, the course was an experiment of sorts, designed to protect us from burnout in the years to come. In contrast to the large lecture halls where most of our classes took place, these evening gatherings parsed us into small groups led by physicians who had practiced medicine and left, or who had taken a turn to a different kind of practice. Led by Rachel Remen, author of *Kitchen Table Wisdom* and eventual guru to a relatively new interest in tending physician wellness, the course directed us to reflect on why we had come to medical school to begin with.

We would sit huddled together in that softly lit room, with night settling outside the windows and traffic slowly receding, and consider our motivations. *What did we fear?* we were asked. *Who inspired us?* Most important of all, we were directed to consider: *How would we ensure that we not lose sight of our ideals?*

In hindsight, it was a little like abstinence-only sex education. No one described the pressure or temptations that lay ahead of us, but we promised to retain our innocence.

That said, I still carried with me the shame of failing my first test, and this exercise in self-compassion impressed me deeply. Only here were we encouraged to honor our former selves.

One evening we were directed to draw crayon self-portraits of who we had been before medical school. Somehow mine has survived all these years: I am smiling, hiking up the side of a mountain in crimson hiking boots under yellow sunshine, surrounded by green pine trees and a cloudless baby-blue sky.

Why had I left the mountains?

On the worst of days, I was not sure. In my medical school application, I wrote of wanting to make a difference in people's lives. I wrote of empathy. I wrote of making a career out of caring; it was something I had always done anyway. And in truth, nothing else sang to me the way studying the human body did. The mystery of how living cells could add up to muscles and tendons and bones and even a whole personality. How a human body could be coaxed into amazing physical feats. How emotions could be lifted by someone's care. Surrounded by swaths of forest and majestic mountains, as I pushed my physical limits, I had felt authentically myself—but also irrelevant. I wanted my work to matter.

The hours of studying only served to make me wish myself back to the idyllic year before, when I hadn't had to mete out only an hour of sunshine between school assignments, when there was plenty of time for reflection, and when I wasn't constantly reminded of my failings. Even if only for a few hours at a time, the Healer's Art class promised that my efforts would matter someday. And that I was not, after all, alone.

Showing none of the reticence I had adopted, Nicole befriended some of our classmates and began studying with them: Elizabeth, Daphne, Anne, and Camilla. At first I wasn't invited, or I avoided joining them if I had been. I had no trouble with exams after that first one, but I still feared that they would see in me the fraud I half-believed myself to be.

"Anne and Camilla invited us over for dinner," Nicole announced one evening, "and to study for the neuroanatomy test."

Nicole seemed unflappable to me then. She studied, but she also spent time with her college boyfriend, who lived nearby. She did not appear to suffer the bouts of panic that flared up for me unpredictably.

I didn't answer right away. I liked Anne and Camilla. I craved company. But what if they found out how little I knew?

"What time?" I asked, stalling. The days were already short, so I could not claim to be planning a walk or bike ride. I really had nothing else to do.

"Whenever we are ready. I said we would bring some veggies."

So it was already decided.

It took time for me to trust my new friends enough to show my failings—and about as long to realize I could learn how to study from them. Each of my friends had their own superstitions about preparing for exams. Unlike the stereotypical "gunner" medical student, who liked to test the knowledge of people around him with obscure facts and medical minutiae, and whom I dated in my second year of school, my girlfriends often shared company more than conversation.

Elizabeth holed up with books and learned the background of the information in addition to what we were supposed to study, which made her a great resource if I didn't understand something. Anne drew pictures and diagrams. Daphne made up songs. I had a different system each quarter, it seemed—making charts sometimes, or taking notes others. I always felt like I was missing something. It didn't occur to me that we *all* were: the bulk of information was too great to swallow unless divided into manageable pieces or mashed into familiar forms, and what worked for one often failed to help another. We had distinct talents, miscellaneous quirks. The real task was finding our own best strategies—not borrowing somebody else's.

Years later I learned what very real struggles other people in my class faced during those difficult years, when I was too worried about myself to notice: financial uncertainty, abusive husbands, unexpected pregnancy, alcoholism. In my insecurity, all I saw was the wall of the hole I lived in. I assumed everyone else was basking in sunlight I could not see.

To return home from Rodeo Valley in the Marin Headlands without climbing an extra hill, bicyclists ride through a half-mile-long tunnel alongside one lane of car traffic. When lit, the tunnel is not difficult to negotiate. There are insignificant puddles here and there, and the walls curve inward to form an arch, but there is enough room for bicycles and vehicles to pass comfortably, and enough light that a biker can keep her sunglasses on the whole way through.

One afternoon, unexpectedly, David and I found the tunnel unlit. According to the detour signs, traffic was being diverted up over the pass. There was no power to the area at all.

As always, we had planned just the right amount of time for the ride. We had neither time nor inclination to backtrack up the hill we had just descended. Our books were calling us. Our legs were already aching. We peered into the dim passage and decided to press on, comforted by the absence of cars, emboldened by the presence of one another.

Just before we pedaled in, another cyclist approached. She seemed unsure whether to pass through, and she turned to look up at the alternate route, winding out of sight.

"You two are going to take the tunnel?" she asked.

When we nodded, she elected to follow us, and we proceeded as a band of three into the ink-black cave. We couldn't see the other end immediately, but once it appeared—just a glimmer the size of a grape—we picked up speed. The light was too distant to reflect off the walls, and it occurred to me, as I tried to aim myself directly toward the exit, that I might be off just enough to crash into the side. Three times I nosed my bicycle to the left, veering toward the middle of the invisible road beneath me. David whooped, and I laughed, my glee hollow-sounding in the chilly darkness. A drop of water splashed on my nose and I shivered, but I kept my gaze trained on the exit.

There was a scraping sound in back of me, and a woman's voice, a soft cry or curse. Then I heard David's brakes, and his voice: "Are you alright?"

She replied, but I couldn't hear her words. David said something about the wall. They dropped behind me. I was afraid to break my momentum or stop in the dark, dank tunnel. I imagined crashing into the sides. I felt the panicky helplessness of blindness. I imagined an earthquake, suddenly aware of the weight of the earth above me. My hope was a pinprick of brightness, and I could not afford to look away. Gradually, the light began to grow bigger, now an apple, then a grapefruit, then a whole sunlit scene with sea, sky, trees, and road. With one more breath, it enveloped me, and I was free. I stopped. David and the other cyclist emerged a few moments later, both smiling with relief.

I thought about her often after that, every time I held my breath and dashed through the tunnel under yellow lights alongside cars and motorcycles. How I hoped never to traverse that distance in the blackness again. How almost-confidently I had pointed myself at the glow on the far side of the tunnel, hoping and trusting, blindly, that I would make it through. How much safer I felt knowing David was there. How I heard that unknown cyclist scrape against the concrete side wall and heard David ask after her, but I had not stopped. I had been too scared, too concerned for my own survival.

What if she hadn't emerged with us?

Would I have gone back?

A bumble bee has miniscule wings, paper-thin, to support its thick body. Its dizziness is palpable as it lifts off with a slight gyration and the puttering sound of an uncertain motor—but it takes wing. And flies.

When the bee crawls from its primordial capsule, slick and new, how does it unfurl its wings from that soggy torso? How does it know to proceed cautiously, allowing a gentle breeze to caress its legs and ever so slowly lift the fur of its body and those tiny, soap bubble wings? The bee waits there for hours, trembling at the novelty of air whirling past, at the thrill of arriving from its larval origins to stand at the brink of this bright, fresh place. Some desire shudders through its awkward body, shaking off the last bit of water from its birth. The bumble bee may stay all day, until that involuntary hum of energy swells with certainty, gradually guiding its fragile wings into a determined fury. And then, beyond any expectation, it rises clumsily, confidently, toward the sky.

How have we lost this faith? The gene map lost in a fold of DNA, an extra arm of information that renders lost our instinctual patience. Standing here blinking at the light, I feel the improbability of flight weighing on my shoulders, keeping my feet heavily rooted in place. What wings could bear these doubts?

Amidst the onrush of information, the brilliant promise of understanding, and the whirl of activity, I am tiny and precarious. I cannot feel my wings, though I imagine—I pray—they are behind me, gently adjusting to the wind currents around me. The only rhythm I feel is the beating of my heart, surging with fear and ebbing with the stability of earth beneath me. Where is the surety that will lift me, breathlessly and helplessly, into the sky?

(SPRING OF FIRST YEAR)

Chapter Three

BALANCE, PEDAL, BREATHE

That March, low clouds pushed down the sky and blunted the passage of time. If the sun cut a path through the gloom, I did not see it. There was morning, and night, and gray. Hours seemed to hover but not pass, then disappear all too rapidly, another day gone and too little accomplished. Too much to know.

It felt like suffocating.

Not all of my second year had been so somber. Steven's striking blue eyes, with his dark hair and olive skin, had caught my attention in our first class gathering, but a year passed before we started making excuses to get together, often for rock climbing, then studying, and finally dating in the fall of our second year. Even our secret relationship fit into the school agenda: we would meet after class for a two-hour stint in the climbing gym, stopping for burritos on the way home, and rounding out the evening with a few hours of heavy reading before bed. Or if the yen grabbed us, we might sit cozily in one of the coffeehouses in the Mission district, sharing a dim lamp and rubbing knees under the table while we studied our texts. It helped that he could wax poetic about viral reproduction and the secret weaponry of certain bacteria. His enthusiasm, and his dancing eyes, egged me on.

"Can't see, can't pee, can't climb a tree?" he quizzed me.

"Reiter's syndrome!" I announced.

"Which is different from being blind as a bat, mad as a hatter, red as a beet, dry as a bone in ...?" He was leaning forward mischievously. He had switched topics entirely, but he loved these little mnemonics.

When I didn't know an answer, he coaxed me into remembering.

"It's a toxidrome," he prompted, drawing out the last word as if extending a lifeline.

"Anticholinergics," we said together, and he cackled in delight.

Long before spring, Steven began studying for Boards, casually absorbing chapters of review books alongside reading material for our regular classes. I knew I would forget whatever I read so far in advance. But as our second winter in medical school rolled toward a wet and silent spring, and Boards loomed ahead of us, I knew I had no choice but to try. The national United States Medical Licensing Exam (USMLE), or Boards, were scheduled at the end of the academic year, in early June. Boards could derail a medical student from the journey out of preclinical, scientific education and into the clinical, or doctoring, years. Still, the mastery of two years' worth of textbooks seemed impossible.

Anxiety started to creep into the muscles of my neck, paralyzing me. Guilt haunted me. What kind of doctor would I be if I could not muster the discipline to learn?

"This must feel like depression," I wrote in my journal, three months before Boards. "No hope of escape, no motivation, no love for the days that are ordered around classes and books instead of love, energy, exercise, friends, affection, fun, dance, music, silence. Even the joy of learning is weighed down by this obligation, this lack of space."

Without time to squander on our relationship—and separated by our feelings about Boards, which he seemed to anticipate with inexplicable excitement, and even joy—Steven and I slowly untangled ourselves from one another. I'm not even sure we broke up. We had bigger things on our minds.

At no point in medical school had I developed the ability to study more than three hours at a stretch—not even with Steven's contagious fervor keeping me company. Always, I punctuated these sprints with exercise, or dinner, or talking on the phone. I would take off on my bicycle and meditate on the significance of a test as I rode. I would review what I knew—if nothing else, the categories I was supposed to study: neurovascular disease, infection, demyelination, degeneration of the brain. There were also tumors, toxins, peripheral nerve disease. For each group I could summon one example: stroke, meningitis, multiple sclerosis, Alzheimer's, astrocytoma, Wernicke-Korsakov, amyotrophic lateral sclerosis. Of these diseases, I had actually studied only three, and there were so many more.

I would push them out of mind, knowing they all awaited me when I returned to my books, and turn my attention back to my surroundings. Something as simple as a break in the cloud cover or the brilliant teal of the ever-changing ocean could make me smile as I pedaled along, just going, not breaking stride, not stopping. *All my life*, I would muse, *is about momentum. There's no stopping now.*

On one gloomy weekend morning I received a phone call from my friend Zeke, whose broad smile and ready chuckle had endeared him to me when we met through friends in college. He was feeling uncharacteristically sad and frustrated. I, too, felt glum. I had just finished a round of exams, but with no sense of relief.

A handful of times since Zeke had moved to the city the previous fall, we had ridden our bicycles together, rushing out conspiratorially when one of us needed to forget everything else. On this particular morning, rain-heavy clouds threatened overhead. The springtime of 1998—the tail end of El Niño, and the end of my second year of medical school—brought storm after storm. Still, biking out of the city seemed the only way free.

"Let's go ride," I said.

He didn't need me to ask twice.

Thinking about the questions he was struggling with—plans for going to law school, and where his relationship with his girlfriend was heading—helped ease the load on my mind. None of my concerns about my relationship with Steven or the upcoming exam were fresh. Just gray and never-ending like the sky above us, or the darkening ocean.

I don't remember whether it rained. Neither of us would have minded; Zeke was the kind of friend you could sing in a downpour with, getting all muddy or wet and just laughing at the way it felt different from other days. The water would have felt good on our cheeks. Maybe it did.

Biking across Golden Gate Bridge, we battled against buffeting winds. Under ominous clouds, we were the only cyclists in sight—which was unusual on a weekend. Still, we pressed on, teetering each time we turned into the wind to go around one of the bridge's enormous supports, and then whipping back onto our path. In the face of our existential challenges, focusing on this small task felt good. Turn, balance, pedal; turn, brake, balance; turn, pedal fast, *breathe.*

On the far side of the bridge, the hills of the Marin Headlands rose sharply from the shore. Below me, the dark blue-green ocean roiled, and a gull coasted at the perimeter of the bridge as I pedaled alongside Zeke. Suddenly we both looked up. A window had opened in the clouds and light spilled through, shimmering against the moisture hovering all around us. We stopped our bikes. Neither of us spoke. We just looked at the hole in the sky where light came through to brush its fingers against our cheeks. It was the only bright spot, and it lasted just long enough that we could be sure it was meant for us.

I studied for Boards—when final exams were over and there were only two weeks left—with three classmates at a retreat center called Commonweal along the coast north of San Francisco. Through the graces of Rachel Remen, who had taught our Healer's Art class during our first year and who led workshops for cancer patients at the center, we were able to stay in a small house perched on a bluff overlooking the ocean, abutting a small grove of trees. It felt like an enchanted cottage, neatly tucked out of sight and surrounded by wild green shrubbery on one side, dark forest on the other.

We arrived to find a bird's nest outside the front door, partially hidden by a broom propped against the wall. Startled by us, the mother bird took flight, leaving four small eggs unattended. After that we used the back porch to enter and leave. We could see the nest from a window, and the sudden arrival of high-pitched, continuous peeping prompted us to look outside later that same day: the eggs had hatched. Scrawny, bald baby birds shivered out of the shells and huddled together for warmth.

I loved the patch of wilderness around us. Every morning I rose early, wandered into the kitchen for a bowl of cereal or oatmeal, and then set to work. I chose a long, narrow table next to an east-facing window and spread out my texts, review books, medical dictionary, notes, pens, highlighters. In solitude, accompanied only by the hush and rumble of the nearby ocean and the occasional twitter of a bird, I would start to read laboriously, poring over the review text and looking up anything I did not understand well. How did T-cells communicate with macrophages? What were the classes of antiarrhythmic cardiac drugs, and how did they work? What caused a macronodular versus a micronodular liver? Why?

In those morning hours, I would luxuriate in spending time revisiting the material we had learned—or crammed—in our first two years of school. I'd imagine myself developing facility with it. I worked efficiently then, after a night's rest and with the promise of a whole day ahead of me. But as the hours passed, once all of us were stationed with books in front of us and the sun burned through the morning fog, my motivation would wane. Words ran together on the page.

My main entertainment at times like this was from the creatures that crossed our front path. One was a small bunny who ambled back and forth, stretching its nose far forward to nibble at a flower, then spooking at its own shadow. Each day I saw it come back, venturing a little closer to the house, testing the space. One morning there was a family of quail feeding nearby. At first both the quails and the rabbit froze, watching one another. Then, tentatively, the birds continued about their business. The bunny—which was smaller than even the quail youngsters—loped slowly over to the group and sniffed. Perhaps slightly irked, but certainly not bothered enough to leave, the quails continued foraging. Eventually the bunny fell into line with the baby quails as if trying to blend in.

Other than the diversions I watched outside my window, my only interruptions were lunch, breaks to go for a walk or ride my bike, and dinner. At night we tried to study as a group, talking to maintain focus on the task at hand. For me it was an exercise in overcoming angst: beside my classmates I felt stupid, slow.

"Okay," Susan said, "cranial nerves: which three are only sensory?"

I had not studied this.

"Trigeminal," I started to say, thinking of the face.

"No," Alex jumped in, "that has motor. It has to be ones for sight, smell, hearing—all the senses."

"Yes! One, two, and eight," said Daphne certainly.

"Okay, another one: where does cranial nerve ten go?" Susan asked.

"Jugular foramen! It causes Horner's!"

"And where does it start?"

"The medulla!"

All of them seemed so confident.

Part of the trouble was that we were not studying the same material. I started with pathology, while others honed in on anatomy, microbiology, pharmacology. Still, it seemed that I remembered nothing. Words tossed out as a clue by one classmate barely lit a dim candle in the back of my mind before others had the answer and could call forth several bits of relevant trivia. Panic rose in the back of my throat. All of this was gibberish to me. None of us took time to reassure or explain areas of confusion—all of us were too stressed. I sank lower and lower with the certainty that I would not pass National Boards. I would make a terrible doctor. And I had just gotten through two years of medical school—cramming information into my short-term memory time after time, pretending to love science and duping myself into sticking with it—for nothing. I reminded myself, over and over again, that this exam was not a measure of what kind of healer I could become. *Then again*, a small voice would pester, *who wants a doctor who can't remember anything?*

The hardest part of our ten days at Commonweal was the fact that we were all so focused on our individual battles against the dragon called Boards, we failed to support each other. Perhaps I imagined the sideways glances when I couldn't answer a question, or the shoulders cutting me out of any conversation I could not contribute to. It could have been my imagination that the others begrudged explaining.

"What are the side effects of a loop diuretic?"

"What increases jugular venous pressure?"

"What is the mechanism of penicillin resistance in staph infections?"

"Which nerve controls dorsiflexion?"

I felt myself sinking, and the only people who could've helped, didn't. I wonder whether I failed them too. Were we all so desperate to survive that we abandoned one another?

My saving grace was biochemistry—a course taught by that same teacher from cell biology whose exam I had very nearly failed. At the start of the course, she had stood up at the front of the sloping rows of newly upholstered blue-and-gray chairs and suggested that we consider acquiring large pieces of poster paper to draw out the biochemical pathways as we learned them. I never took another assignment before or since more seriously. Armed with a new package of ten brightly colored markers, five colors of thin-tipped pens, and a roll of paper, I carefully labeled sections: liver, brain, adipose tissue, skeletal muscle, GI, and "all tissues."

In the liver I eventually drew two mitochondria, and I surrounded this central organ with a strip called "bloodstream." At some point I taped on an eight-and-a-half-inch by eleven-inch piece of paper representing "erythroblasts in the bone marrow." I carefully copied line after line of chemical names: "1,3 bisphosphoglycerate" and "coproporphyrinogen III" among the ones I would come to know well, like glucose, pyruvate, acetyl-CoA. I brooded over the text that accompanied these formulae in my syllabus before drawing, checking, and rechecking to be sure the cycles fit together properly. The map blossomed into a masterpiece of color-coded and accurately graphed tongue-twisters. I recited the words over and over again in the shower, trying to give rhythm to the syllables and envisioning them marching up and down and across the poster.

Before leaving my apartment in San Francisco to study at Commonweal, as an afterthought, I had carefully detached the map from where it still hung on my wall more than a year after the biochemistry class had ended. I taped it above my temporary bed at the retreat center and marveled at it most evenings before going to sleep, standing up on tiptoe and leaning away from the soft yellow lamplight so I could read the details of my handiwork. I discovered something incredible over the sum of those nights: I had been knowledgeable. I had been meticulous. I had been thorough. And I had learned these pathways well enough to note exceptions and make connections where there were none in our class notes. Though I could no longer recite every step of gluconeogenesis, tracing over the names I had written reminded me of the competence that had grown there—even when I was a freshman who had almost flunked her first exam.

Biochemistry was the one subject I knew better than the others did before our ten days at Commonweal were up. Whenever I felt overwhelmed by my classmates' chatter, I went into my little room and shut the door and charted my course across the whole human body with purple words and long, swooping arrows. This was familiar, hospitable terrain. I had been here—and thrived—before.

Every morning I was back in the same uncomfortable wooden chair, studying. Pathology of the lung went down easy, but the liver and kidney had similar diseases, and they were hard to keep straight. Then there were all the other organs: bladder, ovary, prostate, breast, bone, blood vessels, heart. It was like stuffing my mouth with marshmallows to see how many would fit. Past the third or fourth day, I just couldn't put anything else in unless something fell out. I tried anyway. What else, faced with a deadline like that, could I do?

Another of my creature friends during this time was a hummingbird that would come up to my window and hover, its wings thrumming at a pace I envied. I would look up, thinking about different patterns of microscopic kidney damage, and the bird would be there, watching me curiously, inviting me outside. Inevitably, its antics brought a gurgle of laughter to my lips.

I left the house at Commonweal every afternoon. At first, I walked the bluff to a footpath where I could get down to the beach. Clothes flapping in the wind, I trudged along the sand and squinted at the coastline. It was endless. The ocean, whose lapping at the shore might have been soothing, seemed to roar with my own rebellion against this enormous task. I was a shell of myself, dulled and worn by a sea of knowledge from which I had only wanted to take a drink, and in which I was now, certainly, drowning. Discouraged, I stopped walking that direction.

Instead, I escaped the vicinity of our church-quiet house on my bicycle. I rode north alongside rolling hills, and then south to the town of Bolinas, and then north again, along the eastern edge of the peninsula and through forest, farms, neighborhoods. I became anonymous that way, the sum of my muscles and determination and the grin on my face. Normal people didn't hole up for weeks and torture themselves with obscure facts, I reminded myself. People laughed and cried and reached out to comfort one another. Work was supposed to have meaning. Maybe medicine was not my element. Maybe Boards would be the deciding factor steering me away from medicine for good, and after all, it might be a relief. I smiled. *Imagine, not having to memorize the side effects of every antibiotic created. No more pathology slides. No Kreb's cycle.*

But before dinnertime I was always back at my makeshift desk, gnawing on more material. I was too proud to stop trying, too stubborn to quit. I had come this far, and I thought if I could just harness the energy of perpetual progress, I might keep riding it through Boards, through medical school, through life. The part of me that knew how dangerous momentum could be—that it might drag a person far from his or her intended course, lulled by the promise of success and the humming of predictability—had to be silenced, for now. *Give in,* the texts demanded. *Sit down.* There was no other reality than the turning of my mind and the endless road of medical terms and outlines, paving my way to a destination I could still barely see.

By the time we left Commonweal—still with three days left to study ourselves sick before the two-day exam—the baby birds outside the front door had sprouted downy feathers. We could see them stretching up blindly with beaks open, trusting that someone would put food in their mouths, hoping. Whichever parent was feeding them would arrive and distribute bounty, somehow keeping track of which mouth had been fed, which belly was emptiest. And then it would fly away, leaving its young chirping, open-mouthed, reaching.

The day before the exam, my insides were twisted into knots of dread. I reviewed statistics about the exam over and over: The passing score was about 70 percent. Nationwide, some 90 percent of students who take it pass Boards on their first try; it's mostly foreign medical graduates who don't pass. Everyone from the University of California San Francisco (UCSF) passes unless something goes terribly wrong, one teacher had pointed out. All that meant to me was that not passing would be even more pathetic. I had never sat for an exam feeling so tiny beside the mountains of material to know.

This was the fundamental question, to me: did I *deserve* to become a doctor if I didn't love science the way my classmates did? I tricked myself into remembering things, creating mnemonics and charts to bypass understanding—and even for this my memory seemed to have reached overload. I spent an hour learning how antibodies were made and how they differed, only to resort to the backwards mnemonic I had adopted a year before: M does *not* stand for maternal, so IgM is made first and IgG is the one that crosses the placenta.

Smoldering in my heart, burning more furiously as the exam approached, was anger with my future profession. What kind of institution nurtures a healing instinct in its pupils as it throws them to the wolves? Requiring an unknowable mass of information, I decided, could only be intended to demoralize, humble, and separate us.

The Boards exam, we all knew, was irrelevant to our abilities to care for patients. But each of us—stripped to our intellectual foundations—had to get through it. Alone.

The night before Boards, I went with a small group of classmates to see a movie called *The Truman Show*, about a man raised in an artificial world with his every move televised to the real world. The other people in the show are actors and actresses who try to keep him from learning that there is anything outside his hometown. Desperate to get out, he tries sailing away—but even the sea is under the control of the show's producers, and they create a storm to thwart his efforts to sail to the (fake) horizon and escape. At the climax of the generally light-hearted film, the protagonist is clinging to a boat for survival against a raging storm, bedraggled and refusing to be deterred in his quest for freedom. Raising a fist toward the "sky," he shouts, "Is that the best you can do?"

Walking out of the theater, we laughed and clung to each other. We didn't speak explicitly about Boards, but it felt as though some grand false god had laid down this exam to torture us. We talked of getting to bed early, and what time we had to be "there," but the lonely self-doubt we all felt didn't leak out. It would have been too messy.

Then, just before I went to bed, Steven called to wish me good luck. I hadn't spoken to Steven through all of this time because I couldn't bear to see the eagerness in his eyes, his lust for knowledge, and his certainty that he would do well. He always did well; he was the picture-perfect mental giant we medical students were supposed to be. He said he was sure I was ready. *You have no idea*, I thought. But his voice reassured me. Starting in November, we had studied together for almost every exam before this one. Intimidated as I was by how much more he seemed to know, his confidence steadied me. Our romantic relationship may have ended, but no one in medical school knew my intellectual capabilities more than he did.

"Thanks," I managed. My eyes burned with gratitude.

I scarcely remember the exam. I remember paraphernalia: wooden tables, rows of pencils and a good eraser, the ticket to get in and out, my baggies of black jelly beans and yogurt-covered pretzels, the empty backpack, my watch tick-ticking away. Older women read instructions we had all heard seemingly hundreds of times before in slow, precise voices; then, telling us to start, they patrolled the test center on thick-soled shoes. Of the examination itself I remember only agonizing perpetually between the two choices I could narrow a question down to. So close and yet so far. I had to pick one and move on. Too often I knew just enough to get muddled and stuck.

On the second day, before we had to be seated and facing front, our Healer's Art group joined hands and rolled ourselves into a hug we called the "jelly roll." We were eight then: Emma, Nicole, Cathy, Darius, Daphne, Susan, Mimi, and me. A month before Boards, we had sacrificed precious study time to handwrite and decorate anonymous notes to each of our classmates: "You make me smile," we wrote. "Thanks for your unending enthusiasm." "I've always admired your poise and presence." We sensed what we had not yet experienced: people slipping into quagmires of apprehension and self-doubt. Now we were almost to the other side. We could taste the end. We would love one another, and ourselves, again.

After it was all over—pencils down, tests collected, doors opened—Nicole, Anne, Elizabeth, and I headed for the coast, to a hike at Lands End, which we had done only once before.

"As long as we don't talk about Boards," Nicole requested.

"What Boards?" Anne asked, batting her big blue eyes in feigned ignorance. "Oooh, look at that bird!"

I chuckled gratefully.

As was so often the case in San Francisco, the fog still hovered over the western edge of the city, and we arrived at the trailhead wearing hats and sweatshirts. But as if on cue, just as we arrived at the parking lot, it started to dissolve into a thin mist, and we stripped off layers as we walked.

"So where are you going until rotations start?" Elizabeth asked. "And which one do you start with?"

I had hardly given the next step in medical school any thought, but sure enough, in a few weeks we would start our clinical education by spending blocks of time shadowing doctors in designated specialties. I started to wonder whether I would be allowed to continue if I had failed, but I pushed the thought from my mind.

Just then we reached the end of the well-worn trail that hugged a cliffside along the ocean, where most people turn back. I spied a seldom-used foot path that dove toward the shore.

"Let's go down to the ocean!" I called, not waiting for a response.

All these months I had been watching it from afar; it was time to feel the salt water on my skin. Leading the way, I scrambled over and through tree branches and bushes, tiptoeing over rocks and running up small hills. I might not have passed Boards, but on these narrow trails and rocky outcroppings, I was nimble and capable.

All of us came alive as we went, checking out tide pools and shimmying up to overlooks on our meandering way. Sun on our skin felt like the best gift we'd had in months. I thought of Zeke and our shining moment on the bridge. Now that pocket of light had opened up and engulfed the whole sky.

In a small cove, hidden from the trail above, I washed away the weeks of grief. My friends were around me again, the exam was over, and I had answered at least a few questions right. I stripped off my shorts and T-shirt and flopped into the water, laughing with sheer relief. Anne waded in to join me, with Nicole close behind.

We had made it through.

How easy it is to love. The way a sculptress might run her fingers over features of clay, my gaze licks the face of a beloved—some pressure here, a light touch there. A smile at the perfection I could not have created. Every face is that way, if you look at it lovingly. Soft curves and subtle molding belie the amazing capacity for expression, thought, suffering.

Look how the skin has adapted to a smile, folded to accommodate laughing, wrinkled around the eyes. It dips and undulates down the neck, over the clavicles and down the curves of the body, modestly cloaking our inner workings from view. I am fascinated by this. Can it be I love the exterior of a person too much to devote myself to studying medicine?

(WINTER OF SECOND YEAR)

Chapter Four

BABE IN THE WARDS
THIRD-YEAR PEDIATRICS ROTATION

A few days after taking Boards, I flew to Europe to spend two weeks in the Alps with my sister. I coveted the timely limbo of travel, the poetry of feeling weightless and open to whatever small opportunities presented themselves: a new flavor for my palate, taking the train at sunrise, a street market of useless wares and hanging chickens, or the simple joy of having hours at my disposal to squander, to read—or walk, often aimlessly. As a traveler, I felt blank. Anonymous, insignificant, watching the unfolding of lives all around me. There were lovers on the train from Paris who never saw the farms we passed or the crumbling stone building—was it a castle?—that disappeared as quickly as it arrived, making way for hills, for light in the distance, a rainbow too improbable to be true.

It seemed to me that the Alps would be a perfect mosaic of new life and old; ancient, ageless, the mountains were an ideal place to hike away from my book-self and into the wonderland of the clinical self I had yet to know. There, where the horizon stretched all around me, I would purge the memory of confinement. I would return refreshed for the next two years of medical school, which would happily be spent almost entirely with patients.

Both Danielle and I were living in different skins than we had been the last time we saw one another. She had lived in France for the last year, and she spoke the language so eloquently, with such melodic inflection, that I could scarcely believe her voice came from my own sister. Meanwhile, my new medical vocabulary, whenever it sneaked into our conversations, startled her into a shocked stare. We had, in the intervening year, developed into strangers. And yet there was something soothing in our shared travel ideal: to shirk the duty to learn about the cultures of countries we visited and head straight for the highlands, where open skies melted on our tongues and we licked the views from our fingers. We wanted to *feel* the Alps. We were there to float between past and present in nature's playground, in the satisfying purgatory of time that belongs to travelers.

So on the third day of our trip, in Interlaken, Switzerland (a name that fizzles in my mouth even now like sugared candy), we decided to go paragliding. Neither of us had done such a thing before, or considered it, but the literal boundlessness of being in flight seduced us into paying a little too much money and cinching ourselves into harnesses with guides about our age, taking a few pictures, and surrendering control.

"Run!" called Raymond, the man attached to my back.

In fewer than six steps, we were airborne. I sat in a giant swing in the sky and laughed: *Look how quickly the houses shrink to playthings! Look at the minty-blue lake, the peaks below us! The ocean of green on a hillside of trees ... and my sister! Flying too!* It felt so easy. It *was* easy. Just bid goodbye, unfurl a sail, and walk off the side of the planet into a new dimension.

I'm flying.

I returned from the Alps eager to learn the basics of student doctoring: filling out paperwork, starting IVs, drawing blood cultures, understanding the hierarchy of a hospital team. I learned that, from now on, my work would be supervised by an intern, who would answer to a resident, who would answer to an attending, who was the fully certified, actual doctor running the show. Boards had been the requiem of two years of book-learning; the second half of my education would take place in hospitals and clinics, face-to-face with patients and doctors and real-life health concerns. The start of third year was a major turning point in medical school.

On the wards, I imagined I would be rewarded for caring about people. I hoped that earnest concern for others would be enough to lift me off the ground, and I looked forward to learning by doing and being and sensing and feeling. If I truly could be a good doctor—and I still harbored hope that this might be the case—I would find out in the next couple of months.

My classmates were to be scattered among different hospitals and different areas of study. Nicole would start with surgery, Elizabeth and Anne with psychiatry, and Camilla with family medicine. Steven rejoiced at starting with general medicine, one of the cornerstones of our curriculum and a notoriously challenging rotation, although even he confessed to feeling nervous. All of us would be on new ground.

For my pediatrics rotation, I would be sent on a journey to Fresno, a flat, dry city at the heart of California's Central Valley. Alongside my new "professional" clothing, I packed inline skates, hiking boots, my hydration backpack, and biking gear. My new white coat, already pinned with my name tag—CLAIRE UNIS, UCSF Medical Student—and slung with the forest-green stethoscope I had purchased in my first month of school, hung behind the driver's seat of my car. I had carefully selected a reflex hammer and penlight from the bookstore, and I tucked these into a small, black waist-pouch that was hopelessly out of style, along with index cards and brand-new pens. I had made one thoughtful purchase in anticipation of my upcoming pediatrics rotation: a handbook that promised to contain all the information one could wish for when practicing medicine on children. Which was good news because my experience to date amounted to a very round, very open zero.

The drive to Fresno was not particularly beautiful. The freeway dipped through Oakland and then east, past parched hills spotted with windmills and cement-covered spillover from the cities. Heading south, I saw expanses of dry fields, some distant hills, mostly flatland. Fresno appeared like a mirage, irrigation having transformed the dry land with swatches of green. The growth seemed out of place in the arid surroundings.

I did not know what to expect—of the city, of my rotation, of my clinical years. At orientation the previous week, a panel of upperclassmen had talked about what it was like to be a third-year student on the wards. I had anticipated some words of encouragement, fond reminiscence about patients who had changed their lives, a general sense that we were well-prepared for what came next.

"Competitive," the other students said. "Everyone's trying to impress the attending." And: "You don't sleep much." And: "You're constantly being evaluated, and you have no control over your life." Only one woman said something reassuring: "It's way better than second year—you could not pay me enough to go back to second year!" I smiled then. Her offering had preserved only a scrap of my former enthusiasm, but I held onto that hope. The key to enjoying third year, I thought, was not to look down. Optimism alone might keep me from falling.

The coincidence of being away from home at the dawn of my clinical years made the whole six weeks feel much like a foreign-exchange program. In college, I had gone to Spain to study the language after only a few months of introductory classes. When I got into a taxi, I tried to tell the driver where I wanted to go, having practiced the pronunciation for the better part of an hour in my mind. The man tilted his head back toward me and chattered a question in my direction. I froze. "¿Qué?" I asked—the wrong way to ask him to repeat himself, I later learned. He tossed another string of words my way. I repeated my first instructions again, slowly: "Plaza de los ..." In Granada, "z" is pronounced "th"—I had not known this either. Finally, I showed him the words, and he looked at the small map that accompanied them, and we were off.

I had no idea my initiation into doctoring would feel as disorienting.

I had watched Granada spin around me and felt electric. I knew the taxi driver didn't appreciate the historical flavor of narrow streets and bumpy stone roads, or my wonder at street vendors selling hot baked potatoes. There were roundabouts, and fountains, and old buildings stained black from the exhaust. Wrought iron. People walking everywhere. I let the driver pick his fare from the bills I had just acquired and went forward intrepidly to meet my host family. I was about to become someone new: a traveler, an expatriate, a temporary big sister to two boys who spoke Spanish far better than I ever would.

Like Spain, the hospital was its own microcosm, a country with an ancient hierarchy, incomprehensible vocabulary, and a landscape unlike any other. There I would study the natives and consider staying. I did not have the reference points of my friends—or their help. I was alone, a traveler in a strange land, trying not to look the part of a hapless tourist, reveling in the freedom of surviving on my own.

I soon learned that my first three weeks out of six would be spent working at Valley Children's Hospital; my pediatrics rotation would end with another three weeks in the outpatient clinic. After a few hours of administrative arrangements, and a brief greeting by the clerkship coordinator that first day, it was time to meet my resident. I was ushered in by a cheerful woman who seemed to evaporate the moment introductions were made.

I wore my white coat. This had been a difficult decision: I remembered learning at some point that children were scared of white coats. Having received numerous immunizations in their short lives, they learned—much like animals avoid electric fences after they are shocked a few times—that doctor-coats mean shots, and they should be avoided, protested, and if all else fails, spit on. But I was a medical student, and medical students wore their coats unless they were told they didn't have to. Besides, I had a lot of paraphernalia to lug around, and I wasn't eager to wear that bag cinched around my waist in a style that had died before I reached high school.

I was introduced to an unimpressed-looking third-year resident who was in charge of our team. "Hi," she said tolerantly, with a plastic smile that lasted just until my original guide had disappeared. Then she continued her conversation with another woman—an intern, I later learned—about where the latter had vacationed the previous week. I stood by attentively, waiting to be spoken to. Both women were attractive, dressed in skirts, and wearing impractical heeled sandals. Neither of them wore white coats.

They started to walk. I followed. The intern peeled off to take care of something, and my resident kept walking. Not sure what to do, I followed. She kept looking straight ahead, not seeming to notice me at all. Her thoughts were clearly elsewhere. I matched her pace, a stride behind, a half-stride, almost even with her shoulder.

Without a change in step or demeanor, she stated flatly, "We're going to the cafeteria."

I followed.

Once we sat down with plates of food in front of us, Maria seemed to remember that it was my first day with her.

"Our team meets every morning at eight in the call room downstairs," she said. "So you should see your patients before then. That's residents' rounds. Then we have an hour before meeting Dr. Jaffen at ten for attending rounds."

I nodded. The terms were familiar at least—I knew our team would have an attending, a resident, interns, and me. And rounds were the time we got together to talk about patients. But I would see "my" patients? Who were they? What did it mean to "see" them?

"What happens in the afternoons?" I asked.

She shrugged. "We just get stuff done … if we're not on call. Or if it's a call day we might get new patients. I think you meet with Dr. Delgado sometimes too."

Sonia Delgado was the coordinator of the pediatrics clerkship in Fresno. She had said, I remembered, that we would meet to discuss topics in pediatrics a few times a week.

"Yes," I replied. "On Tuesdays and Fridays."

Maria didn't answer, and I decided not to pester her with more questions. She played with the Jell-O on her tray. I noticed the unhappy curl of her lips, molded into a pout. She wore tasteful makeup and had perfect teeth, whose whiteness matched her pearl-and-diamond earrings. Dark, straight hair, stylishly cut, was tucked behind one ear. She didn't look the part of a harried resident. She didn't seem concerned about what went on in the hospital at all. And she definitely didn't seem interested in hearing from me.

After lunch, Maria gave me a brief tour, waving manicured nails at the "heme/onc" (hematology/oncology) ward, the general wards on two hospital wings, our team's usual meeting place, and the children's play area. She led the way into the intensive care unit (ICU), where she told me to "hang on a second" while she went to talk to another resident. While I waited, I took in my surroundings. The room was whitish-blue, very clean, with typical hospital linoleum floors. Lining the walls were large, three-sided cubicles filled with cribs or hospital beds and panels of gauges and nozzles and coils of tubing. I heard respirators for the first time: the slow sighs of inspiration and expiration interrupted by sharp, mechanical clicks.

Next to me were two small cribs, the shiny metal bars placed only a few inches apart and lowered to make access to the patients easier. A motionless toddler lay in the nearer one, her dark brown curly hair startlingly reminiscent of my sister's hair in childhood. I looked closer: there were her lovely, almond-brown eyes, wide open as the girl looked around. She wore a brace on her neck, and below it, her body was chubby. Her skin was the deep tan of

Danielle's sun-worshiping complexion. A tube in her mouth was helping her breathe.

In the quieter corner, a pale-skinned infant lay sleeping with a ventilator attached to a hole in her neck. Her features looked overly pronounced: puffy cheeks, movie-star eyelashes, firmly-shaped nose. Maria appeared beside me, and I asked softly, "What's the matter with that baby?"

"I-cell disease," she replied nonchalantly, leading the way out of the ICU. Then, as if remembering I was a medical student, she added, "Do you know what that is?"

I didn't. I had never even heard the name.

"Her bones have already stopped growing, but the rest of her hasn't. Her heart is pressing up against her ribcage already, and there's no room for her lungs to inflate."

"What will happen?" I asked. I assumed there had to be some life-saving therapy, a way to release the tension in her small chest and let her breathe again.

Maria shrugged and looked at my face—hard—for maybe the first time. "There's nothing we can do. She'll die pretty soon."

I didn't ask about the other baby.

All of Fresno felt like a fever; I had forgotten how sweltering summertime could be. Only in the first hour of daylight, or the last, could my attempts at exercising outdoors be undertaken without leaving me dehydrated and wilted on the carpet of my generically furnished apartment. The rest of the hours of the day shimmered like a strange dream, made hazy by the steam rising from concrete, the desert landscape, watered lawns.

When Javier was brought to the hospital by his mother, after five days of feeling hot to the touch, we didn't know whether to believe the first temperature reading, which put him close to 102 degrees. Children don't regulate their heat as well as adults do, I learned. We had him take off his little-man blue jeans and the long-sleeved flannel shirt that wasn't necessary, even in the air-conditioned emergency room. In his red-and-white briefs, he curled himself up on the paper-covered examination table, fingers touching the hip of his round, protective mother. When we got near him, he whimpered—but he didn't move. Exhausted from illness, the four-year-old boy mustered enough energy to cry only twice: when he got stuck with a needle to start an IV, and when we held him still to look in his ears.

The son of migrant farm workers from Mexico, Javier was the youngest of seven children, but lagged behind the others by at least five years. Everyone else in the family was healthy, his mother explained in Spanish. But Javier had become sleepy and cranky over the course of most of a week, and he had stopped eating. This last bit seemed to concern her the most.

It's one thing to talk to adults in Spanish that might be a little rusty, but quite another to try to console a child. I had learned the language in a combination of college classes and traveling through southern Spain and Central America. Consequently, my accent was all but defined, and definitely not Mexican. Javier's eyes cracked open long enough to see my white coat, and he let out a wail.

"Ja, niño, estás bien," I crooned awkwardly.

He inched behind his mother.

Señora García was indeed the sort of woman a child would hide behind. She was stalwart and unmoving as she answered my resident's questions in rapid, tumbling Spanish.

"Does he have a sore throat?" Maria asked in Spanish.

"Yes. He will only eat soft things. No meat, no vegetables."

"Headache?"

"No, *doctora*."

"Coughing?"

"No, *doctora*."

"Stomachache?"

"A little bit, two days ago."

"Vomiting? Diarrhea?"

"No."

It has never failed to amaze me how much parents know about their children.

My resident glanced at the boy who, with attention directed away from him, lay on his side, dozing. "Has he been irritable or sleeping more than usual?"

"Yes, *doctora*. He doesn't want to eat anything. Usually he tries to keep up with his brothers. Not since Friday now."

It was Wednesday.

"Has he had a rash?"

"No, *doctora*."

"Are his immunizations up to date?"

Señora García stared blankly for a moment. Maria had accidentally slipped back into English.

"Vacunas?"

"Sí, sí."

Maria excused us both from the room, and she led the way to a rack of medical forms.

"So what do you think?" she asked me.

"He seems really sick," I offered.

"What do you think about when you hear his symptoms?"

Oh, God, I thought. *This is going to be one of those rare infections I never learned well. He probably got bit by a weird bug, and I have no idea which one. ...*

"I'm not sure," I started. "It doesn't sound like he has a cold, or gastroenteritis."

"Right," she prompted.

"Seems like it could be strep throat or something?"

"And what's one thing you always have to rule out in a child with high fever?"

I knew this. I knew I knew it. It was just ... so ... hard to remember. ...

"Meningitis!" I said, in concert with Maria.

"So should we do a spinal tap on this kid?"

"Probably?" I speculated. I had no idea what the criteria were.

Maria looked like she was taking my input into consideration— ludicrous, given the fact that she had four more years of experience than I did.

"We'll ask the attending," she decided. "Since Javier doesn't have a headache or neck stiffness, it's unlikely. Here," she handed me a sheet of lined hospital chart paper. "Why don't you write up the admission?"

I took the paper without thinking, and she sashayed across the charting area to answer a page. When she returned five minutes later, I was still sitting there with the blank sheet in front of me.

"Maria?" I asked softly as she walked past.

"Mmm? What's up? You didn't get very far."

"I've never done a write-up before," I admitted.

She sat sideways beside me in a chair and prompted, "Chief complaint."

I wrote, "Chief Complaint: Fever."

"You can just write, 'CC' for chief complaint."

I nodded, and waited.

"HPI—that's history of the present illness."

I wrote the letters, and checked with her again. "Fever for five days?"

Maria sighed and started dictating the note to me, pausing while I wrote what she said word for word: "Four-year-old boy with tactile fever and sore throat for five days, also with stomachache two days prior to admission. Decreased appetite, sleepy, and irritable. No history of bug bite, puncture wound, headache, or neck stiffness. No vomiting or diarrhea—you can just write, 'No V-slash-D'— good—and no recent sick contacts. Previously healthy."

We made it through the whole admission note this way: Past Medical History (PMH), Birth History (BH), Immunizations (Imm.), Allergies (All.), Medications (Med.), Family History (FH), Social History (SH), and Physical Exam (PE). The last category was further subdivided into VS—Vital Signs, like heart rate, blood pressure, breathing rate, and temperature—and then body areas. HEENT stood for "Head-Eyes-Ears-Nose-Throat." Then Neck, Chest (meaning lungs), Heart, Abdomen, Back, Extremities, Skin, and Neurological (which really meant brain function as well as reflexes and coordination). By the time we finished this part of the note, Maria had been on the phone two more times, and she was impatiently bobbing her crossed leg up and down.

"What comes next?" she asked me, testing to see whether I had any idea where this was leading. The challenge felt like it had a slight air of malevolence, but I brushed this thought aside.

"Assessment, right?" I remembered from our orientation that all notes ended with a summary and then the plan. I just hadn't memorized all the steps that came before.

"So write it," she replied.

I froze. What *was* wrong with him? We had yet to figure that out. Luckily, Maria's impatience got the better of her, and she dictated a quick summary: "Four-year-old boy with fever to 102 and history of five days of illness with fever, sore throat, lymphadenopathy, and decreased appetite, presented dehydrated and irritable."

It seemed to me there was a lot more to Javier than that. What about the fact that he had a stomachache? Or that he lived on a farm? What if there were pesticides there? We didn't even know what kind of produce the father picked.

Maria fired off the plan in a spurt of short commands: Admit him to the hospital. Give IV fluids. Throat culture. Blood cultures. Neck X-ray. "Consider" lumbar puncture. Antibiotics.

Then she went back to the phone.

The first test to come back was a complete blood count (CBC), which had been sent when the nurses started an IV, almost an hour before. It showed that Javier likely had an acute infection of some kind: his white blood cell count was elevated, and the kind of cell that was present in highest numbers was the kind that usually fought bacterial infections—polymorphonucleocytes, or PMNs. When we rechecked his temperature, it was still close to 102 degrees.

Javier got a lumbar puncture, a spinal tap to test for meningitis. But not on the first try. I watched one of the interns set up for the procedure, while Javier's mother waited grimly outside the door. The boy was scrunched into a ball on his side and held there, moaning softly, while the intern tried to numb the area with anesthetic, introduced through a small needle. With sudden ferocity, Javier flailed his arms and legs out of the grips of unsuspecting nurses and sent supplies flying. He glared at all of the gowned doctors and nurses with a chilling scowl—the kind that means someone is not going to forget the damage for a long, long time. Javier was clearly a child who was accustomed to fighting off older, larger siblings. He was wiry and surprisingly strong.

But he was also sick, and tired. He could only muster enough strength to fight off the tap one more time, and then it was successfully performed by a more senior doctor who could tell there might be only one shot at it. Javier's mother looked at no one when she was readmitted to the room after the procedure was done. She went straight to her son and held him. She had heard every whimper.

According to Maria, Javier was my patient. I should check on him in the morning before rounds. That said, she started to walk away.

"But what happens now?" I asked. It was about four o'clock in the afternoon.

She shrugged. "He'll get admitted. The nurses take care of it. Sharon called; I need to go look at another kid."

And she was gone.

During my first weeks in Spain, I had to ask directions frequently. I understood the key building blocks of such instruction: *derecha* was right; *izquierda* for left; *adelante* meant straight, or keep going. I knew numbers, but not the words for city blocks, *millas* or *kilometros* to measure distance, though I hoped never to have to go that far. *Edificio* meant building. *La escuela de linguaje* (the school for the study of languages) turned out to be an institution few people had heard of before. I asked directions multiple times to get anywhere, mostly because I couldn't understand a lengthy string of advice, and I was too ashamed to ask for more than one repetition. I would smile and nod and try to look like I understood what I had been told, and then walk onward in the proffered direction until it seemed time to ask again. Eventually, when I saw the bank where I had changed money on my first day, I knew I could find my way to class from there. The days were always like this: a mixture of wordless stumbling between familiar landmarks and brief, polite conversations in a language I barely understood. I couldn't have known how well this would prepare me for being a medical student.

When I arrived in the morning on my second day of pediatrics, an hour before rounds, it was with the full expectation that I would have to ask someone to interpret my resident's request that I "check on" Javier. I suspected this meant I was supposed to examine him and ask whether there was anything new since yesterday. But I had no idea where to find him, or what information I should glean.

Just then I caught a glimpse of Sharon, who was charging into a patient's room with a ready smile. Sharon was one of the interns, or first-year residents, which meant she had just graduated from medical school. Interns are the worker-bees of a medical team. We had two—one who had no idea what was going on, and Sharon. I halted and waited for her to reemerge. She was exactly the person I needed.

"Good morning," Sharon said to me, heading for the nurse's station. She was a youthful-looking Korean American woman who appeared energetic even at this early hour. A small Winnie-the-Pooh doll dangled from her stethoscope, and I resisted the urge to reach for it.

"Hi, Sharon. Sharon—Sharon, can you help me with something?" I felt like a kindergartner who needed her shoes tied.

"Sure," she said, "just let me get one thing before I forget."

She reappeared instantaneously. "What's up?"

"I'm supposed to check on this kid Maria and I admitted yesterday. His name is Javier García. But I don't know how to find him, and I'm not exactly sure what to do when I do."

Sharon checked her watch. I learned later that she had five patients to see, but she scooped me up with a "Let's go in here," and we plunked down in front of a computer terminal. Within seconds, she told me where my patient was.

"Awesome!" I said. "Thanks. Do I just go examine him? Do I write a note?"

"Why don't you follow me when I go see this next kid? I'll show you what I do."

Sharon was in and out of the room within seven minutes, and in that time, she had asked the parents a handful of questions and examined a nine-month-old with a feeding tube in her nose. "Have you ever written a SOAP note?" she asked me.

"Yes, actually!" I was delighted she had asked me something I knew. "I worked in a homeless health clinic, and we wrote them there all the time."

S stood for subjective (what the patient said), O for objective (what the exam showed), A for assessment, and P for plan.

"I don't know if Maria wants you to write in the patients' charts," Sharon reflected dubiously, "but I would get a fresh sheet of paper to write your SOAP note and bring it with you. Don't ever take things out of the chart—it's illegal. But I think it's fine if you don't put your note in there till after we meet."

I looked over her shoulder while she jotted down an ESOAP note. "E is for events since yesterday," she remarked.

The clock read 7:20 a.m. when I peeled away to go find Javier.

The moment I walked into the corner hospital room, Javier started to cry. The four-year-old, curled on an adult-sized bed, looked much like an ant might look floating on a bar of soap. He had sunk into the middle of it on his belly, half-turned in my direction. When he saw my white coat, he wriggled to the far side of the bed, where his mother sat, impassively watching me.

I smiled. I always smiled at strangers. I imagined an earnest grin to be a universal indicator of good will, crossing barriers of language, culture, and trepidation. I nodded my head forward a little bit as I introduced myself and explained that I just wanted to check on Javier and see how he was doing today. Señora García and I both glanced toward the boy. He was peering at me from under his arm, and the moment he caught me looking, he sobbed and squirmed. His mother didn't flinch.

I took off my white coat and draped it over a chair. Heavy with books, pens, and index cards, it clanged against the metal chair side. I apologized in Spanish for the noise, and then I squatted beside Javier's bed. His mother unconsciously ran a hand across his hair. The metallic echo faded into complete silence as they waited to see what I would do. Both of them watched me. I opened my mouth. I made myself speak.

"How is he doing today?" I asked in Spanish, looking Señora García in the eye, hoping she could see I really did care to know. More questions came to mind: Is he eating? Does he still have a fever? Has he complained about anything? I was conscious of the slightest uncertainty in my voice as I tried to transition smoothly between questions, like the professional I was not. I jotted notes to cover the silences while I pondered what else to ask. Gradually I began to steal glances at my little patient, of whom I was possibly more afraid than he was of me. He stopped crying. He watched my eyes crinkle in a smile, and didn't turn away.

Finally, I ventured to speak directly to Javier. I asked something dumb, like "How are you?" because I wasn't sure what else to say to a child in Spanish. Señora García had been able to understand me, but she made allowances for my accent that children might not make. The boy didn't move. I explained that I wanted to look in his mouth, and I showed him the light. No response. I showed him my own mouth. Then I inched closer. "¿Abre la boca?" I requested. He remained lying on his right side, facing his mother.

Señora García came to the rescue, propping her son up to face me and admonishing him to open his mouth. His lips parted about a quarter of an inch.

"Grande!" I exclaimed, opening my own mouth to show him.

That earned me another quarter inch. Again, Señora García helped, pulling down on his jaw so I could look at the back of his throat. It was definitely red. I could see a bit of clear, stringy mucous behind his tonsils. He closed his mouth abruptly. End of exam.

Gradually, with his mother on my side, I coaxed Javier through letting me hear him breathe, listen to his heart, and poke at his belly. We had learned the general principles of a physical exam during our first two years of medical school, practicing on one another. On a patient no taller than my thigh, it seemed much harder to tell if his liver was enlarged. I'd never tried to find a spleen. And how could I explain that I wanted to know if my prodding and thumping caused any pain? When I tried to check Javier's reflexes, he got fed up with me and cried, returning to his ant position on the taut hospital bed sheet.

Good thing—the clock read two minutes before eight. I kneeled back down and thanked Javier for being such a good boy (wondering, as I did, whether I should use the conditional or unconditional form of the verb "to be"). Bidding Señora García farewell, and promising to return soon, I collected my white coat and slid out the door, breathing a sigh of relief that she had gone along with my fumbling pantomime.

Rounds were not what I expected: we didn't talk about our individual patients at all. Instead, residents' rounds were a teaching session. One of the house staff brought in an article about cerebral palsy for the group to discuss. I pretended to be engrossed in reading it and prayed no one would ask me any questions. I couldn't be sure if we had even studied this in class before. All that came to mind was the cardboard stand-up from the March of Dimes that used to be at the dry cleaners when I was a kid.

At nine, Maria rounded us up and addressed each of the interns about their patients before asking me, "How's Javier?"

"About the same," I replied.

"Did you examine him?"

"Yes." I felt proud.

"Why don't you present him to me?"

Deep breath. "Okay. Subjective: Mom said he only ate a popsicle last night and was still irritable. She thinks he still has a fever. He thrashed around a lot in his sleep. Objective: HEENT—"

"Wait. What about his vital signs?"

Uh-oh. "I didn't get those."

"How do we know if he still has a fever then?"

I squirmed. "Mom said he did—and so did the nurse."

"But how high?"

"I don't know." Those three words would eat at me for years to come. Throughout medical school, it became clear that I could and should always know something more than I did. The questioning never stopped before "I don't know," and sometimes it didn't even stop there.

"Okay, tell me the rest of the exam."

When I had finished, she suggested we go together to see Javier. I agreed readily, swallowing my fear that she would tell me I had done it all wrong. She burst into their room without knocking, said a quick hello to Javier's mother, and leaned down to examine my patient. She had already listened to one of his lungs before he took his first big breath and let fly with the tears. When Javier opened his mouth to cry, Maria flashed her penlight in it, prompting him to swallow the wail and turn away from her. Maria frowned as she grabbed hold of his shoulder and rolled him back. She wanted to feel his neck, which was still as tender as it had been the day before. He had a couple of large lymph nodes on one side, but, "They're mobile," she remarked. "So it just means he has an infection."

She didn't bother repeating the other steps of the exam. "Thank you," she simpered to Javier's mother, heading for the door with no explanation of our intrusion.

I followed dutifully, but ashamed. It felt like the time I had spent getting to know them earlier was for nothing; by implication, I was party to my resident's disrespect.

"He's spoiled," my resident surmised when we left the room in the wake of Javier's screams. "Did you get a good look at his throat? It doesn't look like strep."

I agreed, although I wasn't exactly sure what strep looked like.
"What do his labs show?" she asked.
"How do I find out?"

They say that newborns are mostly blind for the first weeks of life.
Their eyes open and strain in a habit that's built into the genetic
stuff that makes us human; they eventually learn not only dark
from light, shadow from glare, but also shapes, faces, features.

I started on the wards with the traits that came without thinking:
curiosity, a desire to learn, the will to please. I smiled and listened. I
filled in what gaps I could with observation and leaps of logic. But
I lacked depth perception. I had no idea how much I didn't know.

I gradually oriented to the way a day worked in the hospital,
how to find out information and write notes, whom to ask when
I was confused (usually Sharon). I checked labs on the computers.
And when Maria wasn't with me, I prided myself on the time I
spent talking to my patients, getting to know their parents. I was
soon lulled by the comfort of knowing my way around and the
mechanics of giving a daily report. But when Javier's platelet count
crept up out of the normal range, I didn't know to call attention to
it right away.

I read the daily CBC in attending rounds in the order Sharon had
taught me: white blood count, hemoglobin, hematocrit, platelets ...

"What was that number?" Dr. Jaffen, the attending
physician, asked.

"962."

"Is that new?"

"Well, yes, sir. It was 778 yesterday. But," I consulted the chart
of lab values I had been making, "it's been creeping up."

"We'll call Dr. Morris," Maria assured him. She had said
nothing about this to me, and I looked at her quizzically. Dr. Jaffen
was still frowning at his notes.

"Continue," he finally urged me.

After rounds, Maria explained that the overproduction of
platelets was unusual in uncomplicated illness. Javier might

have a cancer in his bone marrow, so we should get his mother's permission for a biopsy. Maria gave me the hematology/oncology specialist's pager number.

"Set it up with Dr. Morris this afternoon. You should watch the bone marrow biopsy when they do it. And don't forget to get his mom's consent."

I immediately felt out of my league. I pulled out my handbook and searched for information about increased platelets. I could find nothing. When I called Dr. Morris, she said she would see Javier and talk to his mother about the procedure. I was, temporarily, off the hook.

I read every night when I went home. The pediatrics program had loaned each of its students a textbook, and by the end of my first week as a student on the wards, I was leafing through this book voraciously to understand what went on during the days. I found information about various diseases, and even the parameters of normal, but I lacked an understanding of how to get around in medicine, the nitty gritty of going from symptom to disease and back again. Like any travel guide, my textbook laid out the various diseases like destinations, symptoms like clues to the surroundings, but no way to link them. Each day I returned no more savvy, but incrementally better informed.

For perhaps the first time ever in medical school, I enjoyed studying. Reading about a disease I had seen with my own eyes was nothing like trying to learn the charts I had made the year before. It was more similar to learning the history of Granada from the gardens of the Alhambra; I could envision the city's transformation and the gradual piecing-together of the architectural wonder around me. Dates mattered. Conquerors mattered. All of it felt like I could run my fingers over the stone and hear the clashes of centuries past. I had never had a passion for history before. Now, with Javier tucked into the back corner of the hospital with his quietly enduring mother, I took to the study of blood-related disorders the same way. My learning had immediate application and evident relevance. I was getting somewhere, even if my progress was slow.

When I reappeared in Javier's room the next morning, I was prepared to explain what I had learned about bone marrow aspiration. Though I was more helpful as a translator than as a fledgling doctor, I felt protective of the mother-son García pair. I related to their isolation; speaking only Spanish, they went through each day with gestures and charades, inferring what they did not understand. Señora García began to smile each time I appeared, perhaps because I could convey messages back and forth to the nurse for her, but also because I explained what the other doctors didn't. They came to trust me—Javier a bit suspiciously, but lulled by my patience and his mother's acceptance. Most likely Señora García could see that I was the most optimistic of the group, and the most invested in Javier's well-being. Who wouldn't latch on to hope?

The bone marrow aspiration was traumatic—for me, that is. Javier was given some medicine to sleep for the ten minutes it took to prepare and guide a large-bore, heavy needle into his hip bone with a forceful crunch. Cells were sucked out of his bone marrow, and the moment I saw the mixture of red blood and greasy yellow, I felt like a heavy cloud of smog had settled on my head. The room was suddenly hot, too hot to breathe, and the remarks of nurses and doctors sounded like buzzing, far away and abstract. I needed air. I tried to stay—I was supposed to learn—but one of the nurses caught my arm and sat me down firmly, telling me to put my head down. There was just enough air down there, under the chair.

Javier and I perked up around the same time. He never knew what had happened, and just for a moment, I envied him. Señora García looked to me for a description of the procedure, and I told her about it—omitting details she didn't need to know.

Amazing, I thought as I walked away. Here I had recently arrived, and with only a few key pieces of terminology to my name, already someone had looked to me to explain what had mystified *me* only a few days before. Even if I had been contemplating the hospital floor, trying not to lose my lunch, I had learned enough to translate the procedure for her. I had earned my patient's mother's confidence, but what was the real currency of our interactions? Borrowed information? Or my too-ready, too-optimistic smile?

There is a section of Granada that bears the lasting curves of Moorish artists. The neighborhood climbs in winding throughways up the side of a hill, subtly occupying a corner of the city one might not pass through for weeks after his or her arrival. Tea houses stagger their way up the slanted terrain, their darkened doorways afforded privacy by beaded curtains or subtle veils. The flavor of this quarter is decidedly, if unexpectedly, Arabic. I had not noticed the influence that Muslim occupiers of southern Spain had left in their wake until I stepped across time into the narrow streets of the Albaicín.

With two classmates, I hiked up and around a hill, passing flowers that spilled from one yard into another, and people dressed in slacks, hats, and suspenders, who stared at our khakis. Up into another age we walked, and when we returned to Granada, we noticed that Moorish emblems and shaped arches appeared on converted mosques and gardens throughout the city—only we hadn't known to look before.

So it was with Javier's symptoms. He didn't have cancer. He had something no one had thought of yet, something that wasn't mentioned in the section of the textbook that talked about platelet counts being too high, and the signs were right in front of us. Dr. Morris made the suggestion to Maria, and she casually got around to telling me.

"I think he has Kawasaki's," she said.

"Really?" I wrinkled my nose. I had understood this to be a rare disease, and one that usually affected babies in Japan or Hawaii. I hadn't learned more than a few facts about it when studying for Boards. And in recent days, I had been focused on ruling out leukemia, watching Javier's blood count change, and taking care of his mother.

She nodded. "Look it up," she gestured toward the pediatrics handbook in my pocket.

I read that a patient typically has a fever for at least five days and has at least four of the following symptoms: "bulbar conjunctival injection without exudate ... [e]rythematous mouth and pharynx, strawberry tongue, and red, cracked lips ... rash ... [c]hanges in ... hands and feet ... [and] cervical lymph node enlarged to more than 1.5 cm. ..."[6]

Javier did still have a fever, for a total of nearly eleven days at that point. He had a large lymph node in his neck, which was painful to the touch, and his throat remained red and irritated despite our attempts to treat it. But rash? Conjunctival injection (a term I didn't quite understand)? And changes in the hands and feet that were supposed to be swelling, redness, or peeling? I hadn't noticed any of these things.

"Let's go look at him," said Maria.

As soon as we were in his room, I could see the dryness of his lips, the fine cracks I had not known to pay attention to before. Señora García looked at us quizzically, but she didn't speak. She had grown accustomed to the brusque intrusions Maria made from time to time. I could tell she didn't much relish the after-effects they had on Javier, but she sighed and sat down next to the bed.

Maria pulled down Javier's lower eyelids and nodded. "Red," she said.

So that was what "conjunctival injection" meant. Then she picked up his hand and inspected the fingertips. "A little bit of peeling. Not really swollen."

I leaned closer. He had a few miniscule pieces of sloughing skin next to the nail beds. I wasn't convinced. Javier started to cry. We had exceeded the three-minute limit, and he started to suspect we were up to something more than the daily check-up. Maria didn't try to console him. She ran a hand over his torso and looked for rash there and on his back; then she tugged off his pants and underwear and checked the creases where his legs met his body.

"There," she said. A small patch of redness could indeed be seen, and we could imagine it traveled like a faint stain up to his belly, barely evident, but there. "Rash."

I felt a mixture of disappointment and resentment as I copied down the orders she recited to me. I had failed to see the signs that made the diagnosis, but I also knew Maria had missed them until now. She, who was supposed to be backing up my work and teaching me what to look for, had done less than enough to get to know this kid. And now, after the heme/onc doctor had whispered in her ear, she acted as though she knew he'd had Kawasaki disease all along. I swallowed my reservations as I wrote for him to receive the appropriate medications. It had taken six days to make the diagnosis. Was this kind of delay routine?

Finally, the machinery of treating an illness kicked in, and we had a plan for Javier, a direction. Kawasaki disease was mostly benign, but some children developed heart disease afterwards. He needed an echocardiogram, a new kind of medicine, and a lot of aspirin. While Maria explained this to her, Señora García looked at my face, trying to decide from my reaction whether I agreed with the resident who was four years my senior in the study of medicine. I nodded my assent, relieved to see that she had not lost her faith in me. And in that moment, I felt the lift of mattering to another person. I had not known to see Javier's diagnosis, and I lacked experience in explaining echocardiograms, but the one thing that fell within my abilities—caring about two people who were tourists in the hospital realm—I had done right. Señora García still trusted me, more than she trusted the real doctors, and even if I had to ask for direction at every corner, even if I kept stumbling over my feet on the way, I would live up to that confidence.

Throughout my time in Fresno, I was mostly out of touch with my medical school friends. This seemed appropriate; travel is for venturing out into the world with a handful of possessions and learning to manage on one's own. We go to find out about other places; we go to learn about ourselves. And we return full of promises and insights about life beyond that blurry region we call home.

But there is more to it. I did not have any idea what I would say to them, given the chance. Each day felt uncertain. I woke up at 5:45 a.m. to shower and dress, drove twenty minutes to the hospital to arrive by 7 a.m., saw my patients and latched onto the workday schedule until noon. Then anything could happen. I might have to go to a conference, admit a new patient, see a "procedure" (like a spinal tap, liver biopsy, bone marrow biopsy), or even help perform one. I spent entire workdays nervous I would be asked something I did not know, or that Maria would realize how inexperienced I was. I don't know why this mattered; I had started my rotations expecting only to pass. But as soon as tentative approval was extended in my direction—Maria eventually commented that she was impressed by my tendency to read up on patients and write thorough notes—I leaped at the compliment. Before now, I was not "good at" medical school. I got by. I passed, and that was enough for me when the standard was a number on a test that no one much cared about except the teacher who had written it. "P = MD," we often quipped. It was true: there was no higher grade than P, and no tangible reason to do more than pass. During my pediatrics clerkship, I felt moved to study for the sake of learning, and all of a sudden, other people seemed to think I would make a capable doctor. I longed to make that belief true.

After work, when I was not on call, I returned home around 5 or 6 p.m. to eat. I waited for the sun to sink low enough and the heat to wane enough for a Rollerblade venture up the paved path outside of town, or I went to the gym with another classmate and new friend. And in the rest of those evening hours, I looked up answers to the questions I had been too embarrassed to ask. What color *is* "normal" baby poop? What does formula contain?

I thought about Steven often during my weeks in Fresno, imagining the sparkle in his eyes as he immersed himself in his internal medicine rotation. We had more in common than ever, I thought—the more I got into the groove of seeking knowledge, the more I reminisced fondly about our nights of studying and his all-in approach to medical school. I also missed feeling loved. Who but someone else in medicine could understand my elation over finally practicing at doctoring?

Though I knew he shared my jubilation about transitioning to third year, I also feared Steven would quash my budding excitement with tales of his own successes. With a bit of distance, I could see it now: his passion for medicine was a tidal wave, as destructive as it was awesome. I needed affection, not competition.

Instead of calling Steven, I talked on the phone or exchanged e-mails with friends I had not spoken to in months—people who would not ask me how the rotation was going because they would not know what it was. *I* didn't know what it was. I knew I was in Fresno, in a hot physical and educational purgatory, and it helped to speak instead to people who had once known me as someone other than a medical student. I told them about the heat. I told them about the nearby access to Yosemite and Kings Canyon and Sequoia National Parks. I presented this month and a half as a grand adventure, condensed into postcard-sized reflections and colorful ramblings. My friends laughed. I needed laughter. It seeped into my pores and fed my courage to get up at sunrise and start my smiling, eager, apprehensive, and always-unpredictable days.

Once I started to tussle with the hope of being an exceptional medical student—and doctor, someday!—I took my blunders much more to heart than I had when I started.

Trying to help during another spinal tap, I placed my hands firmly on a child's back, pressing a blue paper towel into place to absorb fluids. A sudden silence alerted me that something had gone wrong.

"I'll get another set," a nurse announced, leaving the room.

The intern, who had been about to do the procedure, sat back and said nothing.

Maria was the one who told me what I had done wrong: the blue sheet, which was cut out in the middle and affixed to a patient's skin, was considered sterile. Only the person wearing sterile gloves—in this case, the intern—can touch the paper or the skin in the middle of it. Otherwise, the tap can be contaminated, and the results can't be trusted. We had to start over.

Disapproval hummed around me in the too-quiet room. I swallowed my shame until the procedure was over and then hurried out. I bumped into Sharon not five paces away.

"What's wrong?" she asked.

When I explained what I had done, my eyes burning with humiliation, Sharon chuckled and gave me a quick sideways hug.

"Everyone has to do that once—it's how you learn. You didn't hurt anyone!"

But such simple errors riddled my time in Fresno. They were the familiar quirks of bridging two languages—just like when I'd assumed "embarazada" meant "embarrassed" (it meant "pregnant"); or that "estúpida" was a mildly self-effacing, benign way to explain my forgetfulness (it was a derogatory term akin to "mentally retarded")—and they were the ever-present reminders that I did not belong. In fact, I often felt more akin to my patients than to the doctors I was meant to emulate. Like the young parents who brought ailing children to the hospital for advice, I was just passing through, drawn in by circumstance, to leave again when my time was up.

As a few weeks rolled by, however, the pace and cadence of conversation became familiar to me. And though I still missed every third word or so, there were phrases I could recognize, gestures to emulate, whole sentences I could form and practice, rolling the rr's all the way home.

East of Sacramento, in the hills west of Lake Tahoe, lie a few small communities that people who aren't fond of cities call home. Redwood trees and rolling terrain provide privacy that can't be found easily on paved streets. Kids grow up knowing the feel of real dirt under their toes, with trees to climb and bird songs to learn. They don't have a lot of contact with other children except maybe for school, where they mingle with neighbors who live twenty or thirty miles away. It might seem like there isn't much reason to immunize children in such a place. Who would they get measles from?

Jack Gordon liked his independence. He had a wife and two children, a house in the woods, and a good-sized piece of property. He was a little suspicious of the government, which tried to over-regulate his life, and he preferred to keep his family away from doctors, who might cause more harm than good. The Gordons were living a natural life, a good life, and as long as they stayed out there, Jack reasoned, they had nothing to fear.

Until his eight-year-old son, Jimmy, developed lock-jaw and began to stiffen into a painful, arched-back pose he couldn't get out of. Jack put him in the car and drove to the nearest hospital, where the doctors recognized that Jimmy had a tetanus infection and could die if they did not protect his ability to breathe. Tetanus causes severe muscle spasm that can affect the diaphragm, and it can be rapidly fatal.

Jimmy was transferred to Valley Children's as soon as he was stable enough to be moved; the original hospital lacked the needed tetanus immunoglobulin and was not equipped with a pediatric intensive care unit. So he came to be the PICU resident's patient, and a few days later, when he started to improve, he became mine.

Thin, giggly, and wide-eyed, Jimmy lay in a darkened hospital room with little entertainment. The spasms of muscle contraction caused by tetanus can be triggered by sudden stimuli—light, noise, movement, what-have-you. The boy had few visitors and was guarded by his father, who grew increasingly agitated with the people trying to care for his son as the boy recovered from his earlier life-threatening state.

When I met him, Jack ushered me outside and wanted to know what I intended to do "in there"—indicating his son's room.

By this point in my rotation, I actually knew.

"Jim is getting better," I explained to the man, "as you know. This means he doesn't need to be in the ICU any longer, and he will be taken care of by a new team of doctors. I'm the medical student with that team, and I've been sent to do a brief physical exam and just introduce myself to Jim, ask how he's doing, that sort of thing. I'll be checking on him every day from now on."

Jimmy's father frowned at my white coat. He seemed unsure whether to let me pass.

I introduced myself and leaned in to hear his name. "How *is* he doing?" I asked.

Jack breathed a sigh. "Much better," he said. "But we're trying to keep things quiet back here, not disturb him, that sort of thing, so he doesn't end up tightening up again.

"No lights," he added sternly.

I could see I had Jack's undivided attention as well as his mistrust, so I decided to spend some time interviewing him before trying to see Jimmy. The nice thing about this kind of admission was that I had been told the diagnosis ahead of time, so I had looked it up, and I sounded much more competent than two weeks on the wards had actually made me.

"Why don't you tell me how this all started, in your own words?"

The only wound Jack could think of was a scrape on Jimmy's hand from a nearby barbed wire fence—presumably the route of entry for the tetanus infection. As we had surmised, the boy had not had the routine immunizations recommended for children in the United States. But until now, Jimmy had been healthy.

I had sensed general ire from the ICU resident about the concept of not vaccinating kids against preventable, potentially life-threatening diseases. That rejection of basic medical advice made me a little bit afraid of Jack. But faced with a doting parent who clearly wanted the best for his son, and who had brought him to the hospital as soon as things went wrong, I decided this omission on Jack's part had simply been a result of misinformation. Paranoid misinformation perhaps—but I could relate to his yearning for a simple life. Isn't that why I had moved to Mammoth a few years before? This gruff-looking man in sagging jeans, hiding behind a bushy red-brown beard, was trying to hold on to an innocence that was hard to achieve in modern society.

When Jack said, "He's not used to all these people and machines and things," he wasn't just referring to Jimmy. These were a man's feelings projected onto the most trusting and lovely little boy I had ever seen. Just being touched made Jimmy titter timidly. He watched everything with guileless curiosity.

I felt more like Jimmy than like a doctor myself.

We developed a kinship, this half-a-family and I. When it came to the clash of mountain values and the bustling, humming hospital, I was the perfect emissary between the two. Jack wanted information about tetanus, and sitting on an empty gurney in the hallway beside him, I drew a map of the nerve endings, showing him how the toxins of *Clostridium tetani* worked to keep neurons firing and muscles contracted. We talked about immunity and how vaccinations worked. Jack looked in my eyes and nodded his head to show me that what I was telling him made sense. He agreed to let us give Jimmy a tetanus vaccine before leaving the hospital. We scheduled an appointment for him to come back to our outpatient clinic in three-and-a-half weeks for a last booster and final check-over. I would be working there in the last week of my rotation, so it seemed to work out well.

I watched with a mixture of pride and envy as the two of them left. I had formed an alliance with the formidable Jack Gordon. I had understood his fears. In turn, he listened when I took time to explain our medical approach, and he consented to the protective immunization for Jimmy. This felt like the real stuff of doctoring—and I had managed it all on my own.

As they walked down the hall, the blond boy bumped against his father gently and looked around at the other hospital rooms, children with their parents, and the bright colors splashed around the playroom. But when they approached the door and Jimmy felt the glance of daylight, he fairly skipped outside into the sun, loosening himself from the protective hand on his shoulder. His father followed readily behind.

Almost a month later, when the day and hour of Jimmy's clinic appointment came and passed and the boy did not appear, the residents grumbled about neglectful parenting and child endangerment. I thought the "no-show" was merely a misunderstanding—a clash of cultures that maybe a phone call could set right. I copied their home number out of the chart and dialed it. *They might just be late*, I thought.

Jack's voice on the other end of the line was cautious. "Yeah, I remember you."

"I'm just calling because Jimmy missed his appointment today, and I wanted to check with you about rescheduling it."

Pause.

"Jimmy's just fine," the man said. "I don't think we'll be needing to drive back down there."

My voice faltered. I knew the social worker, sitting beside me, was listening intently to what I said.

"Y-you do know that Jimmy needs one more shot."

Another silence.

"Otherwise he isn't immune to tetanus, and he could get it again."

"I said he's fine now. He's happy here. I don't want to subject him to that … that … drive, and more medicine. It's hard on a kid."

I took a deep breath. This was harder than I had thought it would be. "Sir, I realize it's difficult for you guys to get all the way out here. I'm just worried about Jimmy's health in the future—"

"You just think you know everything, don't you?"

"N-no, sir, I definitely do not think I know everything." The irony of his remark would have been hilarious, if he only knew how I really felt. "As you know, I'm a third-year medical student, so I have a lot to learn." I imagined the smirks of residents and nurses behind me. "But I do know some things about tetanus—and you do too—and part of this—"

"You're going to tell me that the only way to parent is to let you inject my kid with toxins that could kill him, because the government says so. Well, I'm not going to let you."

"Sir, I understand your worries, and you're right—vaccines can cause side effects. But it's far more rare to have a bad reaction to a vaccine than to die from the infection itself. Otherwise it *would* be a terrible idea to immunize kids."

I was being diplomatic, wasn't I? Still, my voice sounded hollow.

"I think it is a terrible idea."

"I'm just thinking about Jimmy, and the fact that he could get scraped again—"

"*You're* thinking about Jimmy? Let *me* think about Jimmy. He's my son, and I don't want anything bad to happen to him, and I'll take care of him, and you can just leave us alone now because we're fine. He's not going near that fence again neither."

"You won't even bring him in for an exam if we don't give the vaccine?"

"What do you need to examine him for? He's fine. I know my son. If he's not okay, I'll bring him back."

It was a lost battle. Jack Gordon, who had been scared when Jimmy was in the hospital, who had been willing to hear what the doctors had to say, was now safely ensconced in the hills far from the reaches of the kind of logic I had embraced. He could say, "No," and hang up the phone. He could hug his son and wake up to the birds and feel reassured by the familiarity of his own house. He wouldn't be back; nothing one said when far away from home could be trusted. I should have known this. I forgot.

When I hung up the phone, I was afraid to turn around and find out who was there to witness my defeat.

I felt a hand on my shoulder.

"Nice job," the social worker murmured. "That was a hard phone call to make. You kept your patience really well."

"Thanks," I mumbled.

My gut was still wrenched in dismay. I knew the other doctors had thought that reasoning with Jack Gordon was beyond hope, but I had to try. And I thought I was going to succeed: I had envisioned myself soaring above the bounds of what the others believed possible, fueled by the ridiculous hope that I was going to be an extraordinary doctor and could reach anyone with the right mixture of patience and understanding.

Suddenly I felt very, very young.

In contrast to the careful structure of the inpatient wards in the children's hospital, the pediatrics clinic was loosely organized: some patients had appointments with specific residents (or occasionally students), but many just needed to be seen by someone. It was a grab bag—thick charts usually described a child with complicated medical or social issues. Thin ones could be anything.

I was in clinic with one other student from UCSF, and she and I split up to see patients with the residents or take an occasional appointment on our own. The format was clear: after talking to a parent ("taking a history") and examining the child, we excused ourselves to talk to an attending physician, or sometimes a senior resident. Then we "presented" our patients. This was structured much like an admission note for a new patient, or a SOAP note if they were there in follow-up. We were to start with why the patient was there, tell all the relevant background, and in an organized fashion, describe what we found on physical examination (starting with general appearance, then progressing top-to-bottom). More senior residents cut to the chase—"Normal physical exam except for tonsillar exudate"—but since our understanding of "normal" was iffy, we students were expected to provide as much detail about our patients as we could: "atraumatic, normocephalic, with clear tympanic membranes bilaterally; extra-ocular movements intact; pupils equal, round, and reactive to light; nasopharynx with small amount of clear mucous; oropharynx erythematous with cobblestoning; neck is supple without cervical lymphadenopathy …" All those words to say the toddler appeared healthy except for drainage at the back of the throat. Compared to this cumbersome medical lingo, Spanish rolled effortlessly off my tongue.

Most days lagged a little bit. I took away some gems of information: that tonsils can look beefy and be normal, for example, and that any time you see a kid with lice, even if you don't catch it, you feel itchy afterward. But each clinic brought in a patchwork of visitors I would never see again, families temporarily detained by Dominic or Kelly or Brittney's sore throat (or stomachache, or school problems).

Sometimes I negotiated my way through whole afternoons without seeming like a total newcomer. More often my ignorance showed through. As long as I was honest about the limits of my knowledge and got the help I needed, no one seemed to mind. I started every appointment saying, almost apologetically, "I am a student." And the more that other people took this fact in stride, the more comfortable I became with my role in the clinic. They *expected* me to ask for directions. That's what travelers *do*. If I didn't need much assistance, it was a pleasant surprise for all of us.

And then, on my last afternoon in the clinic, I looked up to see Señor and Señora García shuffling their way down the hall. When I saw Javier sandwiched between them, I scarcely recognized him. He wore the benefits of his mother's cooking, his cheeks now full and pink. He clung to her pantleg with one hand and held a small truck in the other. I welcomed them gladly, excited to see my first little patient looking so well at his follow-up visit.

The elder Garcías said nothing, but I recognized the relief in Señora García's abashed smile. I knelt down to play peek-a-boo with Javier. He looked at me expectantly, registering my face with none of the anger or fear I had seen there before. He seemed to recognize me. His eyes squinted ever-so-slightly, and his cheeks plumped into a coy grin. Then, with a sudden swoop of the plastic toy, he giggled. I was so surprised, I almost fell over backward. He laughed out loud.

I've never known another sound as sweet.

Like most of the core, required clerkships, my pediatrics rotation ended with an exam. As soon as it was over, after saying quick goodbyes to the residents and doctors, I left town. Everything was packed: clothes and stethoscope, white coat, bicycle, note cards, relief. It was time to go home.

Sun-scalded hills hovered outside the windows of my car. It seemed that the hours floated in midair, the whole afternoon, and I was still suspended on the drive back. How could three hours stretch and coast for so long?

I looked forward to reuniting with my friends. I wondered if they welcomed the change in our lives with as much enthusiasm as I did, if their rotations had treated them as well. I planned to see Steven, from whom I still hadn't completely separated, despite our evident differences. And Danielle, who had returned to France after our travels, now lived in San Francisco, less than two miles from my own flat. We could walk and bike and even travel together again.

But even more than yearning to return to the way things were and the comfort of old routines, I felt the breath of a fresh start, a new confidence fluttering in my chest. Not the ease of complete competence, but the promise that I might get there, a hope I hadn't dared believe in too strongly before this point of departure from a book-learning life. It was part delusion. My safety had depended on the doctors who backed up everything I did, who taught me how to act, who encouraged my attempts to learn, and who kept me out of the ICU, where my heart might have broken before I learned anything. They harnessed me to themselves and swung me out of harm's way; they let me believe I could fly with no more than earnest desire and a smile.

Home is never the same when we return. But even with my friends scattered to different hospitals, on schedules that rarely melded well, and though Steven and I soon broke up for good and I was often alone even back in San Francisco, I wouldn't ever have to go back to second year.

I had tasted flight. I wanted more.

"True" is a word used to describe a mathematical equation that fits rules of addition or subtraction; it is a descriptive term thought to hold weight, a banner of logical acceptance applied to statements or conclusions. "True," to me, is less definable: it's the matching of heart-pounding, deep-seated belief with a thought or realization. It may be a rule by which I operate, or a hope I hold tight to my chest as I fall asleep, but it is rooted in feeling and meaning that can no more be summarized with a word than with an equation.

(FALL OF THIRD YEAR)

Chapter Five

"POOF: THE PSYCHIATRIST"
THIRD-YEAR PSYCHIATRY ROTATION

The words would remain etched into the soft, gray wood of a cabin door. My best friend from summer camp wrote them with a black, ball-point pen while I watched her do it. Caroline smiled proudly when she was done, with the mixture of conviction and rebellion that guided everything we did when we were fourteen. But even then, the words had made me a little uncomfortable.

"POOF: The Psychiatrist."

In a list of summer nicknames, that one was meant to represent me. Had I not loved her, I would never have tolerated the name "Poof" to begin with. Caroline had been referring to my flyaway curly hair that I was trying to grow long, and that at this stage created something of a woolly cloud on top of my skull. As was the fashion, I occasionally swept part of it over into a side ponytail, but the style did not diminish my hair's height or breadth. I had always longed for straight, controllable hair like Caroline's, and I hoped that mine would be calmer when worn long. Nevertheless, Poof I was.

Caroline and I had met the previous summer, as thirteen-year-olds in the youngest cabin at Hi-Camp. I had short hair then, and wore iridescent lip gloss and big metal earrings with my T-shirts and Bermuda shorts. She had shoulder-length straight hair and a sweet face, and her clothes were more preppy than mine. I was excited to be at camp; she had been sent against her will. But in our very first walk around camp, headed by a big-boned and serious German counselor named Bron, we struck up a conversation—and didn't stop for the rest of the session. We both, it turned out, loved to psychoanalyze people. Especially, but not limited to, boys.

After that summer, we wrote confessional letters to each other throughout our first year in high school. I still have a binder of our correspondence—mine photocopied before I mailed them, and hers as I received them—in something like chronological order (though our letters frequently overlapped). "I wish I knew what he was thinking," I wrote about my freshman-year crush, with whom I shared a locker. "My parents are driving me crazy," Caroline penned. When the loneliness of being at a new school got to me, I wrote Caroline from class: "I am so depressed today." For her, home was a harder place to be than school. "I almost ran away yesterday," she told me once.

By the time we arrived at camp for our second summer, Caroline and I felt ourselves to be soul sisters. We tirelessly sought to understand people, and we speculated about moral truth for hours. Not to be mistaken for overly brooding teenagers, we also raided a boys' cabin and ran underwear up the flagpole. We basked in the security of having a close group of friends. Camp was ours.

I'm not sure when Caroline dubbed me "the psychiatrist" for the first time. I know she told a girl from another cabin to come to ours before lights-out, to talk to me about her boy problems. This started a trickle of visitors to my bunk bed, where girls I had never seen before poured out their worries to me. I answered with Dear-Abby-like sincerity, unsure whether they would trust a stranger, but surprisingly sure of myself. Except for a three-week tryst at a summertime academic program the previous year, I had not yet had a boyfriend myself. But with Caroline's encouragement, I was invincible. We had the gift of understanding, Caroline and I.

Psychiatry is considered by many physicians to be a "soft" specialty. Even in our preclinical years as medical students, a mild derision permeated our collective attitude toward psychiatry classes. Based partially on human interaction and intuitive sense, the course couldn't garner as much respect as the hard sciences like pathology or pharmacology. Some students acted indignant at being taught how to interview patients. Others just avoided the class whenever they could. Anything having to do with the brain that couldn't be evaluated under slides prompted more discomfort than a hot day in anatomy lab, but we were still required to learn the material and, yes, pass exams. The lectures were terrific. The material was relevant. But the conditioned response of my classmates, inherited from classes of medical students before ours, was stubbornly difficult to overcome.

Part of the uneasiness, of course, bloomed from the fact that in every symptom of disease, we could see something of ourselves. I could empathize with depression. I could believe that paranoid behavior was sometimes normal. Obsessive-compulsive behavior? What medical student doesn't possess a few of those traits—or even the whole stock diagnosis? I could barely discern the line between normalcy and madness.

One night while preparing for National Boards, I sat down with a summary chapter about personality disorders. By the end of the hour, I had diagnosed acquaintances with many of them. Jason was definitely narcissistic, based on the definition: exaggerated sense of self-importance, believed the rules didn't apply to him, craved excitement to ward off boredom. Bingo. For compulsive personality disorder: a preoccupation with orderliness, perfectionism, and mental and interpersonal control at the expense of flexibility, openness, and efficiency. Yes, that was Allison! Or obsessive-compulsive: excessive attention to details ... trouble with authority figures ... Uh-huh. That suited Larry. The other characteristics of these disorders didn't fit, but the beauty and danger of psychiatry was how pliable an interpretation could be.

Psychiatry had a way of tapping into personal affairs. It was in psychiatry class that I learned the major developmental struggle of people my age, described by Jan Erikson: *intimacy versus isolation.* Once resolved in this struggle, we would then be on the cusp of *generativity versus stagnation,* but there was supposed to be time for that yet. First, we were to figure out whether we would be alone or find companionship in this life. Intimacy was obviously the goal; isolation worried the rest of us.

When I started my clinical psychiatry rotation at the Mt. Zion campus of UCSF, I was twenty-five and newly single again, with no dating prospects on the horizon and a full-time occupation developing every minute. Who could say if I would fall in love before the age of thirty? How was I to meet anyone while cloistered in class or the hospital or the library all day? Time was already working against me.

I had been away from my Healer's Art group for two months by this time, and I rejoined them with some trepidation. My sense of triumph in clinical pediatrics burned as tenuously as a single candle, and I felt hesitant to reveal it to anyone, lest it flame out. While I had been away, my roommate's new relationship had blossomed, and I greeted this news with some mixture of jealousy and loss. I still feared the results of Boards, which had yet to arrive, and which could yank me back into the dank years we had just left behind. In all, it was an awkward to time to open Pandora's box of unsettled feelings—but our group had pledged to meet every month.

Nicole arrived in scrubs, which was a first for our group. Darius wore slacks and a collared shirt, and looked both grown-up and comfortable in his new clothes. Susan arrived grinning broadly, although she had to leave her pager outside with our watches and shoes, and her fair skin revealed evidence that she had perhaps not been sleeping well. Emma, our ballet dancer *cum* medical student *cum* ballet dancer again, was the only one to arrive in casual clothing. Daphne, usually early and always even-keeled, snuck in late. There could be no doubt that a transformation had begun in all of us. The mere presence of this cadre of classmates served as a potent reminder to each of us: though we were following separate paths, we were still in this together. And though I might not have found intimacy, I did not exist in isolation.

In the weeks and months ahead, I would struggle to hold on to this feeling. My roommate got engaged and then married. Other friends found their lifetime partners. Some had already started their families before medical school was half-finished, and I couldn't even fathom dating yet. I'd had enough relationships before medical school to appreciate the freedom of not planning around someone else. But there it was again: affection versus freedom. Intimacy versus isolation.

Was something wrong with me?

Before medical school, I had thought I understood depression. I would have called it a sadness that does not go away, pervading and saturating the hours and days so they never dry enough to flap carelessly in the winds of time and change. I would have blamed it on losing a friend in a car accident, or feeling lonely, or the meanness of others. I was too sensitive as a child, and I cried frequently at injustice and brute unkindness. By the time I started high school, I thought I was endlessly empathetic to others' troubles.

Jenny's personality filled about a quarter of our eleventh-grade classroom by itself. She would ask embarrassing questions a little too loudly—"So, Dave, I heard you got some this weekend?"—just as class started. She made faces that would cause a classmate to laugh, which made Ms. Coleman accost him. When he deflected to Jenny, she giggled guiltily, but she was too cute to bust. She flirted maddeningly with the same boys I had crushes on, but she'd win back my favor by the end of class. That was just the way she was.

The morning Jenny walked into class pale and trembling, too dazed to speak to anyone, I think most of us didn't know she was there. I had just put my bookbag down when I noticed her standing uncomfortably beside me, her eyes glazed and distant.

"Claire," she said softly, urgently, "I need to talk to you."

I picked up my bag and followed her outside automatically. She had nothing with her.

"I'm numb," she said when we were twenty yards away from the classroom, standing in the empty quadrangle under a sunless sky.

"What happened, Jenny?" My voice was coaxing but firm, like a parent's hand in a child's.

She looked despondent. Sadness weighed down the corners of her eyes, the muscles of her smile, even her chin. Not even tears animated the blankness of her gaze.

"I didn't think I would wake up," she complained in her little-girl voice. "And then my mom was yelling I was going to be late for school, and I got sick on the way and had to throw up."

"Do you feel sick like you need to go home?"

She shook her head slowly. "I don't feel anything."

I wanted to ask what she meant, but instead I waited.

"Last night my mom and my dad were fighting and my brother was being an asshole and I just didn't want to deal with it anymore." Her voice was plaintive. "I had a headache the whole time and I decided to go to bed and I took some Tylenol and then I just thought I might as well take more and I thought I wouldn't wake up."

Suddenly a bird started fluttering wildly in my chest, and I felt a surge of panic.

"Jenny, how much did you take?"

Her eyes, trained on me, still seemed uncomprehending. "I don't know. I think the bottle was almost full."

"Oh my God." I was fumbling for my keys and starting to cry; I didn't know where to take her, but I knew it was not the school nurse.

"I'm numb, Claire," she said again. "I'm scared."

I put my arm around her and guided her out to the parking lot, murmuring reassurances and thank-God-you're-alives, then made sure she was seat-belted before I roared out over the speed bumps and into the street. I raced to the only hospital I knew because my father worked there: a county hospital whose emergency room I had never visited, nor knew how to find, but there were signs to guide me. I parked hurriedly and half-dragged Jenny out of the front seat, into the box-shaped, cream-painted building where an unimpressed nurse informed me that Jenny could not be admitted without permission from a parent or guardian.

"She took a whole bottle of Tylenol," I repeated incredulously. "She needs help!"

I could have screamed, for all the good it did.

Then I was on the phone to her house, to her mother's work, to my father. Minutes later, Dad strode into the waiting area with eyes wide and signed that he would take responsibility; then Jenny was backed through swinging doors in a wheelchair, still looking at me vacantly, desolately.

With my father there, and Jenny gone, I crumpled. Dad walked me out to the car.

"She's going to be fine, physically at least," he reassured me. "You did the right thing."

I blubbered a string of nonsense and questions. "I just can't believe she did that ... Is she really okay? ... What are they going to do? ... Should I not have told her mom? ... Why didn't they know? ... Maybe I should stay. ..."

"Honey, it's going to be okay. Jenny's going to need some professional psychiatric help," Dad said. "But you did everything you could do."

I slumped tearfully against the side of the car.

"You should go back to school."

I stared at him in disbelief.

"I'll be here. I'll keep checking on her. Didn't you say her mom was coming too?"

I nodded slowly. I had failed Jenny. Friends were supposed to be enough, I thought. We should be able to tend one another, offering nourishment and support when life got hard. By the time I knew about Jenny's desperation, the problem had sprouted into an unruly tangle. I imagined adults who wouldn't really understand trying to trim it back, hacking at the tendrils of a tree whose roots went deeper than they knew.

But I did go back to school. I ghosted through my classes with my heart buried deep, shame sealing my lips for days to come. I had known Jenny was prone to feeling moody, but not this. I had not seen this coming.

Clinical depression is not sadness. It's not the normal response to loss, grieving giving way to denial, anger, bargaining, acceptance. It isn't a cloudy day making you move more slowly, a little bit of fog slipped through a crack in the window and muting feelings for a day or two.

Real depression lingers. Two weeks is the cut-off, the DSM (*Diagnostic and Statistical Manual of Mental Disorders*, which defines and classifies psychiatric disorders) criterion by which depression is diagnosed. Two weeks of persistent depressed mood, maybe tearfulness or loss of interest in activities. Sleep loss or sleeping too much. Change in appetite. Loss of energy. Withdrawal, cognitive impairment, pessimism or shame or guilt. Many people ruminate on death or suicide. Less typically, there may be anxiety, or hallucinations of voices criticizing, cajoling, commanding.

Was Jenny depressed? In retrospect, I still don't know. Her weight changed often, but she only rarely seemed sad. She didn't complain of sleeping overly much or too little. Her energy, whenever she was surrounded by her friends, was high. But voices? I don't know whether she heard voices.

The first time a patient described the voice in his head, I felt my arm hairs stand on end. Nineteen years old, he heard a man's voice telling him how "lame" he was. Sometimes it told him he should kill himself. When he was brought in to the hospital during my psychiatry clerkship, he had been preparing to do that: with gasoline and a match.

It wasn't the first time I'd heard about voices—but this time I understood how dangerous psychosis could be.

My ex-boyfriend from Mammoth did not have the protected childhood I knew. Son of a woman who was clinically depressed and a man whose best defense was avoidance, Sean was neglected for years. There were reasons for him to be sad, explanations I could make up for his episodic moodiness. Late one night, after we had argued bitterly about his mistrust of my friendship with another man, our conversation softened, and we lay together on my bed, still talking.

"You have no idea what it's like," Sean said, "to have voices inside your head telling you to just end it all. Telling you, 'You're stupid. You're worthless. You might as well just *get it over with.*' Over and over, like a tape recorder you can't shut off."

I could feel the weight of what he was telling me, but I didn't know what to say. Who can't remember feeling insecure as an adolescent? I had spent a few years convinced I was ugly and untouchable. I had starved myself to be more attractive. I had hidden behind makeup. I had changed schools. If my family had been fragmented, maybe I would still—in my early twenties and just out of college—have felt the same way. I reached my arms around Sean and rocked him through a long winter night while he apologized for his rage, talked to me about his stepfather, cried about feeling hopeless.

"I don't know. I'm sorry I get depressed sometimes. I can't really help it. I know it's hard, and we fight over stupid stuff. I really don't want it to be that way. Sometimes I think I should go ahead and *do it,* just make the voices go away."

My voice came out thin, like white breath in cold air. "Do you really think you might try to kill yourself?" These last words were punctuated by my heart knocking at my chest. How on earth could I stop him?

"I don't know," he said again. "I've thought about it. Just get a gun and—" he made a soft explosion noise, "—then I can sleep."

"Oh, Sean," I gasped. He still wasn't looking at me, just out the window at the clear night sky. I tightened my embrace. "But think of all the reasons to be alive."

He was quiet.

I reached out to all the reasons I loved life in Mammoth, loved life in general, and I offered them to him one at a time, like feeding quarters to a slot machine: each one was a chance to hit the jackpot and break him free from despondency. But each fell with an empty, echoing clank.

"You're the only thing that matters to me," he said.

The intensity of the moment anchored me there, my leg twined around his, chest pressed up against him, tucked under his arm like I belonged there. I felt tiny beside his depression, but my heart swelled with surety that love would heal him. My love. My energy, the *joie de vivre* he needed.

It would be months before I learned that love wasn't enough.

Snorkeling with Sean during a six-week backpacking trip through Central America, I felt out of my element and intimidated. He had grown up near the ocean, and now, as our guide brought the small motorboat sputtering to a stop near Caye Caulker, Belize, where the clear Caribbean ocean was just deep enough that I could not see the bottom, Sean readied himself to dive in. *Sharks*, our guide cautioned. *Rays*. My boyfriend took a deep breath through his snorkel and plunged.

The first time I tried to follow him, I came up spluttering. Gradually I learned to hold my breath when I went under and clear the snorkel when I came up. I kept Sean always at the corner of my vision. His long limbs waved with the ebb and flow of the ocean, and he cruised around the shadowy underwater world as though unaware of its dangers. Even with practice I could not go as deep, or stay down as long. I choked on the brine water. He didn't seem to notice.

Away from home, we were all each other had. As my mood became complexly reliant on his, as he veered from contentment into the darker crevices of his mind and stopped talking to me except in anger, my sense of self crumpled more and more with each passing day.

"I understand if you want to go on without me," Sean said, in a rare apology. He held his head like it might swim away while he studied the dirty linoleum in our hostel room. I envisioned surfacing without him, following the plans we had made and continuing on to Tikal, then Honduras and Costa Rica. I spoke Spanish well enough, I thought. I could do this.

But no sooner did I take a breath than he finished his statement: "I can't promise I won't kill myself though."

I stayed.

Coaxing a smile from him was like dragging through miles of sand and not being sure of the way. But it was better than sinking. *I'm strong enough to do this*, I told myself. *We'll make it back.* But sometimes it felt like I was the one drowning in depression. The boundaries blurred. I began to believe we were meant to be together, my emotions a continuation of his, our pathetic symbiosis the greatest achievement of six weeks of travel. The rare good days seemed blissful.

When my parents picked us up from the airport, Sean barely spoke. I chatted garrulously, trying to distract them from his brooding silence. Having witnesses to our interactions was like walking out of the water with him on my back; I felt the full weight all at once, and it was staggering.

Though we broke up soon after that, it took months for me to truly realize that Sean's depression, and whether or not he acted on the voices in his head, had had nothing to do with me. Even two-and-a-half years after that journey, when I could first diagnose his mental disorder and knew it as an organic, brain-chemistry-related phenomenon, I felt very real sorrow for him. I had loved Sean, and I had been loved by him, and part of me—naïve, hopeful, but painfully earnest in the desire to heal him—was irretrievably lost when we parted.

As a third-year student, I spent six weeks in the required clinical psychiatry rotation. I started out fearful, constantly feeling that I might be reckoning with ghosts. Straddling the span between what I thought was true and what my patients said, I inhabited a kind of purgatory in which I could scarcely decide what to believe. Empathy was little help to me. In fact, it was potentially my greatest weakness; I hadn't realized how permeable the boundary between reality and delusion could actually be.

As is true for depression, there are diagnostic criteria established for every psychiatric malady: schizophrenia, personality disorders, bipolar depression, autism. Normal grieving has a time limit. Mood has parameters. A charming woman with a tragic history of loss and betrayal turned out to be a manipulative patient with borderline personality disorder—and I thought we had just had a constructive heart-to-heart. An exuberant young man, filled with elation about the wonders of love, turned out to be in the manic phase of bipolar disease. As with my ex-boyfriend, the boundaries of "normalcy" wavered dangerously, and I felt myself disoriented.

What I had never realized as a preclinical student, ever confident that psychiatry was an intuitive field, is that you have to dissociate yourself from patients to do them any good. You have to work at becoming immune to charm as well as insult, objective in the face of strong emotion, removed when you are asked to be most involved.

I sucked at it.

Mr. Edwards limped into my borrowed office on a scarred wooden cane, his badly atrophied legs barely filling the stone-washed jeans he belted with purple nylon. He wore a lopsided black beret over grizzled gray hair, and his blue eyes stared at me above a scruffy beard as we greeted one another. A plain silver hoop earring adorned his left ear, and he wore a clean, bright T-shirt under his jean jacket and rainbow-striped suspenders. Seating himself delicately in the only available chair, he waited for me to speak.

"Before we start," I offered, feeling uncomfortably like a made-for-TV psychiatrist with my three-days' experience in that role, "I just want to make sure you understand what this program is about. I am a medical student, and I will meet with you several times over the next four weeks to get a clear understanding of why you are here and how we might best help you. I will share what I learn with Dr. Shimaya, whom you met on the way in, and she will continue to see you after I am gone. We will make any treatment decisions together."

I had been told that setting forth clear boundaries and expectations made a therapeutic alliance more productive.

Mr. Edwards nodded, and in a drawling British accent said, "Yes. Yes, that's fine."

I smiled politely and leaned forward a little bit in an attentive and interested pose. "So," I asked, "what brings you here today?"

He tilted his head curiously, and I almost expected him to call my bluff. Instead, he said, "Well, it all started when my mother abandoned me. I was nine, and I felt the sharp end of that sword."

Here, I thought. *Two minutes into the interview, and already at the heart of the matter.*

Half an hour later, I wasn't so sure. Mr. Edwards was a dramatic storyteller with a yen for stopping before the punch-line. He told me he was an artist with the desire to return home to England before he died—yet there was no discernable reason why he would expect to die in the near future, as he seemed convinced he would. He claimed to have been depressed for a year, more or less, but had no clinical symptoms of depression other than sadness, and only off and on. He had been arrested during his teenage years "for effeminacy," but would reveal no actions on his part that prompted his arrest. His list of complaints (which he had printed carefully by hand and borne to this first meeting) included such disparate concerns as noisy neighbors, difficulty finishing projects he started, and sorrow. I spent most of the meeting chasing these clues: what's *wrong* with your health? What happened a year ago that made you sad? What did they charge you with when you were arrested? Why do the neighbors concern you so much?

Like the craftiest of con artists, Mr. Edwards steered me away from the emotional content of his stories into other topics, so that at first I believed that his chief concern truly was where to store his artwork once he died.

Finally, I tried to hone in on this worry. "Mr. Edwards, why do you believe you won't live much longer?"

"I'm terribly weak. And I'm getting weaker."

I looked on his intake sheet for a diagnosis that would explain this symptom. "Is that from the tertiary syphilis? Or is this something new?"

"I don't know, really."

I asked a string of questions to assess what he was able to do for himself, and what required help. He was afraid to take the bus anymore, he said, because he felt fragile in large groups of people. But he rarely allowed anyone to drive him around.

"I'm a very dependent person," Mr. Edwards said.

"Very *dependent*?"

"No, *in*dependent. I dislike waiting around for other people. I'd rather walk than sit around half the day waiting for someone to take me to the market when it conveniences them. It messes with my schedule."

"In what ways are you dependent?" I asked.

"Well, I live in public housing. And I receive SSI." Supplemental Security Income is a federal program providing monetary support to people with long-term disabilities or age greater than sixty-five years.

"Have you needed more time to get around recently or found that there are new things you can no longer do?"

"No."

A phone call to his primary physician later in the day was no more revealing. She chuckled and told me he was prone to somatization—he had physical symptoms for emotional ills—but that his state of health had not changed in the five years she had been his physician. She had prescribed antidepressants for him at one time, chiefly because he claimed to have lost his appetite and admitted to feeling down, but they had not helped.

The next time I met with Mr. Edwards, his story had grown more robust—and disturbing. His mother, he suspected, had had lovers other than his father, and had left her family to run off with one of them. Then my patient's father, until he remarried, shared a bed with my patient, sometimes fondling him at night. This was only a starting point for a string of very personal revelations: how he had performed fellatio on a sailor in front of onlookers at age thirteen; how he had swallowed needles at reform school and poured acid on his hands at military school to get his mother's attention; how he had tried to kill himself with carbon monoxide upon learning that he had contracted syphilis from a lover. One attempt at psychotherapy in the 1970s had brought him to a primal scream therapist, who would literally crush him to make him scream. Subsequently he had found a therapist to help with alcohol problems and "trouble with a companion." This therapist died from AIDS, however, and my patient had gradually stopped going out much at all.

About these elements of his past, he was only mildly reluctant to talk. About the present, however, Mr. Edwards remained stubbornly vague. There were no significant relationships in his life, he said at first, except one that had been ongoing for thirty years and was not physical; the "significant other" was a man he saw rarely, though they both lived in San Francisco. About alcohol his story changed as well: he drank only wine, only sometimes, only with friends, only because he was used to it. And he smoked marijuana "occasionally"—which he later defined as every night for the past thirty-five years. Repeatedly, the suspicion that I wasn't getting the whole story stopped me from trusting his answers. How could it make sense that he could walk no more than a few blocks but refused to let anyone help him get groceries? Why did he pine to return to a country that was the stage of so much abuse in his life? What did his mysteriously beloved artwork consist of?

Each night after our sessions I tried to piece together a whole life filled with experiences that were not my own. My task as a student was to do exactly that: create something called a "psychodynamic formulation," or formal postulation about my patient's formative life experiences and current psychological struggles. By the end of our fourth session, I was to assign him a provisional diagnosis and be able to discuss him with the psychiatrists in a coherent manner.

I sat down and tried to imagine being Mr. Henry Edwards. Then I leaned back and tried to analyze him. Donning my writer's cap, I started by describing him in detail. Under my pen, he became a character in a novel: events led to actions, and turmoil, and resolution in a logical, if slightly fabricated, way.

But when it came time to assign him a diagnosis, I felt stuck. Mr. Edwards had a litany of complaints, but he denied most symptoms. He couldn't express why he had come to the psychiatry clinic. Medication for depression had not helped him, and he didn't want to participate in group psychotherapy. If he had a burgeoning substance abuse problem, it had not yet interfered with his ability to tend his daily needs and make his appointments. The only clues to his current malady were in recent events: death of his estranged mother three years before, and that of an admired "friend" less than a year ago. My patient's most significant problem, it seemed to me, was loneliness. What could we prescribe for that?

Loneliness isn't a diagnosis in the DSM. In medical terms, it would be more like a common cold than pneumonia. There are no medicines that help, no salves to make it go away. All one can do is tell a patient to take care of himself, and use whatever remedies seem to work. Though I provisionally called his problems dysthymia (longstanding depressed mood without other symptoms of depression), chronic pain disorder, and "rule-out" cannabis dependency (meaning I wasn't convinced), the supervising psychiatrist agreed: Mr. Edwards fell into the uncomfortable no-man's land of the medically undiagnosable.

At the end of our last meeting, Mr. Edwards left abruptly. I had been accustomed to his lingering reluctance to depart after each session, as though he would be content to stay and reminisce all day. From the window, I watched him hobble down the bustling street with surprising agility—he was not as hindered as he had intimated in our earlier session. Had he wanted only sympathy from me? Or the ear I lent him for an hour a week? Either way, he was on his own now. With the number of truly ill patients in psychotherapy at the clinic, there were no resources for the well patient who just wanted someone to listen to him. That was what our sessions had revealed: wellness, crippled by lack of support.

He had to look elsewhere for empathy.

When I first arrived at the psychiatric emergency ward of San Francisco General Hospital for my assigned night "on call," the physicians and nurses appeared relaxed. It was dinnertime, and the evening shift staff sat at a long table, joking with one another and nibbling on food either brought from home or purchased on the way to work. I was introduced by a young attending with whom I worked on my clinical rotation.

"I'm trying to convince her *not* to go into psychiatry," he joked about me. "But I'm not sure I'm doing a very good job of it."

A writer at heart, Dr. Berman spent evenings typing out stories, meeting with a group of other writers, and sending submissions out to journals and magazines. When he learned I had majored in writing and that I dreamed of taking time off to write, he encouraged me to do so. As for psychiatry, he was happy enough in the field, but it was a job. A job that enabled him to write, but not one he would entice me toward. Or so he had explained one afternoon when I sat in his office, having sought him out about a patient and then been happily sidetracked to find a kindred spirit in the midst of this confusing, disorienting profession.

"I'd love to write full time," he had said, "but it's just too hard to make a living as a writer." And we both agreed that medicine kept us in touch with the real world, real people's lives. Balancing science and creativity was refreshing.

"Unfortunately, residency sucks," he had commented, "but it gets better after that."

But since I was still a student, and ever agreeable, I found myself replying by telling the others at Psychiatric Emergency Services, "It's just that Dr. Berman is an example of why I *should* consider psychiatry."

Dr. Berman flashed me a look of incredulity. "Really? Are you considering it?"

I nodded to stall for time. *Would* I consider becoming a psychiatrist?

"Well, I think hearing people's stories is a big part of why I enjoy medicine, so I might like the focus on interviewing and actually spending time talking to patients."

It was true I had thought about this, but my own words took me by surprise.

Dr. Berman opened his mouth to answer but was interrupted by the explosive entry of a young African American man accompanied by two police officers who hoisted him into a padded cell. The man was thrashing and hollering about things we could not see. A nurse materialized with a liquid-filled syringe, and the other psychiatrist gave the man a shot of haloperidol while the policemen were still there. Then they locked the agitated patient in the dark room, stripped of anything that could cause harm, and waited for the sedating effects of the anti-psychotic medication.

The vision shocked me: how, like an animal, this young man was injected and locked up—no time for an interview, no full assessment, just shoot first and ask questions later. I learned that he had been floridly psychotic, shouting at people who weren't there, irrationally terrified. But more than that, he was strong, frantic, and threatening. All it had taken was an injection to restore calm in the psych emergency suite.

I spent the latter part of the evening interviewing a homeless patient who had been there all day. Mild-mannered and dulled by medication, he was nevertheless deemed potentially aggressive, and our interview was set up in a room with windows bordering the staff room. His chair was in the corner farthest from the door; mine was set within reach of the exit.

The interview has faded in my mind. More exciting than anything this man said was the possibility of danger, but this turned out to be overblown. My patient spoke calmly of his hallucinations, denied knowing he was schizophrenic, and admitted to having tried crack cocaine (the most likely trigger of his current bout of psychosis). He showed no emotion while we talked, no expression that would fix him in my mind. I had the sense that he wasn't really there, and perhaps that's why, in the collection of patients I have spoken to and faces I remember, he seems to have disappeared.

I doubt I was any help to him at all.

A significant percentage of homeless people are "mentally ill." The term is vague. What I know of these individuals is what I have seen: disheveled men and women talking to no one in particular, shouting at people they don't see, howling their distress and being walked past, not acknowledged, left to flounder in the fickle tides of their mental chemistry. A bottle of medication might be tucked away under layers of clothing or in the bottom of a backpack, but people whose thoughts are disorganized often forget to take their pills. Someone who goes on a drinking binge, or gets high, isn't going to remember either.

But there are so many less obviously ill in our midst. I have a friend whose mother is schizophrenic. She was a married physician with two children when the symptoms first started. Over time she started to come undone, gradually slipping from living mostly in the present-day to succumbing to hallucinations, persecutory thoughts, lack of cohesion in her own mind. She lives in a psychiatric care home now, but sometimes she escapes and comes to my friend's door, her lips working over words from the past, her own certainty of home and place askew. This isn't new to him. He understands the illness behind his mother's erratic behavior. He is no longer surprised if she doesn't recognize him. He still visits her, manages her affairs. Sometimes she strikes up an ordinary conversation about his job as a lawyer and remembers the names of his pets. Other times he might as well not be there. The hardest part is something he doesn't talk about: with a mother who's schizophrenic, he might turn out to be schizophrenic himself.

None of us are immune. In my family tree there are ancestors who killed themselves, others whose eccentricities are still the stuff of hushed speculation. I'm sure there were a handful of alcoholics. Depression runs just under the skin. Anything can happen, and it is our very vulnerability that makes empathy so dangerous. Without the objective eye, who could recognize the threads of mental illness that weave into the fabric of a person's life? No category of sickness has a greater propensity to be ignored for a long time because it seems like something that can be treated at home, smoothed over by spouses or parents or children. After all, feelings are the most personal aspect of self that anyone has. If these can be tangled by a process beyond our control, what is left?

When I broke up with Sean, it was because I had nothing helpful to give him. I had been a crutch; I had allowed him to pretend everything was all right. I had tried to normalize his outbursts and his episodic despondency. I dreamed with him about a peaceful life. I connected to the person he was most of the time, but sometimes he was unreachable. Finally, desperation plunged me into the same miserable melancholy that held him captive, and then I was no use to either one of us.

What remains after all that has passed is the memory of helplessness. No amount of love could have fixed the turmoil in my ex-boyfriend's head. He didn't want to go to a psychiatrist. He didn't want medicines. All he wanted, so he said, was me. And in the end, the most caring thing I could do for him was to take that away. Only after we broke up did he finally seek professional help.

Poof, the curious and imaginative teenager that I was, has grown more cautious now. She still exists, still finds satisfaction in listening to friends and offering advice and promising to be where she's needed. Still loves to stay up late talking about intangibles like intuition. Still lets herself believe that the world works in a magically, mysteriously karmic way. She even appears in me when I listen to some of my patients, whose emotional needs I do my best to handle.

She is—I am—not suited for psychiatry. The difference between medicine and psychiatry, to me, is in the depths of empathy. Who can conceive of having voices intrude on their thoughts if it has never happened to them? Who dares to admit she might understand the tides of insecurity and breathtaking sense of worthlessness? In psychiatry, you learn to dive just deep enough. You stay near the surface, eyeing the landmarks that allow you to make a diagnosis. Beneath that uppermost layer, the water is too deep, too unpredictable. I keep wanting to dive in and put my arm around the person who is drowning, drag that struggling form up for air. I should know better—but I still jump in. The only way to save myself is not to go there anymore.

There are tools, medicines, that can change lives, bringing the almost-lost back within reach. I am glad there are people who can do this. Nothing makes this more true than knowing someone who has needed, and who has benefited from, psychiatric help. As a physician, I can recognize signs and symptoms now. I know what a world of difference treatment can make. But I still fight the current of my own irrational fears, and the unforgettable memory of choking in an implacable sea.

For myself, I had better stay on shore.

He sits at our Thanksgiving table and talks of his wife's death. His love for her is a crisp edge to his thoughts—they all come right up to it, dance close, teeter there. This is how I feel, watching him: like we are all balanced precariously there with him, drawn to the brink, breathless, fearful.

(FALL OF THIRD YEAR)

Chapter Six

GESTATION
THIRD-YEAR OBSTETRICS & GYNECOLOGY ROTATION

The first thing I noticed about childbirth was the nakedness.

In the delivery suites of a middle-class hospital, once the ruffled bedspreads were laid aside, all attention was focused between a pregnant woman's legs. A mother-to-be conversed with family as though this were normal, to have doctors placing two fingers in her vagina from time to time, as though it were no surprise to her parents and friends to see her naked, as they certainly did if they were there for the birth.

I was impressed.

That eddy of time, before she actively started pushing and after the nurses had already set the stage for a new arrival, felt panicky to me. I would generally try to gauge what was appropriate to say then, whether I should hover in the room or check on another patient, when it would be time to put on shoe covers, a gown, mask, and gloves, and feign confidence that I would help deliver this baby safely.

I would introduce myself. "Hi, my name is Claire, and I'm a medical student working with Dr. Hunter this month. I'll just be helping out with the delivery."

I wanted them to know why I was lurking around the room. The words "medical student" were the thin sheet that protected me from any expectations.

I felt naked too.

But perhaps I was the only one who felt so vulnerable. I do not remember shame in the delivery rooms, no nervous snatching of covers to protect the privacy of patients—or the innocent eyes of a medical student.

I had thought it did not exist in our society, this communal comfort with women's bodies. Many of my female friends were obsessive about fat, burdened by the distorted body image of most white American women. Now it was all before me: thighs jiggling with excess flesh, belly buttons protruding under pressure, stretch marks like purple streaks of lightning across swollen abdomens, hemorrhoids pooching tenderly beneath it all.

When I presented myself to the private office of Dr. Hunter and her three partners, located in a wealthier area of San Francisco called Laurel Heights, I felt conspicuously out of place. They took one medical student every year, under great persuasion from UCSF, so there were no well-established ideas about what to do with me. Tucking my backpack into a discreet corner of Dr. Hunter's office, I followed her in and out of examination rooms the first day, just getting accustomed to the flow of patient appointments and watching my preceptor for cues.

Tall, blond, with a pleasant face and a very even demeanor, Dr. Hunter seemed to glide through her patient list without a change in expression. Then she coasted across the street to the private hospital and showed me around. We visited a small handful of gynecology inpatients, checked the labor and delivery (L&D) ink board for names, and cruised through the post-partum area. Wide-eyed, I took mental notes on where we were and what we did in each area.

During my rotation, she explained, I would be coming here alone to watch and participate in deliveries. I wanted to be sure I could find my way back.

We chatted about the upcoming six weeks, about which clerkships I had just finished, and what I thought I might want to do (I had no idea). She nodded and grinned and said little. I managed to ask how long she had been in her current practice (about twelve years), but I was too intimidated to ask much else. She appeared to use words, like time, very efficiently. We arrived back at her office before lunch.

Every day involved some combination of clinic appointments, rounding in the hospital, attending deliveries, watching surgeries, and going back to school for meetings. I rarely knew what I would be doing until I was doing it.

At least once a week, I scrubbed my fingers, hands, and forearms alongside Dr. Hunter. I had been taught to "scrub" the day the rotation started; taking a plastic sponge-brush, a doctor strokes every surface of the fingers and hands at least ten times with antibacterial soap. She touches nothing else after this presurgical preparation. Water is turned on and off with a plate at knee-level. Arms up, hands dripping, a surgeon (or assistant) backs through the operating room doors and waits until a sterile towel is offered by the scrub nurse. If, perchance, one were to touch something (the water spigot, sink, door, an eyebrow), one would return to the sink and start over. Such are the rules of sterile procedures.

We were usually in the operating room to perform one of two common procedures: a hysterectomy, in which the uterus is removed entirely, or a scheduled Cesarean-section (C-section). In the latter surgery, a low, horizontal incision opened the pregnant abdomen to permit access to the uterus; cutting through this thick muscle allowed a delivery that could not have occurred via the birth canal. Babies were born this way routinely. Occasionally, they were also removed this way urgently, as when something went wrong with a vaginal birth.

What I loved about being in the OR with Dr. Hunter was her calmness. I could tell when she was worried by a furrow in her brow and a reluctance to speak, but tension never erupted as harsh words or impatience. In an emergency, I might not be invited to scrub in; or I might scrub and then stand just out of the way, at most offering a suction catheter when asked. But in the relaxed early mornings, when she operated with one of her colleagues and they swapped stories about their kids' soccer games and teachers, I felt included in a sisterhood of sorts. An operating room staffed only by women was not common. But here in the small group practice in which I had been placed for six weeks, I had the benefit of learning primarily from female doctors.

In general, I felt ambivalent about the OR. Cutting was done using an electrical knife called a "bovie." Cauterizing as it cut, it left a foul smell in the air. I was grateful for the surgical mask that covered half my face, hiding my displeased expression from view. Having been given the job of suctioning, I took it upon myself to try and suck the smoke away as well.

During one procedure, Dr. Hunter smirked at my efforts.

"Remember," she asked Dr. Wells, "how much that smell bothered us when we were pregnant?"

"Ohhh, it was awful," her colleague agreed. Turning to me, she explained, "We were pregnant at the same time. You should have seen us in the OR together!"

They both chuckled. Dr. Wells finished cutting through the layers of skin and the yellow fat underneath, and they now each pulled on respective corners of the incision. A metal flat-edged hook called a retractor was placed on the skin edge to open the field of view more. "The problem was reaching the table," Dr. Hunter continued a moment later. "We both had bellies out to here—"

"—and we had to pee every five minutes!" Dr. Wells added.

"It was bad timing," Dr. Hunter said. "And then Cindy got pregnant too."

"All three of you were out on maternity leave at the same time?" I asked.

"No, Cindy's was later, but Molly and I had our kids within a few weeks of each other. That was rough for the other two."

"How did she get so many adhesions?" asked Dr. Wells, referring now to the patient. Tacky extensions of thin tissue stuck the uterus to the abdominal wall around it, and they worked blunt-nosed scissors through the webs to release them. Watching, I was impressed by how casually they worked, how smoothly their fingers reached for the next instrument, scooped sutures around bleeding vessels, and kept working, almost automatically, as they talked.

"There's her uterus," Dr. Hunter showed me. "These lumps are fibroids. That's why we are taking it out. And here—" she reached around the balloon-shaped organ through a field of moist structures I could not identify. She pinched an edge of membrane, and I realized that she had cupped the small gray ovary, no bigger than a goldfish, in her hand. "Round ligament, fallopian tube, ovary."

"The uterus should be much smaller than this," Dr. Wells contributed.

I nodded, grateful for the explanations but still not sure I could ever find these landmarks on my own.

"I remember going into labor at the end of clinic, and asking you to check me," Dr. Hunter reminisced.

"That's right! You were already three centimeters dilated."

"Dr. Wells delivered my son."

"And you delivered Betsy!"

So the conversations would go, introducing me to the life I might look forward to.

I don't think I realized what a gift those mornings were until much later. I hadn't expected the privilege of shadowing Dr. Hunter. I tried to emulate her easy-going style and plied her subtly for more stories. Until this point, I had not found a female role model in medicine. Nor had I realized I wanted one.

What I needed wasn't career advice—yet. What nagged me when I went home at the end of the day was something I couldn't say out loud: the more educated I became, the more I worried I would never find companionship. I wondered if focusing on medical school meant I would never meet anyone and never become a mother myself. Was I wasting my twenties? Simply by the fact of having families of their own, Dr. Hunter and her colleagues offered hope that I would not remain alone.

Obstetricians often cite a disturbing fact: women age thirty-five or higher have a markedly increased risk of having children with chromosomal anomalies, like Down syndrome. There is also an elevated risk of complications with birth as women get older and infertility rates increase. Thirty-five, then, is the cut-off for "advanced maternal age" (AMA). Women are advised to have their babies sooner.

This tidbit of information gnawed at me. At only twenty-five, I felt far from getting married. I would want a few years to play after residency, before having children. At this rate, I would just barely finish my training in time to have two children two years apart—assuming I found someone to marry. Mulling over the men in my life, I imagined them as fathers, myself as a mother. I tried to imagine what sort of relationship could last. Maybe I just needed to try harder, to think toward the future. *Yeah, right,* I thought. *I don't even know what I want to do, let alone who I want to be with.*

Talking with Dr. Hunter one afternoon about the AMA designation, I was surprised to learn that she had borne her first child at the age of forty-one.

"I thought I didn't want to have kids," she said. "And then later I changed my mind."

She shrugged. This was old news to her; her two school-aged children had both turned out beautifully. But to me, a student who had yet to separate absolute rules from relative dicta in medicine, this information about her life provided an immense sense of relief.

I learned from my patients too. Like many twenty-somethings, my only doctor visits were to gynecologists, so talking to women about their menses and birth control and breast self-exams felt quite normal to me. Perhaps because I was female, Dr. Hunter's patients often agreed to see me—meaning that they let me ask them about symptoms and do a pelvic exam and pap smear, only to have Dr. Hunter repeat the pelvic right after I did. Some of them gave me feedback, many encouragement. I was everybody's student.

There were some surprises. For example, I had never thought about taking a sexual history from a seventy-two-year-old woman. I had never thought about people having sex above a certain age. I don't know what age, exactly—it just wasn't something I had thought about. And then, once I started thinking about it, I realized I probably had quite a lot to learn.

For the most part, I related to patients easily, seeing myself in young mothers as well as college students, sexually active eighty-year-olds and middle-aged women who weren't sure what were symptoms of menopause and what might be worth reporting. I could feel the awkwardness of coming in for a gynecologic exam, as well as the relief of having otherwise taboo questions answered. At some stage, I might be any of the patients who agreed to share their stories and bodies with me. I felt grateful for their gifts of trust.

Many nights, I thought about the assortment of women I had met in clinic: shy, brazen, in house slippers, or lavishly adorned, mature, nervous, pretentious, kind. I tried to imagine their lives and constructed snapshots from what they told me. Some had had many lovers, of either sex or both; others, a lifetime of celibacy. Most seemed to have children. I invented their careers and pastimes, colored in companions and house decor on a hunch. I felt a funny kinship with these strangers, maybe stronger because we talked about concerns we had in common. I don't think I had ever talked to so many different people about being female before, never heard about relationships at so many stages or long-term birth control decisions or breast cancer risk and family planning. All of these issues were central to being female, with choices I, too, would have to make. Learning took on a personal dimension every day.

Most of the deliveries I watched were not attended by Dr. Hunter. Many obstetricians sent their patients to this hospital and rushed in for deliveries on a moment's notice. As instructed on my first day, I introduced myself to families and asked permission to be present for a birth. No one seemed to mind. By the time their doctor arrived, I was already in the room, alongside the nurse, helping with whatever small tasks would make me unobtrusive. Few doctors objected to the help.

Whenever a uterine contraction came, the energy in the delivery room built. The mounting anticipation captured my emotions and those of anyone else privy to the scene. Often, I had no sooner introduced myself than I might be positioned holding a woman's leg, echoing a mantra of encouragement and praise. I watched a pregnant belly hunker down as the enormous uterus knotted itself in effort, trying to make the impossible happen.

Our voices rose as the contractions intensified. I could watch the bedside monitor, the unmistakable up-slope signifying a muscle starting to tighten. As the line escalated, so did the chanting of mothers and labor coaches, midwives and nurses. *Okay, here we go. Breathe-two-three-four. Lift your head and push. That's it, that's it, that's IT!*

We kept up this chorus with every contraction for up to an hour before anything seemed to change. Then what had been a mere tuft of hair poking out of her vaginal opening would become, at least while she was pushing, an ovoid patch of scalp. Tightly drawn skin would shine. The contractions would come more and more often. And a labor and delivery nurse, well-trained in the timing of such things, would call the obstetrician, wheel in a tray of instruments, and lower the foot of the bed in preparation for a new arrival.

Then the real pain would start—at least for those who had opted out of an epidural (an anesthetic "block" of pain sensation for the lower half of the body). The baby's head had reached the lower part of the vagina, and getting that head to emerge was the hardest and most agonizing part. I learned to think of this as the "stretching" phase, though no textbook alludes to such a stage. The pushing was the same, but now a doctor or midwife rubbed the skin around the outlet, using two fingers to pinch and smooth the taut drum of skin the baby's crown pushed against. Over and over they massaged that edge, encouraging the stretching the mother's hormones had begun. I found it a soothing gesture, though none of the women seemed to notice. The hope was to keep her from tearing. My hope was to keep her from needing an episiotomy too, but to the OBs, such a procedure wasn't a big deal—just a little cut to keep her skin from ripping in the wrong direction.

Standing back now, gowned like the obstetrician, I watched the faces of these women. So different before this moment, they seemed to develop a surprising likeness. Between contractions they accepted praise and affection from husbands or lovers gratefully, buoyed in their exhaustion by this attention. But all of them, in the grasp of a strong contraction and the need to push, wore a far-away look of intense determination and complete oblivion to those around them. Lips pursed, face scrunched, perineum stretching slowly under immense pressure—in the process of giving birth, each one, it seemed to me, was really alone.

I harbored many expectations about what it would be like to see a baby born: magical, emotional, amazing. I hoped to be dazzled. I could hardly wait.

But watching a delivery felt nothing like I anticipated, until I got past the initial shock of it. I was impressed by the messiness: a gush of amniotic fluid, a trickle of blood, white vernix caseosa coating the baby's skin. The astounding fact that a new person had developed inside another seemed almost too bewildering to comprehend.

The baby always came faster than I expected. We could be in a delivery room for hours beforehand, and the arrival of a newborn still seemed startling at the end. Suddenly there would be a head poking out between the woman's legs, bluish and puffy from the neck upwards, like a twisted balloon with air in the end. One more push and the shoulders could get free, leading the rest of the body like an afterthought into the world.

No one spoke until the baby cried, proving it could breathe.

The nurses usually took the newborn to the corner of the room to be cleaned off, wrapped, and presented to its parents. I was torn between following the infant and tending to the mother. The obstetrician waited patiently for the placenta to separate from the uterine wall, concerned with the baby only enough to know that it was alive and well. But I could not abate my curiosity. Each time, I snuck over to the warming table to see. There he would be: a half-blind creature, more confused than I, kicking and reaching out into thin, unfamiliar air. When he opened his eyes though, I believed he could see much more than any of the rest of us would ever know. That was the moment of enchantment, for me. Those windows revealed a vital soul.

Everyone around me swooned. Fathers cried, mothers beamed in triumph, and couples whispered and gazed at one another, holding their new offspring like fragile and unbelievable gifts. Young families, surrounded by grandparents and well-wishing friends, radiated a sense of completion. As long as I stayed in the delivery room, I felt myself anointed by that warm glow. Leaving, it turned into a kind of lingering wistfulness, a longing to create and share something of my own.

When I arrived home at the end of each day, my little apartment would feel too quiet, yawning its dusty emptiness around me. The medical student life had its own contractions: pressure building before every test, anxiety at the start of each rotation. Between these bursts of focus, life barely returned to a sense of normalcy. The involuntary, increasingly forceful rise and fall of intensity had moved me along through school. But for what? So I could give birth to a career and nurture it alone?

Silent so much of the day—following doctors around, smiling mutely at patients in the background—I came home brimming with words I had swallowed and thoughts left unsaid. All around me were these incredible sights, and I wanted so badly to share my feelings at seeing a blush of color turn a newborn into a life, or watching the pain of a mother dissolve into relief at the sound of a squalling cry. Who would want to hear the ideas that crowded my head, the images of life-changing instants stacking up and sprouting into whole stories in my mind?

I tried dating. During the weeks of this rotation, a college boyfriend resurfaced, a climbing partner expressed interest, an old friend came to visit, a stranger asked me out. I still felt lonely. Next to the intense adoration I saw in delivery rooms, dating felt unsatisfyingly awkward. I could not relate to people out in the ordinary workday world, and I struggled to communicate the complexity of my life to them. We ended up talking about less challenging topics, like one of the few movies I had seen in the last three years, or a rock we aspired to climb. Empty hours could be filled with male company but remained unfulfilling. At the end of an evening, I was relieved to say goodnight and retreat home.

Lying in bed with my journal propped up and my pen looping across the page, I imagined myself pregnant. Gestating another life immersed inside me, I would talk so she would know my inflection, read out loud and whisper my hopes through my veins. I catalogued what it would take to raise her properly: the books about parenting, piles of clothes and clever toys, my mother's assistance, someone to hold her all the time and listen with enraptured attention as she tried her voice. I would want her to have all my affection, want to breastfeed her and warm her with my own body, raise her to know only love and comfort and company—not the threadbare carpet of my apartment, the heater churning grime from the basement, me trying to balance my career with this unexpected gift, and failing. Badly.

No, I did not want to be pregnant then. The loneliness that kept poking at me was not a maternal yearning, not yet. I paused. Rolling the pen in my fingers, I admired the even rows my writing had made. I could think of only one other thing I craved at this point: it was the comfort of knowing my own voice, the reassurance of putting words to how I felt.

I wrote that down.

After a few weeks of assisting with deliveries, I no longer felt so unnerved by them. As I had watched only births that went well, obstetrics did not seem difficult to me. We were accessories in a process that had historically taken place without a physician, there more to assist than to direct the show. Or so I believed.

I wanted to deliver a baby myself.

Dr. Hunter suggested I ask one of the other doctors who had a patient waiting to deliver. She doubted the likelihood of one of her families consenting to the prospect of a medical student delivery. This was a downside of training at a private hospital; whereas my colleagues at the county hospital might be delivering babies regularly, Dr. Hunter's patients had chosen her specifically. What she didn't say outright is that there is also a lot of liability involved in practicing obstetrics. Who would take a chance on a student?

Just then, Dr. Rosenstein happened past. I knew he had a patient in labor who had been progressing slowly. I jumped at the chance.

"Dr. Rosenstein?" I asked as he strode through the nursing area. "I'm a medical student working with Dr. Hunter, and I wondered if you would let me help with, or, um, do a delivery?"

He had a bald pate and a smile that reminded me a little of Jack Nicholson—not quite a leer, but not really a smile either. As I was thinking this, he squinted at me and looked away, then fired a question over his shoulder as he continued on his way. "Do you know what to do?"

I stammered. "I-I've watched a lot of deliveries."

"Have you practiced with the doll?"

I winced at his dubious tone of voice. "I don't know what doll you're talking about," I admitted.

"Well, don't bother me if you haven't prepared!" He turned to go.

Hadn't I been here for three weeks already?

"I want to learn," I spoke to his back. "I've been here every day. It isn't my fault if no one has taught me."

He halted in his march down the hall.

We regarded one another for a moment before he spoke.

"Do you know which way the baby rotates?"

I paused before I slowly shook my head "no." Though I had read about deliveries, it was hard to recall such spatial details. And in the deliveries I had watched, I had not noticed. I could not remember.

Dr. Rosenstein must have seen the dismay in my face. "Wait here," he said.

A few short minutes later, he was back with a life-sized baby doll, which he pressed against his belly feet first. He created a make-believe orifice on top of its head with his fingers. "Now," he said. "Look which way the baby turns as it is born."

He showed me a few times, then told me to put my hands out and grasp the baby the way I would in a delivery. No sooner had I placed a hand under the doll's head than he barked a loud "No!" at me.

"If you do that, you'll drop the baby! You have to put a hand up like this." He held his hand up like a gesture meaning *stop*, except his thumb pointed off to the side. "You have to *control* the baby as it's born, and to do that you have to get a secure hold like this and *don't let go*. Now, see how I can rotate my wrist as the baby turns? You keep contact the whole time. If you go the other way, you have to readjust."

He demonstrated how to support the head while maneuvering to free the shoulder from under the pelvic bone—the last step before delivery of the infant.

"Now, you try it."

I fumbled twice, grasping the neck underhanded and then reaching up with the wrong hand, but then I started to feel what he was showing me.

"Now turn ... good!" he coached. "Do it again."

Three more times and I had the hang of it. Dr. Rosenstein still did not smile, but nodded emphatically. Then he whisked away the doll and bolted for a meeting, leaving behind an unspoken promise: the next time he had a delivery, I would go with him.

I delivered eight babies in the remaining three weeks of my OB/GYN rotation, always with an attending at my side. Like the obstetricians I had watched, I stroked and thinned the skin in the stretching phase, willing it to extend and give so it would not tear. I felt the fetal crown to check head position. The first few times, when the baby came, Dr. Rosenstein guided my hands, keeping his own hovering over mine as I went through the movements he had shown me. Before I could reach for an umbilical clamp, he had one in hand and ready. So, too, the scissors to cut the cord, the towel for the baby, gauze for its mother's perineum. He helped me deliver the placenta, and to repair the lacerations caused by birth.

One afternoon I walked into a room to see a familiar face smiling at me from the delivery table: a nurse from the emergency department at San Francisco General Hospital, where I had spent a few shifts as a second-year student learning to suture. Bright-eyed and unbelievably calm, Kate had complete command of the delivery room from the moment we arrived. She positioned her husband next to her head, with firm instructions that he not watch the birth of his son (he had a history of fainting at the sight of blood). To me she granted consent to deliver her baby, knowing of course that I would be closely supervised. Meanwhile she talked and laughed with the nurse, displaying almost no discomfort with her early contractions. I was impressed.

I also found, when the time came for her to give birth, that I wasn't nervous. This was only my sixth delivery, so I was certainly no professional. But Kate trusted me, and somehow that was enough confidence for two of us.

I watched her face as she labored, serene and concentrating, youthful yet resolute. She emanated resilience. After each contraction, she locked eyes tenderly with her husband, reassuring him with her smile that all was right. Attractive before we started, she somehow looked even more beautiful as she surrendered herself to childbirth. I was surprised to find myself envious, both of her bond to her husband and her own individual strength.

While she navigated the waves of her contractions, and the attending scrutinized my work, a healthy baby boy made his way quite uneventfully into the world. "Uneventful" in this case means that nothing went wrong. In fact, a whole lot went right. Enough that—after all was done, and the husband hadn't fainted, and the baby was bundled, and Kate was cleaned up—when I went back to check on them, she greeted me with a shining smile and a generous thanks. Then she asked the question I had been mulling over after every successful delivery: "So are you thinking of being an obstetrician?"

"I don't know," I replied, adding an enthusiastic "Maybe!"

Being part of other people's gladness, delivering their love into the world with my two hands, seemed a strong salve for my loneliness. My days swelled with the rewards of caring for people I could relate to, who were not really sick, and not unhappy. Only when I left the hospital did I feel that twinge of regret, the reminder of my aloneness. If I might always be a midwife to others' devotion and not ever own it for myself, would that be enough?

I did not realize until the fourth week of my rotation that abortions (called "D&C" for dilation and curettage) were offered in the small office that served as my home base. Had I not asked, I might never have known. Only one of the doctors performed the controversial procedure, arriving before usual office hours when there were few patients or nurses who would know what was going on. When I arrived on an appointed morning to hang my bike helmet in the closet and change into my short white coat, there was only one person in the waiting room, one at the front desk.

I had expected our patient to be young and single, maybe close to my own age, probably nervous. Mrs. Emory was none of these. Our patient was an attractive white woman in her late thirties, impeccably dressed, with gold-buckled loafers and a wide wedding band. She answered questions without emotion; she never looked us in the eye. While she changed into a cloth gown, I tried to imagine what circumstances had brought her here: Did she have enough children already? Had she talked it over with her husband and decided together to let this one go? Was her career taking off, leaving no room for a baby? Or perhaps she'd had had an affair;

it was not her husband's child, and she had sneaked in to have the abortion so he would not find out. Whatever the case, she had decided early; she was just over four weeks along in her pregnancy.

The procedure was not complicated, and our patient remained stoic and uncomplaining. A medication was inserted to soften her cervix. Then, looking down a speculum at the opening to her uterus, Dr. Sanders dilated the mouth of the cervix (the "os") with metal instruments of gradually increasing diameters, a few millimeters more each time. Pain medication must have made this stretching bearable; our patient's gaze never wavered from the ceiling. When the os was dilated enough, Dr. Sanders introduced a suction curette into the uterus and gently, but thoroughly, removed the inner lining—and the early embryonic life that clung there. It took only a few minutes.

At four-to-five weeks, there is not much to see. Dr. Sanders gestured at a collection of cells the size and consistency of a blood clot and nodded that we had successfully removed the "products of conception." He placed it in a small dish and looked for proof: fimbria, tiny projections of tissue that had attached the conceptus to the uterine lining.

I don't know how Mrs. Emory felt about the abortion. She remained aloof—whether from regret or fatigue or determination, I will never know. I know I felt better having seen it done. Media hype and political controversy had led me to expect it to be so much worse than what it turned out to be: an unwanted clump of cells, removed more easily than a uterine polyp. It looked nothing like a baby.

I had been thinking about the fact that a fertilized egg—just one cell—can become a whole, living baby. That one cell becomes two, and two becomes four, and eight, and sixteen, and then somehow those microscopic packages of DNA start to differentiate into the precursors of almost-identifiable elements of the creature that might emerge nine months later. That was a true miracle, to me; something no bigger than an idea could take on a life of its own, if protected and nurtured long enough to get there.

A fetus leaches what nutrients it needs from the bones of its mother, saps iron and protein from her cells. To become a life, it pilfers small gifts from hers. A woman's body changes and expands to accommodate this growing idea. She sleeps more, or sometimes less. Her body is hijacked by this conception, and no matter how much she wanted it, she sometimes resents this coup over her previous existence. All this for the hope of what may be: a healthy, living abstraction come to life.

Many ideas never take shape at all.

In the lingering afternoon sunlight that accompanied me home each day, I felt a deep-seated sense of unrest. My belly felt queasy, my breasts heavy. My mind swam with images of the day's events: conversations with Dr. Hunter, a sixteen-year-old screaming as her body gave birth, a fifty-year-old former ballet dancer with malnutritional scoliosis. In those introspective hours, checking in with the pulse of my life, I sometimes imagined that I felt two throbbing heartbeats instead of one. A second cadence, off-beat from my own, clamored *do, do, do.* Faster than mine, almost anxious, it reminded me how quickly the moments scooted past me and were lost. In that sweet, auburn light, shadows stood in stark relief. Beauty seemed almost unbearably temporary. I hurried to write down the flutter of ideas that unsettled me, to try and pin a finger on fleeting self-discoveries. *Do, do, do,* it insisted. I loved my hours in clinic, felt pleased as I grew comfortable performing breast exams and deliveries, sharing new-found knowledge with other women. The throbbing was little more than a murmur, my own voice humming contentedly. Maybe I *was* pregnant after all, with an occupation that grew silently most of the time, but thrashed inside me when I lay down to think. *Do, do, do!* Stubborn, excited, sending me out of bed to work each morning with increasing confidence and purpose. At the end of this gestation, of course, there would be no newborn baby. The life I carried inside me was my own.

In the infertility office, the darkly paneled walls felt secretive. A desk huddled to one side unobtrusively, and an elegant couch lounged against one wall, showing scarcely any sign of use. The only hint that this was a doctor's office was the file of papers on a glass coffee table around which three comfortable chairs were arranged, and a gray-haired man jotting notes while he talked to a couple about their attempts to conceive, their desires to start a family.

I was allowed to lurk behind him. We asked each couple for permission when they came in; they did not care that I was there. They did not notice me even when they started sharing details of their sex lives: how often, what time of day, even positions they had tried. Some had kept calendars. Some had tried medicines. The doctor asked them about sexually transmitted diseases, previous pregnancies or paternity, surgeries, menstrual history. Questions that must have been hard to answer honestly in front of one's spouse. He was careful not to blame either of them for the difficulty. Their hopes blazed in the awkward silences between questions. No question would be too personal if he could make this one wish come true.

"Infertility affects about 15 percent of couples," he stated. "There is an 85 percent chance you will be able to conceive with our help."

They held hands as he talked, in anticipation of what he might say. Well-groomed, poised, and steadied by one another, they always looked picture-perfect to me. She would be wearing pearls and an elegantly tailored dress. His designer button-down would be loose at the neck, where tan skin advertised time spent in the sunnier parts of San Francisco. I imagined the waiting house, the baby room, money enough for truckloads of diapers and maybe starting a trust fund too. I suspected this was their only roadblock in a life of relative successes.

"Of the causes we can identify, about half are male-factor, and the other half have to do with either the ovulatory cycle or female anatomy. Let's start with a physical exam. Then I am going to send you home with a chart I want you to fill out until we see each other in a couple of weeks. I'll arrange for semen analysis and tell you where to go for that. And we'll send you to radiology for a few studies."

Whatever he said, they nodded. If he suggested medication, they swallowed that too. Surgery was okay. Artificial insemination. Anything.

A downside of assisted reproduction is that sometimes it works too well. One of Dr. Hunter's patients, pregnant with triplets, was restricted to hospitalized bedrest when her blood pressure skyrocketed. They kept her confined as long as they could, until steroids could be given to help the babies' lungs mature, but her hypertension proved difficult to manage, and a decision was made to deliver the babies by C-section. Excited to be present for such an unusual delivery, I took my place in the operating room alongside three sets of nurses, two obstetricians, and a pediatrician.

Initially this was no different from other C-sections I had watched: with a drape hiding the mother's head from view, and her legs covered, she became only her expectant belly, a vessel carrying precious cargo. Dr. Hunter and the other obstetrician went about their work quickly. One after another, the babies were handed over to a warmer, dried, and examined by the pediatrician. At just thirty-one weeks along, they were tiny, but vigorous. Our patient slept through the birth but awoke to find herself the mother of three incubating babies. Not exactly an ideal delivery, but she and her husband were elated. No matter how they had gotten there, they now had the family they had so desperately wanted.

The drive to procreate—not just to have sex, but to create progenitors—is about as basic a need as human animals have. We need food, and sleep, and shelter, but we also feel compelled to make our DNA survive. Some people can substitute a life's work for procreation. Most cannot.

I watched these couples struggle and realized uneasily that I might one day be there, once my career was finally established and I was in my thirties—if I had met the right person yet. But one cannot hurry some things in life; if I were not meant to have children, I reasoned, I would have to face that fact when the time came. Worry would not help. At least, for the time being and while I awaited the perfect circumstances to start a family, I could focus on other yearnings that had already taken root.

It was easy to forget that I was fortunate to have conceived of my career early. I often focused on how quickly it had swelled into a burden, but I forgot how many of my contemporaries struggled instead with that first inception and still drifted uncertainly in the working world. With only four months of clinical experience, I had already delivered babies, managed hospitalized children, counseled people, and learned more than my mind could hold. Maybe my other interests suffered as this one endeavor took precedence, and maybe I lacked a spiritual equal with whom to share my development, but I had been blessed with this one starting point. All I had to do now was keep growing.

My experience in obstetrics and gynecology was cushioned by its setting: in a private hospital with insured patients. The rotation became a meditative time for me, weeks of relating to educated patients who could afford to provide what their children would need. In this idyllic environment, we did not see many complications. Mothers-to-be attended their prenatal appointments, did not take drugs, and had supportive partners or spouses to help them through rough times. Occasionally a vaginal birth was converted suddenly to a C-section, but this happened smoothly, and both moms and babies turned out okay. It was easy to believe this was always the case; I never saw otherwise.

Not until more than a year later did I see what could happen when women are ambivalent about the lives they carry in their wombs—and about their own. Shrunken infants born addicted to crack, misshapen faces from poisoning by alcohol, and premature babies delivered someplace unsavory all made their ways to the county hospital. Their mothers were always blamed. No one asked who had fathered these children. No one asked if the baby had been forced upon her. I now know from statistics that some of the women I saw in our hospital, whom I envied for having doting and ever-present lovers at their bedsides, must have been abused women too. I never recognized it then. But there was a lot I didn't know.

After my OB/GYN clerkship I began to take "women's issues" personally again. Watching the feat of childbirth, it was easy to develop immense respect for the capability of a woman's body, just as it was inevitable, witnessing others' praise and adoration, to feel these sentiments myself. The more kinship I felt with my patients, the more I felt it my duty to protect them—looking for signs of mistreatment, checking for symptoms of eating disorders, screening for depression. I imagined a vulnerability much greater than I observed.

In the month and a half that I emulated an obstetrician/ gynecologist, women's bodies had transformed. Whereas I had started out vaguely embarrassed by brazen nudity, that shame had been eclipsed by awareness of how lovely, fragile, and powerful we inherently are. I had watched in amazement as the purpose of childbearing took over and then eventually released a body from its temporary captivity. Uncomfortable as it obviously was to be nine months pregnant, or laboring to bring new life into the world, the pain was transient. For better or worse, women's lives were defined by the propensity to conceive, nurture, grow, give birth—and then do it, a little differently, over again.

Perhaps that is why my favorite part of this rotation was rounding on women in the post-partum unit. The morning after giving birth, even after staying up late with a new baby, the women exuded such enviable bliss. There was no recollection in their faces of the travails of the day before. Not even a shadow of memory cast doubts on their pleasure.

I have heard that adrenaline blocks the mind from knowing how deeply the body has suffered in childbirth. This adaptive phenomenon makes sense. Bringing life into the world should seem worthwhile. Labor is universally remembered as "painful," but the word is said in the bland tones of common knowledge, not the anguish of personal agony. Encircled by family, new mothers seem never to have labored alone.

So, too, I had heard doctors speak of medical school as a far-off thing, a faint recollection of an awkward time, best forgotten alongside puberty and first dates. What part of us is trained in forgetting? Would I one day neglect to recall stretching myself around this profession, and the solitude of these days?

How do I love? Arms wide open, heart exposed, with the excitement of winter air tingling on skin and the desperation of knowing my time is limited. The minutes march away the day; for hours I am confined indoors not learning and not living, and I keep this love in a box in my chest for just those moments that I get out of the hospital and am free! Until then I am to work on my armor, compartmentalizing: Here are the patients. Here the other doctors. Locked away here are the people I love, and I have to keep them away from my hospital life—lest the air here make them vulnerable to the same almost-losses that are breaking me apart.

(FALL OF THIRD YEAR)

Chapter Seven

WINTER'S PROMISE
THIRD-YEAR ADULT MEDICINE ROTATION

Back in my second year of medical school, just as February had arrived with a flurry of storms, I could have died. I woke up with a belly full of pain unlike anything I had felt before. I tried to study—this being a Saturday before a week of four midterm examinations—but the ache gradually came into focus. Sharper, insistent, it grabbed a corner of my abdomen and pulled until I rolled to my side, possum-like, and gave the pain my full attention. It didn't go away.

I picked up my notes again. Twenty-four years old, always healthy, I trusted that nothing too unusual could be going on. But after six or seven hours of agony, I gave in and let my roommate drive me to the emergency room.

There I waited with half-a-dozen unconcerned-looking people, all watching television. I leaned sideways against Nicole while she studied for our pharmacology exam, quizzing me on anti-hypertension drugs that all sounded the same: propanolol, metoprolol, labetolol. What were these other people doing here? No one else looked like their insides contained a sharp instrument skewering them to one side.

Finally, a door opened.

"Ooo-niece?" A nurse in a pastel-patterned scrub top mispronounced my name.

I nodded gladly and rose to my feet, steadying myself against the pang that resulted. I passed grimly into a scrubbed hallway and was motioned toward a gurney to lie on.

"Doctor will be with you shortly."

Though it hurt to move, and I was starting to believe something was truly wrong, I played the role of a "good patient." I waited quietly. I smiled at people. Wanting to befriend the doctors—with whom I felt a kinship I could not yet substantiate—I minimized my concerns when they finally interviewed me.

"I just can't sit up," I said sweetly.

After a brief exam, including a pelvic by a resident who was not a gynecologist, and a negative pregnancy test, I was sent home with pain pills and reassurance, and—when I insisted, realizing late that my brave act had worked too well—the promise of an ultrasound exam to be performed the next morning. I took some of the medicine and slept through the night.

I awoke with the same, stabbing side ache on Sunday morning and hauled myself into my roommate's car for the short drive to the hospital. As promised, a radiologist materialized at 9 a.m. Soon he had me propped on the ultrasound exam table, with warm gel smeared across my belly.

"Looks like a dermoid," he remarked, squinting at the screen.

We had just studied ovarian tumors, including dermoid cysts, the previous week in pathology class. When we saw a dermoid in a glass jar in lab, I had commented to a friend that they were about the grossest thing I could imagine finding out I had inside of me. Filled with various kinds of tissue, sometimes even hair and teeth, they caused pain by either leaking irritating fluid or twisting the ovary and cutting off its blood supply. Mine was most likely doing the latter.

"It's about eight centimeters by nine," he announced. The size of a grapefruit.

To be seen again in the ER, I would have to sit in the waiting room again (having been there two-and-a-half, painful, hunched-over hours the first time).

"What are the chances they will do anything about it today?" I asked.

The radiologist called someone who said it could wait until Monday. Home I went.

Bed-bound, sleepy from codeine, and unable to think clearly, I emailed my instructors to tell them I would be unable to take my Monday exam. Then I crawled back under the covers and dozed. When I awoke the next morning in the same position, still held captive by an invisible knife in my side, I accepted that there would be only one way to get rid of the pain: someone would have to remove the cyst.

I called a gynecologist's office on the recommendation of a friend of a friend and secured an appointment for later that afternoon. Then I decided to shower. Standing took effort; reaching up to wash my hair caused the hurt to radiate outward and grow fangs. Instead, I tucked my head down toward my chest, letting the water cloak my shoulders and glide in rivulets over the unmarred skin on my abdomen. Suddenly a wail rose up from somewhere within me. I had been able-bodied and healthy. All at once I was plunging from being fit enough to show off my stomach to ashamed, falling from the ease of youth into the world of age and illness. I had thought myself impenetrable to such catastrophe. But the surgeon would cut out of me the self-image of strength I had held too dear, and my skin would bear the proof. Soon it would be interrupted—forever—by an angry scar. I would never see myself whole again.

The gynecologist was furious.

"This should have been taken care of immediately," he said. "You could have gone into shock!"

Shock describes collapse of the body's ability to circulate blood; had the cyst ruptured, I could have bled into my abdomen and, if I didn't make it back to the hospital, might have died.

A large, gruff-looking man with thinning dark hair slicked straight back, Dr. Collins spoke in a booming, authoritative voice. "Now, when was your last meal? You're going to surgery."

He explained laparoscopy to me, saying they would be able to look around inside me with a camera and possibly remove the cyst that way—using only three tiny portholes in my skin. If not, they would have to make an incision over my lower abdomen to take it out.

I stammered when I asked him about the ovary itself. "Can it be saved?" I wanted to know, thinking about the fact that the normal one hadn't shown up well on the ultrasound. The surgery might inadvertently leave me with none.

"There's no guarantee," Dr. Collins replied. "We'll do our best, but we don't know how much ovary is there."

I had been distraught about seeing myself disfigured by surgery; now, still curled on my side from the belly pain, the anticipated scar seemed to tear across my whole future—and any dream of having children. I sobbed uncontrollably, not caring to be brave any longer, not wanting to relinquish my fertility along with my self-concept of being strong and physically whole. There were no words for my profound sense of despair—only tears.

It took three people to calm me down: Dr. Collins, the chief resident, and my roommate. When I could listen, the doctors explained that I would certainly have at least one ovary left, and it would be enough to have children. "We are going to do everything we can to save the ovary," Dr. Collins proclaimed.

"You're going to do very well," the chief resident added. "We'll take good care of you."

"It's going to be okay," my roommate soothed, brushing my hair from my forehead.

I felt like a child, but I clung to her. My identity as a young woman who had expected, without thinking about it, to be a mother someday was suddenly in question. Only the pain in my side remained consistent and sure. Numbly, I signed the consent forms.

All I remember from my day and a half in the hospital was how grateful I felt to have my mother there with me—she arrived in my last minute of consciousness before the surgery—and to look around and see friends' smiles of encouragement after the surgery. The other memories are there too: searing pain, being ignored by nurses when I needed one of my medicines, the noisiness of a hospital at night, being awakened to have blood drawn, trying to sit up with my abdomen stitched together. And then my father, arriving by taxi and distraught to see me, the patient, standing up clinging to an IV pole for support.

"This will make you a better doctor," promised the chief resident, an attractive, cool-headed, and sincere woman who had won my immediate trust.

I nodded and smiled weakly. Anything beyond getting home from the hospital seemed far away.

That weekend my parents took care of me, while my friends went on the skiing trip I had organized for all of us. It would be weeks before I could think of skiing, too late for this season at all. Instead, I watched the winter Olympics on television while my mother coaxed me through eating soup and taking pain pills, and I waited for my bowels to start functioning again. Beneath the bandage, my wound puckered and started to seal over, granulating into a fuchsia scar that I would someday learn to accept.

All my life, I had thought of illness as something that happened to someone *else*. The truth hit hard but squarely: I was no more exempt from being a patient than I was immortal.

Winter has always been a confining season in the city. Darkness stains the late afternoon, blotting out any chance of a run in the park, or even a sunset bike ride, after the workday is done. But there is hope in the worst of weather. After a storm, we know the mountains will glitter with fresh snow. If time can be cornered for a three-hour drive to the Lake Tahoe area, the chance to ski will combat the winter doldrums with a special kind of treat, the kind that tastes like fresh air and free time and escape. Even with the drive home to contend with, and all the other weekenders who appreciate a day of high-altitude capering on skis and snowboards, the literal and physical high of a wearying day on the slopes offers enough reward.

Still smarting from the lost ski season the previous year, I started winter of my third year in medical school with frozen air on my cheeks and skis on my feet as often as possible. Immersed in the cold tingle of that mountain air, launched by adrenaline into swooping down as many runs as I could fit into a day, I felt myself recharged and ready for one of the most challenging rotations: adult medicine.

January and February are the busiest months in hospitals. Spending the heart of winter as a student of internal medicine, I met some of the sickest people I had ever laid eyes on. This rotation's coincidence with the shortest days of the year seemed fortuitous: I hungered less for release from the hospital. Little distracted me from my medical life, and I fell into this world much the same way I had started as a ski instructor in Mammoth a few years before: I pasted on a nametag and an enthusiastic smile, and I copied the behavior of people around me. The one notable difference was that I remembered being a patient myself. And this time, people were dying.

My first patient was a frail but good-humored woman in her late fifties who had recently undergone surgery for esophageal cancer. When I helped admit her to the hospital, Laura Belham complained that she'd had a cough for some time, and it didn't seem to be getting better. Many of my patients that wet, dark January had come in with pneumonia, and I assumed she suffered the same. Though Laura was thin with sallow eyes, looked twenty years older than her age, and took shallow, quick breaths, her mirthful, quick wit distracted me from her ill appearance. It didn't occur to me that she might die the following night.

Her chest X-ray suggested otherwise: the cancer had spread.

Two sisters, a cousin, and a neighbor gathered at Laura's bedside when her condition started to worsen. She tired quickly and needed an oxygen mask almost right away. The sisters—one short and hunched over, the other taller and shy—begged my attention in the hall. Their eyes were already red-rimmed. They saw what I had not yet accepted.

"We're not quite sure what to do. Should we stay with her tonight?" The shorter sister asked as soon as introductions were made.

I sighed, wishing I knew what to say. I reminded them that I was a student and would have to ask the other physicians what they thought. All of us knew the real question: *Is she going to die tonight?*

"I do need to talk to you about decision-making for Laura," I said.

Our discussion—about whether she would want mechanical ventilation to help her breathe, and what we should do if her heart stopped—was easier than I anticipated. My patient, mercifully, had been clear with her family that she would want no drastic measures taken in these circumstances. Her primary doctor had instructed them in preparing papers that conferred on one of the sisters full decision-making power, and when I asked, the scoliotic woman produced these for me to see.

"Is she in pain?" the softer-spoken sister asked.

"We are giving her a little bit of morphine," I explained, "because it helps her breathe without tiring. I can ask whether she needs more than she is getting, but I think she is pretty comfortable."

I went in to see Ms. Belham and the sisters flanked me, watching as I tried to wake her (unsuccessfully), listened to her lungs, patted her hand. None of what I was doing mattered, I knew. But I suspected it would be a consolation to the two women who hovered behind me, watching their sister tenuously connected to this life by an oxygen mask and an IV.

I could not go home that evening, not at five, or six-thirty, or seven-thirty. Passing her room, I saw the gathering grow: another good friend arrived, another cousin. They spoke in murmurs at the entryway. My patient slept on.

The attending physician—who supervised our team of residents and interns and students—documented a plan in her chart: steady IV morphine to keep her from feeling the strain of breathing, but not enough to slow her respirations drastically. No resuscitation was to be tried, except medicines to keep her blood pressure high enough. As the doctor signed the orders, we heard a cry from our patient's room.

"Laura!" her sister exclaimed. "You're awake."

It was true. Laura looked around at everyone gathered there and pulled the mask off her face.

"You all look like you expected me to die or something," she chuckled.

When I finally went home around eight o'clock, there was still an animated buzz surrounding my patient. Someone had brought pictures to pass around. Laura was telling jokes, and her loved ones were laughing before the punch-lines.

"It's not uncommon for that to happen," one of the doctors explained to me later. "Often patients have a brief period of lucidity before they die."

I stood outside my patient's empty room early the next morning and wondered how this could be true. What signals that the time has come? Is there no promise in exuberance, in laughter?

I could be dying too.

On an evening that smelled like snow, when an icy rain kept most people from driving to the hospital, John Turner stumbled into the ER. Thirty-three years old, homeless, alcoholic, he wore filthy clothes that stank of urine, sweat, and other bodily fluids. Evidently intoxicated, he seemed to be complaining that he had vomited blood. He also had a cough—pneumonia, we later found out. Lice leaped from his stringy hair. Aided by drugs prescribed for "the shakes" from alcohol withdrawal, he soon became stuporous.

"We see a lot of patients like this at the county hospital," my resident said. "He would be a good one for you."

A skinny intellectual with Ronald McDonald hair and thick glasses, Tim wasn't much impressed that this patient would turn out to be "interesting"—meaning complicated. But he was right that I should learn to treat alcohol withdrawal sooner rather than later. Here at Moffitt/Long Hospital, the academic center of UCSF, we rarely treated the uninsured patients who populated San Francisco General Hospital. Based on the aroma coming from John Turner's room, I didn't think that was such a bad thing.

I gulped and then shrugged.

"Sure," I said. "I'll go talk to him."

Neither that night nor during the month that I would care for him could Mr. Turner ever give a clear story of why he had come to the hospital, though I did manage to find out how much he usually drank, that he smoked a pack a day, and that he slept in the park rather than in a shelter. When asked a complicated question, however—like, "What made you decide to come to the hospital?"— he would drift off.

"Patients like this just sleep for a few days on benzos [sedatives given to treat alcohol withdrawal], get their antibiotics, and walk out of here," Tim promised when I expressed concern about not being able to talk to my patient. "This is classic."

He seemed right, at first. And then, suddenly, John became the sickest patient on our service and was shuttled to the Intensive Care Unit (ICU) overnight, unable to breathe well without the help of a machine.

And that was only the beginning. In the weeks to follow, he turned yellow from liver failure; his kidneys stopped working; he had a high fever that failed to get better with antibiotics; he developed a rash; his lungs stayed congested and he had them biopsied; and two CT scans each of his head, chest, and abdomen failed to show anything definitive. Different teams of specialists were asked to evaluate him: infectious disease, renal, pulmonary, interventional radiology. More blood tests were sent. His liver was biopsied. No one could explain what was wrong with him. Bloated, jaundiced, with lines in his veins and arteries, Mr. Turner slept through almost all of it.

Concerned but helpless to do anything for him medically, I spent my time coordinating his multiple tests and the opinions of different doctors about his condition. Third-year students didn't usually follow patients in the ICU, but I had assured Tim that I wanted to try. After all, I knew my patient's history better than anyone else, and when the month rolled from January into February, and all the other members of the team had switched places with new interns, a resident, and an attending, I was well-positioned to ensure John Turner's well-being. And I made myself useful: I looked up rare diseases that he might have (for a while, I was mistakenly convinced that he had an infection called trench fever, passed by a tick bite and exceedingly rare in San Francisco). I called the county hospital for his records, which didn't show much. Finally, in hopes of learning more about him, but also searching for someone to consent to the multiple medical procedures that had been proposed to find a diagnosis for him, I called his mother in Florida.

She cried on the phone.

"He's a good boy," she said. "But he has a problem with alcohol. Neither my husband nor I could stop him from getting on a bus to go out there to California, but I couldn't help thinking we might never see him again. He usually calls us about every week or so. I think he's always been pretty healthy, but he's a grown boy, so he doesn't involve us in his affairs. You know, his birthday is in a few days. ..."

I didn't halt her meandering story at first, but gradually I nudged her to answer some questions. Did he have any friends out here she knew of, or other family? Did she know if he had ever been HIV tested? Did she know if he ever used drugs other than alcohol? Had he been sick recently, or complained about anything to her?

"Let me put my husband on. He knows more of this medical stuff than I do."

John's stepfather, a retired paramedic and very Christian man, instructed me to tell it to him straight: just how sick was his stepson?

"Well, sir," I stammered. "I'm the medical student taking care of him, and you'll probably want to speak to one of the attending physicians about how they think he'll do. I can tell you what we know right now."

"Yes, please."

"John is in the Intensive Care Unit," I began. "There is a tube helping him breathe, and he appears to be fairly ill. We know he has pneumonia, but he's had fevers for about a week, even with antibiotics. We haven't been able to locate another source of infection. There are a few tests the doctors would like to do, if you and his mother consent—"

"Is he going to live?" The man asked solemnly. His words buzzed and echoed in my head. I could sense the tension with which he gripped the phone, pictured my patient's mother sitting nervously, watching his face for a reaction to my answer. Who was I to make a prediction like that?

"I think there's a good chance he will. He's young—he has that going for him. And we're certainly doing all we can for him. But we don't know what's wrong yet."

He sighed. "Well, his mother and I sure are glad he is in such capable hands. Any tests you all need to do are fine with us."

Every morning, I poured over the panoply of lab tests, my patient's temperature and heart rate, the nurse's notes. I went into Mr. Turner's room and examined him by rote: eyes, mouth, heart, lungs, abdomen, skin, reflexes. Each time, I spoke to the unmoving form that was my patient, unsure whether he could hear me at all but certain it couldn't hurt to be talked to. He had been thick-bodied and muscled when he first came to the hospital. A month later, his cheeks hung sallow and he had lost his paunch. His skin changed from pale and flea-bitten, to yellow, to speckled with rash. The smell that had first repelled me was long-extinguished by baths and talcum powder, and while he slept, I could imagine he had a sweet, gentle nature. I liked the person I imagined he was.

"Hang in there, Mr. Turner," I encouraged. I squeezed his arm, patted his shoulder. Sometimes he opened his eyes. But as the weeks passed, he just didn't seem to get better.

Time after time, I called to get his parents' consent for different tests, each time representing a powerful group of physicians whose expertise was widely known and respected. But his mother was more interested in knowing I had personally read her letter—full of faith in God and prayer for his well-being—to him.

"I'm just so glad you are taking care of him," she said to me. "Thank you for understanding how hard this is."

Meanwhile, my patient was approaching his nadir, and after a seventh or eighth failed diagnostic test, it occurred to me that he might die after all. Nevertheless, the doctors wanted to try more invasive procedures on him, particularly something called ERCP, or endoscopic retrograde cholangiopancreatography, which involved passing a small camera down his throat, through his stomach, and to the opening of the bile duct in the small intestine. The ERCP was unlikely to reveal the cause of his illness, and I knew it could cause him to become much sicker—but I felt painfully powerless to stand up for my patient. I knew his parents would say it was okay, blindly trusting "us." But it seemed to me that Mr. Turner was almost no longer a person to these seasoned physicians. He had become "an interesting case," and the pursuit of a diagnosis was hurtling full speed ahead.

"He'll probably die anyway," a trainee on one of the specialist teams said casually. "We might as well try to find out what's wrong."

I walked grimly to the women's restroom, where I locked myself in a bathroom stall and screamed.

All the caring, the long conversations with his mother, the attention to detail in trying to figure out what his lab results meant and predict what might help, the blind faith I had that talking to him would make a difference were for nothing: after all this, he was going to die. Sobbing, I kicked the door a few times. Worse yet, it might be at the hands of a team of physicians whom I had proudly represented when I spoke to his parents, and whom I now suddenly despised. I had thought the doctors could fix him. I had believed they would find the answers.

Disillusionment soured in my throat. I wanted to be his doctor. I wanted the power to heal him. And it hadn't occurred to me, until this terrible moment, that one doesn't always make the other come true.

One of my favorite attending physicians from that clerkship worked primarily in the ICU with critically ill patients. The ICU is a depressing place: patients are mostly unable to communicate; they struggle against pain, injury, and infection with all their measly might. Immobile bodies with multiple lines in their veins, arteries, urethras, stomachs, and lungs lie beneath fluorescent lights under a barrage of medical equipment. Alarms sound every few minutes. Many patients never make it back out, despite the multiple interventions to keep them alive.

I can scarcely imagine a more precarious existence. In hospitals, we can often prolong dying for weeks and even months, but when the moment comes, even the expected happens too fast. Fate churns forward with ruthless determination, leaving a semicircle of physicians watching in helpless fascination. At first, she feigns nonchalance, spurring doctors to do all they can for someone who may or may not survive. But on that very cusp of mortality, fate takes such resolution from our hands. We cannot pretend to wield control over such otherworldly decisions.

Americans rarely welcome death. Doctors are charged with preserving life at all costs—even exorbitant costs—and every loss is a failure. We are to value each life equally and fully, and the marker of such behavior is doing all we can to postpone expiration. Sometimes it makes sense. With others it is a futile exercise—but we try anyway. Dragging with us the weight of people we have lost, or those who survive in a state closer to death than life, it would be easy to lose heart. But my attending, surrounded by the mystery and liminality of the ICU, loved his job. Every day he weighed the value of life against disability, the chance of recovery against the possibility of failure. Sometimes, rather than prolong the torment of mechanical life support in the face of miniscule chance of recovery, in an act of greater kindness than intervention would be, he consented to let patients go. But he never took the decision lightly, contemplating the available options with a furrowed brow, talking to families, conferring with colleagues.

"I still cry every time we lose a patient," my attending confessed to me.

In that instant, he rekindled my affection for medicine. It was possible to keep caring, keep feeling love—and confront mortality every single day. All that remained was to figure out how.

One morning as my team rounded in the ICU, we heard singing. Solemn, calming voices chanted and soared in a language we could not understand.

"They're withdrawing support from Mr. Dorjay," my classmate said, by way of explanation. He meant that a decision had been made to stop trying to keep the patient alive with machines and medicines that had to be adjusted several times an hour. Mr. Dorjay was dying.

In the small, glass-walled room, the lights were off. Around the bed were gathered robed Buddhist monks and the patient's family, all of them with their eyes closed, singing an ethereal incantation to the shrunken Nepali man before them. We tiptoed away, not having distracted from the lovely ceremony taking place, and not wanting to.

The prayer songs continued until dark. No one disturbed those assembled around Mr. Dorjay. Patients were ushered in and out of the ICU that day, each with an individual entourage of attendants and bleeping boxes. But the room in the corner was sealed off by the cadence of human voices, coaxing and soothing the passage of a man's soul away from this life.

Secretly, I think we all welcomed the invocation. All day the hymns rose and fell like hard moments and joyful ones—at times low and mournful, others elated. A lifetime was summed up with devotion and breath, uninterrupted until the sun sank in a winter sky over the Pacific Ocean. So ended an odyssey rich with the textures of survival, triumph, and sorrow. Underlying was always a familiar refrain, the undulating current of human spirit that carries one through days that feel too burdensome to bear, and finally on, over the seas to the next resting place, wherever that may be.

I found myself calmed by the softness of such an approach to death. There were no tears or protests, no last-minute heroics against the inevitable loss of someone beloved. Just a circle of affection and a day of song.

Loss changes everyone. Some part of us that sailed on the breath of another person falls heavily to the earth, where its weight is nourished by groundwater and sadness. At first it roots us in place; eventually, we step gingerly over it, nudging the old feelings to the side a little bit with a toe, smoothing the edges, letting them gradually seep back into the soil. The pain trickles away. We take a few more steps, testing our own vulnerability. We leave. Even coming back to that same spot, we eventually cannot remember how very much the loss hurt at first, if grieving has worked its magic.

But sometimes this process takes years.

And sometimes, when one loss follows another, and another, we stop letting parts of ourselves out to balance precariously on the lifeline of another person. Then there is no falling down, no heaviness, no grieving. There is also no flight.

What I learned, during my two-month internal medicine rotation, is that many kinds of loss exist. Only a few of my patients died. Most of them lived. But they did not march out of the hospital and go skiing for the weekend, like I did after my clerkship was over. Some went home in wheelchairs. Some didn't go home—they needed nursing care, or long hospitalizations. The broad landscape of living under a changing sky and feeling seasons groan or flutter or glide past was taken away, maybe for weeks, maybe more.

There are gradations of death. One might be plucked from life and die quickly; or wilt gradually over years; or be forced to change shape and live another, totally modified and maybe even unpleasant kind of existence.

On my medicine rotation, I was surrounded by people in limbo, healing or dying, loving, crying, hoping. I tried to offer them my best self, the one shining with compassion, woven in and through with a medical student's attention to detail. Often, I could do little more than listen and care. I squeezed a hand, smiled, and turned away in the end. Their pain was not mine, and I had other peoples' pain to tend to.

I am dying too.

I suspected this in the way medical students were expected to: I became too aware of my body's fragility. I poked fingers into my flesh until it hurt and rubbed the skin raw with my worry.

But there! See, I am losing myself.

If I play back the images, I can see my smile growing thin and hard, lips pursed against the ache of another soul weeping. I was a student. I could do nothing concrete to help. Many patients knew this, and they took what love I could lend them, for whatever time I could offer. My job was to empathize without crumbling, to mourn without neglecting those left behind.

I am a student, learning how not to care too much.

Two of the best physicians I know are neurologists. Theirs is an admirably pliable concept of what it means to live and thrive. Their acceptance of sudden mental or physical deficits—like my grandfather's loss of speech and right-sided paralysis after his stroke—is strangely, warmly encouraging to the patients they care for. These doctors are comfortable thinking about life for someone who is paralyzed or silenced, and they adjust to a patient's new self with ease, inviting that patient and his or her family to follow suit. These neurologists grasp in a moment what it takes us mortals weeks to learn and accept. Perhaps this is a function of the relative irreversibility of most neurologic injuries: there is no room for denial. The best thing to do is revise our conception of the world around us.

I think these doctors know something greater, something most people learn only if they have to: the soul keeps living. The soul keeps reaching out as the body dies.

In my first year of medical school, I received word that my uncle had been in a skiing accident in Mammoth, and after having been helicoptered to Reno, Nevada, he was conscious, in an ICU, and unable to move his legs or arms. As it turned out, he had a permanent spinal cord injury, and he was told that it was highly unlikely he would walk again. The news was devastating.

After that, life had an entirely changed construct. Physical therapy, mostly performed in his own house—without the supervision of a therapist (because insurance would not cover prolonged rehabilitation)—was one of his most important pastimes. His wife cared for him in more basic ways than he ever would have expected to need. Previously a high-functioning, very independent engineer, he saw that the road before him would be littered by multiple episodes of frustration and searing disappointment. Nevertheless, he learned to use his hands and arms enough to feed himself. He could embrace his family, work the television, and hoist himself up to standing. He walked again, with a walker, and used the phone. All of that superseded what he was once told he would be able to do.

But something else changed after his injury.

Though he was my godfather, my uncle had not been easy for me to get to know before his accident. He was good-humored but distant, with a tough exterior that didn't lend itself to close conversation. We chatted about what I was doing in school, and he would say he had a lot of work, but that was all. Self-sufficiency was an unspoken assumption for his children, himself, and me.

But he could not be independent now. With that unhinging of a core expectation, and a deep wound to his pride, came a torrent of emotion unlike anything we had ever seen from him. Suddenly he was able to express his sadness. He talked about the small triumphs that, with great determination, he eked out over time. And he listened, more than I remember he ever had before. His new desire to communicate was an unexpected blessing from an otherwise tragic, life-bending event.

I couldn't help but think about my uncle when I went back to Mammoth on vacation after my medicine rotation concluded. I knew he had fallen near the top of the mountain, on a run called Cornice, and when I wandered the mountain on my skis, delighted by the crispness of the snow beneath my feet, worried by winds that gusted at the chairlifts, I avoided that area.

Cornice was the first black diamond I ever skied. At nine, I had been a fearless skier, eager to try an advanced run. Back then, snowcats couldn't make it up the steep top of the mountain, and a lip of snow formed and curled like a frozen wave at the entry to the run. An instructor had led the way in and then stopped to wait for me, ever ready to grab on to my slippery ski bib if I fell. When I made it down safely, he told my parents to buy me the tight-fitting stretch pants that were in vogue for skiing back then—he said if I took a tumble in my slick snow pants, I wouldn't be able to stop. And Cornice is a long run. At that moment, I graduated from being just another kid skier to being "advanced." I begged to ski Cornice every time we went skiing. And for the most part, I did.

But this time I went a different way instead, satisfying myself with the similarly exhilarating blast of snow crystals that sprayed my face as I slid over the edge into other ski runs. Now that Cornice was mowed over by snowcats on a regular basis, the routes I chose—Dave's Run, Climax, Scotty's—posed a bigger challenge than the relatively benign, but slightly icy, slant of my first favorite. Still, every time I went to make that initial turn, I felt my heart grabbing for the snow edge I left behind. The first turn is always the hardest. When I summoned enough courage to inch forward, reminding myself to lean-forward-boots-against-shins-don't-hold-back-be-confident!-hands-downhill-rise-up-slide-forward-swoop!-right-ski-balance-go!, I felt my body respond by rote, schooled in the motion of turning skis for more than twenty years already. But still, there was the magnetic pull of gravity, over a thousand feet of hill, and just my two legs locked into skis to fight falling. How does anyone survive?

As the week passed, I gained back my confidence. The whole ordeal—lift passes, goggles just in case, mittens and sunscreen and thin socks and how to cinch my boots just right—became as routine as it had been when I lived in Mammoth and taught others how to ski.

"It's 90 percent mental," I had told my pupils enthusiastically, as though the number had been scientifically determined and proven beyond doubt. "If you're confident on your skis, and you stay on top of them, they'll go where you want them to go."

It all seemed so easy back then.

When I finally skied Cornice, near the end of the week, I didn't enjoy it. The slope had been scraped over, leaving a slick sheen of snow too hard to sink into. I remembered my mother saying it had been icy when my uncle fell backward and blacked out. I conscientiously positioned myself on near-tiptoe in my boots. When fear pulled me back, I cursed and stopped. And started over. With each rise-step-swoop, I angled uphill enough to control my speed before the next turn. I imagined going from the tingling cold and breathless adventure of dancing with gravity to chilling paralysis. One minute feeling my thighs burning and pushing myself to focus and be smooth, graceful. The next knowing my body only as an uncooperative appendage that ached like something remembered— and gone. With each loop of my ribbon track down Cornice, I wondered: *Will it be this turn? The next one? The next?* Surely I could not be so lucky as to keep feeling the thrill of danger, and never fall. *It will be one day when I least expect it. An accident might happen any time.* But I could not give it up. I went back up Chair 23 for another run.

I sometimes wonder how I would adapt if I were paralyzed. A girl whose early life was filled with sports and running around outside, I have grown into a woman who cannot sit still for more than a few hours, who prizes her time outdoors, who grows sullen if an injury hinders her for even a full week. Could I find the mental courage to keep living if physical activity were taken away from me? Would I be doing it because I wanted to, or for the sake of other people? What would I cling to as my new source of joy?

Life demands that we re-create ourselves from time to time. I became a medical student, a swing dancer, and a biker/climber with a lengthening list of orthopedic injuries. I used to be a ski bum. Before that I was a feminist activist on an Ivy League campus. Before that I was a weight-lifting, sun-tanned Southern California girl—after I was a tomboy, a self-professed poet, and a six-year-old avocado-selling entrepreneur.

But we don't choose everything that happens to us; the most life-changing events seem to be those that happen while we are looking somewhere else.

Every minute, every hour, cells in our bodies are dividing. The lifespan of these microscopic packages of our heritage varies—skin and hair cells die and are replaced constantly. Blood cells last four months. Neurons may never regenerate if they are destroyed. But while we go about our days, cursing at the news or laughing with friends, falling in love, walking familiar streets in a foul or numb or ecstatic mood, this intricate process might easily slip. Not to worry—our DNA has built-in plans to destroy cells that misbehave. On the other hand, if the error involves a fault in the self-destruct mission, or sneaks by unnoticed, a renegade cell might divide more rapidly than is its due. It might not stop dividing. It might take over whatever space around itself it can fill, chew into other structures, and ever-so-insidiously, before anyone can guess what it has done, plant its missives throughout the body. Not all cancers do this. But many do.

I was lucky, during my third-year internal medicine clerkship, to spend an afternoon at my attending physician's oncology practice. I was not naturally drawn to the study of cancers, which involves intricate recollection of that ill-fated cell biology course from first year, but when he suggested I might like to see the office and observe him with patients, I accepted readily. It was rare that we saw attendings in their full dealings with patients, and role models like Dr. Clark were precious.

Some cancers are treatable, he reminded me as we walked over. The armamentarium against these Napoleonic cells continues to expand, and my attending was skilled at keeping well-informed about what was available: chemotherapies, surgery, radiation, combinations. Much of what he did in his office was talk to patients, address concerns about their options, and listen. There was never a one-size-fits-all approach. Together they would decide on the best course of action.

"It's really about the relationship," he said.

One of his patients was a woman in her late thirties who had been through a long list of chemotherapy trials. Pulling out an article on the treatment of breast cancer, Dr. Clark showed me each of the agents that had been tried. Each time, Bonnie had relapsed just as another drug arrived on the scene, and each time it had seemed that perhaps the cure had been found. She had been his patient for about six years already. This time an MRI had revealed bad news: a new metastasis (a relocated clump of cancer cells) had appeared in her brain.

When we entered the exam room, Dr. Clark introduced me to Bonnie and her husband, Chris. At first the appointment seemed quite normal; he asked Bonnie whether she had experienced any unusual symptoms, how her appetite had been, how she was sleeping. He asked about her most beloved pastime: photography. He asked both of them about the clarity of her thinking. Casually, he performed a physical exam while talking to her, and secured

Bonnie's permission for me to examine her as well. There was nothing unusual save for the dual mastectomy scars on her chest. She was thin and athletically fit.

All the while, Bonnie seemed slightly nervous, looking frequently at her husband while Dr. Clark talked with them. There was one more drug they could try, but the doctor was skeptical that it would have any lasting effect. Dr. Clark was unapologetically honest with them, and I didn't know, at first, whether to cringe or be relieved. Had he left the room immediately afterward, I have no doubt that he would have been perceived as callous. But because he stayed, leaning against the table near Bonnie, looking both Bonnie and Chris in the eyes, waiting for his words to seep through the veneer of fear and worry, I had no doubt he cared about them. To him had fallen the unsatisfying task of being honest about Bonnie's prognosis. From him had to come the words they feared most, the sentence: *It's probably time to think about how you want to die.*

When they left his office, Chris asked Dr. Clark, "Saturday afternoon?"

"See you then."

I looked at my attending quizzically. He waited for them to leave before explaining, "We go golfing when I can get away. It's the only time Chris ever cries. Usually around the tenth hole, he starts to cry, and we talk about what it is going to be like to lose her."

I could have dissolved into tears, right there in front of him. To have the strength to not only accept death as inevitable, but also to continue extending compassion and support to patients and their loved ones despite the predictable loss—to not have to protect oneself from grieving—implied a tremendous, almost impossible capacity for understanding. To Dr. Clark, dying was another stage of life.

John Turner did not die. He was still only semi-conscious when my rotation ended, but I came back to visit him a few weeks later. I had heard from a classmate that he was recovering, though not because of any of our interventions; he was a classic case not just of alcohol withdrawal, but of the benefit of supportive care when all else failed. I found him propped up in a chair, hunched over and dozing, breathing on his own.

"Hi, Mr. Turner," I greeted him enthusiastically. "You look terrific!"

Opening his jaundiced eyes, he looked at me uncomprehendingly. His cheeks looked gaunt.

"I took care of you for a long time here, but you might not remember."

His stare remained unchanged.

"Anyway, it's nice to see you out of bed."

He nodded, and his head dropped.

I ran into one of the interns who had cared for him with me. "Doesn't he look rosy?" the intern asked.

"Amazing," I agreed.

Mr. Turner disappeared from my attention for almost a year after that. There was a question of whether his kidneys would recover completely or whether he might need dialysis. I couldn't imagine him, homeless, drinking every day, coming back for dialysis, but I was no longer taking care of him, so the arrangements would not be mine to make. I never forgot him—he was my most memorable patient, even if we never diagnosed anything but pneumonia and alcohol withdrawal—and I knew no one on his medical team would care nearly as much about him as I had.

A year later, as a fourth-year medical student doing a sub-internship at the county hospital, I would admit Mr. Turner to the hospital again. This time, he would comment that I looked "kind of familiar" to him. I explained that I had cared for him in another hospital the previous February.

Twice he would say, "Thanks for caring."

To anyone else it might have felt casual. At two o'clock in the morning after I had admitted him to the hospital as my very own patient, with the strong memory of how deeply I had wanted him to live despite all indication that he would not, it brought me to tears.

As it turned out, he *was* a classic alcoholic, and though his personality was edged with graciousness, he was not easy to talk to or at all interested in stopping drinking. This time he caused the expected amount of havoc for someone in withdrawal, got better quickly, and walked out of the hospital within a few days.

I don't know what twist of fate brought him back to me, but I think some divine being intended me to hear those words. *Thanks for caring.*

I went skiing after my fourth-year rotation ended too. I have had to keep skiing in my life, even as I kept biking after my broken hand, as I kept camping after my time with the Search and Rescue team, as I keep driving and crossing streets and daring to care about other people who might depart. I know I might die at any time. I might lose any part of myself. But I am in love with the flight of spirit that makes it worthwhile to be alive.

We are all so temporary, I wrote in my journal during my internal medicine rotation. *How would I know if I, too, am slipping away?*

Out on a winter slope, I feel whole again, and strong. I crave the exhilaration of being surrounded by mountaintops and gulping wide-open sky as I tussle with gravity and the drifts and moguls of a substance more ancient than medicine. My fear of falling blurs into an exuberant consciousness of living, as it has since my first time down Cornice; and by the time I return safely from one ski run, I am ready to take on the next, to be lifted up to the summit, to plunge down again. I come back exhausted each afternoon; morning shines with possibility once again. This is, it seems to me, what it is to live: to know that loss is coming, and to take the risk—of caring, or skiing, or just plain showing up—anyway.

When I returned to the city, to the hospital and my books and the night arriving thick and early, I held on to how it felt to be up there. I missed my mountain life, but I realized I didn't need it every day; I was becoming someone else. I could be grounded, mired in responsibility and medical paraphernalia, serious and pensive—but still flourishing inside.

It's all about making that first turn. I take a deep breath, envisioning gracefulness, and I jump into the soul-bending work of medicine, knowing we only get this chance, this ski run, these few moments in the grander vista of life's many uncertainties to make a difference.

Might as well try.

Sometimes I think I can trace everything about myself back to riding horses.... When I use tone of voice to convey reassurance, empathy to figure out how to respond next, touch to demonstrate gratitude or shared triumph, I wonder if I didn't learn these from riding... People, like horses, are sensitive to your behavior and attitude, especially when confronted with something new.

(APPLICATION TO MEDICAL SCHOOL)

Chapter Eight

TOUCH
THIRD-YEAR SURGERY ROTATION

A memory: in a hard-packed dirt lot behind a small ranch in the foothills of Southern California, I stopped my pony and watched the older riders on their well-trained mounts. Makeshift obstacles had been set up in the brickyard area: a pile of branches, a small ditch with water in it, old wooden poles, and an accordion-like snake of stacked railroad beams. Young women guided their horses over them in graceful succession. At the age of ten, I had jumped almost all of them at some time or another, but today I had my eye on the largest one: a pyramid of cut telephone poles that stood about three and a half feet high. Starr only stood about four feet at the withers, but he was usually game to leap over just about anything. We'd never tried a solid obstacle that big.

I ran through the steps in my mind: take him to a fast-paced canter, point at the middle, don't waver, count the paces. Then there was the approach—rein and leg to place him in a good take-off, weight off his back, give him his head and squeeze, sail, pray....

Starr was a bit wild-eyed and stubborn, with a propensity to speed up to a dead run in the middle of a dressage ring and keep zooming in circles until I let him hop over the foot-high piping that marked the show field. I had spent many an evening riding in the closed practice ring, listening to my instructor call out, "Relax your seat! Calm your hands!"

Once Starr started to take off, getting nervous only made things worse; he could feel the tension in my legs and chokehold on the reins. Then all control was lost—unless I could coax my thighs to lie heavy on his flanks, relaxing my hands to give and take with the working of his neck and crooning, as calmly as I could, "There, boy. Good boy. It's okay, eeeeeasy. Easy." When he listened, his pace would lose its frenzied panic, he would slow, gradually, and we would be back in touch, working together again.

With a deep breath, I squeezed his sides and steered him into a wide arc around the brickyard. We cantered around the jump. An older girl's horse refused.

I lost my nerve.

When another horse finally cleared it, I regained some of my courage. I wanted to jump it when others were around, in case something went wrong. Also, they had to vouch for me when I bragged to my instructor—if I made it.

I took a deep breath and started Starr toward the jump. But he was still trotting when he should have been cantering already, so we circled. Loping in a rocking see-saw rhythm, we approached again. Nice-smooth-pace, I counted. Five … four … three … two … Starr dug in his hoofs and stopped, popping me onto his neck.

I slid back into the saddle and circled. I hadn't given him any indication that we were about to jump. I had hoped he would figure that out himself.

Here we go, I murmured, and patted Starr's neck. My heart was thudding in my skull, but I reminded myself not to show the pony I was nervous. I sat in the saddle while we cantered and practiced slowing him by relaxing my seat. Leg pressure sped him up. His neck was bowed; he was listening to my reins. It was time.

Aimed straight at the center of the log pile, I fiddled with the reins a little bit and pushed my seat out of the saddle while still keeping pressure on his sides. He perked up—he had seen the jump. Again, I counted down the paces, but this time I looked up, squeezing with my legs as we approached. We half-stopped before he sprang into the air, improbably close to the tar-stained poles. Then we were landing, Starr's legs bending beneath him and reaching forward into a cantering stride. We had cleared the pyramid! And I had stayed on.

That night I fed him extra carrots and some oats and molasses, stroking his neck proudly as he ate while I waited in his stall for my mother to arrive. Evenings when I finished riding early, I often sneaked into the gelding's stall and crawled onto his back while he was eating, feeling his warmth seep through my thin riding pants. I wasn't supposed to be there. But I trusted Starr in a way I could not explain to grown-ups. We were attuned to one another. All those lessons about rein grasp and leg pressure and adjusting to the horse's gait were really about one thing: empathy. Horseback riding taught me early on the give and take of caring for another being. Communication is often intricate, subtle—a squeeze with the fingers, a settling of the seat. And calm. Careful, composed calm.

Richard Selzer wrote about making rounds in a jail with his father, a family physician who was saddened by the lost souls he found locked up and in ill health.

"You have to touch them," the elder man told his son. "Sometimes it's all you can do."

Starting in the first year of medical school, many of my classmates and I volunteered our time in a health clinic for homeless people. Uninsured and accustomed to being disregarded, our patients would wait hours while we bumbled through taking a history, examining them, and then bringing in the doctor to check over our work.

In these cramped, make-shift cubicles, I asked strangers shyly about the drugs they used and whether their needles were clean;

and if they had sex with men, women, or both; and did they use condoms sometimes, all the time, or never? They shrugged and answered me straight, without a trace of shame. When it came time to examine them, few hesitated to remove articles of clothing and wait while I spent a full five minutes listening to lungs, and at least as long listening to their hearts.

Joe was a Black man in his sixties, thin, with scruffy facial hair. He had a hospitality kit with him, and he had obviously scrubbed his face and brushed his teeth just moments before coming in to see us. The most remarkable thing about his exam was that the tracks on his forearms had collapsed all of his veins—sometimes, he admitted, he would shoot heroin into his jugular because the other veins were "used up." Scars from old abscesses marked his arms and thighs. I ran my fingers over the firm tissue blemishing his limbs before finishing the exam and excusing myself to get the doctor.

The supervising physician accompanied me in trying to get our patient to consider a substance abuse program.

"You're getting old to be living on the street," the doctor said. "And your body can't take much more of this abuse."

The man shook his head. "I appreciate what you are trying to do, doctor, but I'd rather die on a good high than try to get through the withdrawal."

Nothing we said convinced him otherwise; he remained respectfully resistant. All we did for him was diagnose a cold and hand him some decongestants, but he thanked us graciously for checking him over. He came back regularly for the same routine: the concerned questions, a stethoscope placed tentatively on his chest, and inexperienced hands exploring his neck and abdomen, thumping on his back. Sometimes he didn't have any symptoms prodding him to seek medical attention. He said he just liked being examined once in a while.

Later in my education, as a fourth-year, I examined a patient I'll never forget. HIV positive since 1984, homeless, and on parole for crimes he preferred not to tell me about, Tom was a fifty-six-year-old white man who came to the emergency room with a fever and a hacking cough. Acting as an intern, I asked him a litany of questions before admitting him to the hospital. He had tried to overdose on crack cocaine on New Year's Eve, he confessed. It hadn't worked, but since then he had had very little appetite and had been getting sicker and sicker. He was mostly alone in the world, though he had a few friends in a nearby city and a daughter his ex-wife wouldn't let him see.

"It ain't easy," Tom said. "In fact, it's hard a lot of the time, especially when I start to get sick. But I ain't afraid to die neither. Says right in the Bible not to be afraid."

I washed my hands before touching him, even though dirt was caked into the creases of his skin. He let me check his eyes, nose, mouth, ears. There was a good chance he had tuberculosis, so both of us wore masks over our mouths and noses (except during the exam, when I lowered his). When I pressed my fingers into his neck to check for swollen lymph nodes, he closed his eyes.

"I think you're the first person who wasn't afraid to touch me in at least a couple of years," he said, and sighed. "I know I've got a good doctor now, because I can tell you care."

I said nothing, trying to concentrate on listening to his heart and willing myself not to notice his stench. Between heart sounds I heard a squeal and a whoosh, and I looked up in surprise to see him sobbing.

"It just feels so good to be touched."

At San Francisco General Hospital, abscess patients are a dime a dozen. Every other patient in the emergency department is transiently housed, if at all, and about as many have substance abuse problems. Injection drug users come to the hospital nightly to have abscesses drained. Hair matted, malodorous, ill-kempt, and often grouchy or claiming a litany of other aches and pains, these patients are automatically admitted to the surgery service.

Typically, during my time as a student of surgery, if I evaded loitering in the ED, I did not hear about these admissions until the morning. Working alone, the second-year resident would do a cursory interview and then take the patient to the operating room, where a simple incision into the abscess would release a foul-smelling mixture of pus and blood. This had to be suctioned out thoroughly, and then the cavity was packed with moist gauze. The patient was admitted to the hospital and given intravenous antibiotics and a bed to sleep in. Our duty, as third-year medical students, was to unpack and repack the wounds every morning.

Which would have been simple, if the procedure were not so painful. Every time we went to remove the gauze, patients would whimper and demand more pain medicine—and because they were heroin users, their tolerance to morphine was astronomical. It didn't help that many tried to convince us they were reliant on higher doses of methadone than they usually took (methadone being a substitute for heroin that relieves withdrawal symptoms and helps patients detox—and can cause a high in large enough quantities). Nor did it help that these were disenfranchised, mostly homeless men and women who had self-inflicted their abscesses, albeit unintentionally. These patients were uniformly, and not inaccurately, considered "drug-seeking" by both residents and nurses. No amount of morphine seemed enough to them—but it was also possible that even high doses weren't sufficient to relieve their pain. We students weren't sure who to believe. The medical staff felt used: for a place to sleep, good drugs, attention. Patients hollered and cursed, but rarely, even after demands for morphine were appeased, expressed appreciation. This kind of patient care seemed thankless.

Each morning, the ritual was the same: our team of residents, interns, and students visited ten to twenty hospitalized patients as quickly as possible, to finish with time to grab breakfast before an 8 a.m. surgery or 9 a.m. clinic. We students were supposed to get to the rooms of abscess patients first, to "take down" the wound dressings and remove gauze from the cavities that had formed on arms, legs, buttocks, or shoulders. We carried a "bucket" (actually a plastic caddy) filled with wound dressing supplies: gauze, tape, tweezers, bandages, scissors, sterile water, gloves. Under the impatient gaze of our superiors, we asked, begged, cajoled, and ultimately forced our patients to submit to the stripping of their abscesses. I could feel each time the dressing caught on underlying tissue and had to be peeled away—not only because I felt the resistance to my pull, but because some patients expressed themselves with each tug.

"Oh! OW! Huh! Ouch!" some shouted.

And then they trained their accusing eyes on my face. I frowned sympathetically, apologized routinely. The stares were relentless. By the time I had begun stuffing a fresh length of moist gauze into the raw pink pocket, my team had departed for the next patient's room, leaving me alone with an angered man (or less often, woman).

I loathed this duty. I felt deeply ashamed of my disgust, but no amount of training blunted the fact that it took all of my concentration not to grimace at the smell of the wounds. Repelled by the odor, disconcerted by my gut reaction, and sleep-deprived on top of it, I had what felt like a terribly shallow pool of patience from which to draw. Mornings went on and on with abscess after abscess to dress, all of them attached to patients painfully similar in demeanor though different in appearance (Black, white, Hispanic, man, woman, older, teenaged). Heroin abuse had altered whatever personalities lay beneath, leaving behind hulls of physical hypersensitivity and disordered emotions. The hope of actually making a difference in the lives of these patients was almost nil; they would all shoot up again, and most would come back with another abscess. This would, in turn, shake another resident out of sleep and torment more medical students, who would swallow their repulsion every morning to change the dressing and try not to cry when the patient turned against them for inflicting pain in the process of trying to help. Almost none of the abscess patients were comforted by a pat on the back or a soothing voice. We were instruments of torture to them, and they understandably did not welcome our arrival.

This was not the model of patient care I envisioned—or wanted to practice.

My good friend Anne and I had both been assigned to the county hospital, and we were placed on the same surgery team. When the rotation started, we thought this stroke of luck would help us cope with the notoriously long hours and the humorless supervision we expected. She was the first to notice that our team couldn't—or didn't bother—to tell us apart.

"Clairanne," she mimicked, "Where's that presentation on antibiotic use in appendicitis we asked one of you to do? Oh, that was the other student?"

Apple-cheeked with large blue eyes, Anne would be easy to peg as sweet and compliant; she was often underestimated and never failed to notice it.

"Clairanne," she continued, "Where were you? I told you we would round at seven-thirty!"

We giggled, enjoying the freedom to speak uncensored in the women's locker room. Most of the attendings and all of the residents and interns were men. Presumably exhaustion and lack of concern allowed them to confuse us. My brown eyes, Middle Eastern nose, and curly hair should have made us easy to tell apart.

That first week of the surgery clerkship, we reveled in our anonymity. We poked fun at the austerity of the surgery patriarchy. We even practiced dance steps when no one was looking.

But a few weeks of abscess service changed everything.

Anne was part of my circle of female medical classmates whom my high school friend Max called "The Huggers." He named us with a sneer, a sarcastic discomfort with our tendency to embrace as a greeting, a reassurance, a thank-you, a good-bye. He didn't dislike my friends, but he seemed to consider us a species for anthropologic study; no one in law school behaved this way.

I can't explain how the phenomenon came about. I was normally fearful of the overniceness of strangers. My roommate, Nicole, had no such hang-ups, however, and before I knew it, our household and another were linked in friendship. Then a woman who lived alone became part of the posse, and sometimes a few of our other classmates. We met to exercise, to make dinner, to study. Soon we depended on one another for companionship. I can't remember when the hugging began. It must have been early; until Max commented on our behavior, I wasn't aware of the reflex at all.

Inevitably, whenever this group assembled in part or whole outside of school, we exclaimed in pleasure—high voices chiming and clashing "*Hel*-lo!" and "How *are* you?" and an extra-emphatic "*Hi-i!*"—and then enfolded one another in glad embraces. The most petite among us, Anne would nevertheless end each hug with pats on the back, as if to say, *You're okay, I'm here now!* To an outside observer, we would appear to be good friends who had not crossed paths in months or years. More often, we could measure the separation in terms of hours.

Those warm squeezes glue together my memories of the first two years of medical school. Our hugs marked a pact against competing; our promise to care for one another; our acceptance of one another as people deserving of love and affection. None of this was spoken, but it was clearly, kinesthetically implied. When I hugged Anne, I welcomed news about her long-distance relationship in addition to greeting a study partner. Camilla brought her calendar bursting with overcommitment, and we helped her sift through the appointments. I embraced Elizabeth's fiery political convictions. Nicole was always late, but caring. They all accepted my obsession with being outside. We soothed each other's academic worries by studying or taking breaks together. Our embraces were the supports that propped us up, day after challenging day.

When our rotation in surgery began, Anne was weighed down by a recently failed relationship. Though we were supposed to follow the surgery residents around and diligently do their bidding, I remember Anne hanging back more and more, just getting through each day. I raced around the wards in a panic, trying to do the work of two. Meanwhile, her discomfort with our role as medical students made her feel dissociated, watching me scurry to keep up with our team. She remembers me trying to reach out to the patients we breezed past in rounds, getting frustrated by a structure of care I could not alter—but she lacked the energy to care. Previously so well-matched in our observations and priorities, we were soon divided by the chasm in our responses to pressure: whereas I adopted the efficiency of our team, eager to finish and be excused as early as possible, Anne resisted and retreated more into herself. I grew frustrated with her slower pace of wound-dressing. She felt betrayed by my implied alliance with the others.

Even now, I don't know how we ended up in such different states. Our friendship crumpled as our surgery rotation went on, not because we stopped caring about one another, but because we couldn't bridge the differences in our approaches and still stay afloat ourselves. We still spoke, but we didn't hug. We didn't go for walks anymore or study together. I started to go out swing dancing as often as I could. Most nights she stayed in and studied, or slept.

It would take months to build our friendship back to what it was.

Swing dancing saved me.

When I became a student of surgery, I had been swing dancing for seven months or so. In the beginning, there had been the challenge of learning the steps. Could I fit my body to the eight-count rhythm of lindy hop? Could I do it over and over without failing or falling? Shyly, I would hover at the edge of the dance floor, hoping to be asked to dance so I could try. Ever so gradually, I became acquainted with some of the dancers around me, in my classes or workshops. We looked for one another at events, relieved to find familiar faces and sure-fire dance partners. I yearned to graduate from being a true beginner, being at the mercy of brand-new leaders whose sometimes jerky, offbeat, or potentially hazardous leads made a whole three-minute song something of an endurance test. I watched better dancers with envy, how their hips moved with the music, feet stamping out the rhythm, spinning elegantly in place. Some part of me believed I could do it—if I just had the chance to practice.

And then, just before I started the surgery rotation, I felt something click. It was the essence of partner dancing, and it was missing in the repertoire of most beginners: connection. Two bodies moved the same way to music when the leader led and the follower responded. Part of it was intuitive—like sitting on a cantering horse by relaxing into the rhythm. Part of it had to be learned: balance, frame, just the right amount of resistance. Each dance developed like a conversation, and no two were exactly alike. When I surrendered control and let myself be spun and dipped, moved back and slid forward—assuming I could keep up, and my partner knew how to lead me where I was supposed to go—each eight-count was a surprise. I laughed when I danced: at myself, at the awkwardness of holding hands with people I didn't know, with joy and satisfaction at fitting moves to the music.

Perhaps most of all, I loved following, and not having responsibility for how the dance would unfold. The leader strung it all together. Eventually I would learn how to add my own flavor, but in truth, I didn't want to yet. It was enough to just feel a gentle hand on my back, touch on my wrists, and go with the flow.

Meanwhile, I spent my mornings trying to cope with the wound bucket, premedicating our patients, and getting in and out of each abscess patient's room as gracefully as possible.

No amount of niceness softened the patients toward me, and I often felt like a beast afterward. I learned that I could not get through these mornings of curses and histrionics and still treat the abscess patients with the kind of care and compassion I wanted to be capable of. My empathy weakened. I could feel my armor sliding into place, blocking out the malicious glares and cries for pain relief, and for once I did nothing to stop it. The hours passed more smoothly when I learned to do it all by rote.

"Hi, Mr. So-and-so, sir, we're here to change your dressing. Can you just put your arm out here?"

It would be reluctantly offered. He would remind me that this was going to hurt.

"The nurses told me you already got some morphine, sir. It won't take all the pain away, but if you hang in there, I'll be done in just a minute."

There would be a sigh, a plea to wait until later. The arm would shiver under my touch, or jump.

"Yes, we have to change the dressing ... I know it's *uncomfortable* . ..."

We both knew it was a hell of a lot worse than that.

My lies went unnoticed by all of my colleagues—except one. I imagined she could see the guilt I held between clenched teeth, as though I had screamed it across the room. No one else knew this was not my personality. No one else really cared. But all I had to do was catch Anne's eye, and the lack of recognition there spoke volumes of accusation that never had to reach her lips.

One Sunday after a night on call, nearly delirious from lack of sleep, I collapsed on my bed at noon and did not wake up until dinnertime. I awoke feeling completely disoriented and deeply troubled.

I had dreamed of horses, but this time instead of being empathetic, sensate creatures, they were obstacles. In the dream, I drove a familiar road to get to a cabin where I was planning to vacation with friends. A small child ran in front of my car, and I almost hit him. I recovered quickly, but coming around a bend I had to swerve again, this time to avoid a dead, black foal. Soon the road became unpaved. I drove around another motionless horse, then a clump of two. They were newly damaged, not yet assaulted by flies or the heat of the sun. My way was blocked when I got to a group of three horses. Although they seemed to be dead, I was unwilling to run over so much as a hoof. Suddenly, one of the clusters rose and limped away, for which I was relieved—*not* because it was alive, but because I could now pass through and go see my friends.

Knowing that horses have long been my subconscious stand-in for people, I was horrified.

What does it mean, I asked in my journal, *that I passed by, superficially sad for them, but accepting the destruction of these beautiful creatures and moving on? Is this what I have learned?*

Constantly sleep-deprived, episodically panicked over truly life-threatening emergencies, we students soon began to understand our surgery residents' apparent lack of sympathy, and even callousness, toward patients who were not in critical condition. The surgery team doubled as a trauma service, admitting motorcyclists with fractured legs, a man knocked into a coma by a bus, car accident victims, gunshot wound survivors, people bleeding into their guts and slipping into shock. So if our residents ignored someone hollering about what kind of pain they were experiencing, we knew it was because these doctors took indignation as a good sign: frustration, after all, is a sign of life. And yelling means someone is breathing.

I never wanted to adopt that attitude myself. Still, it seeped under my skin when I was too tired to resist, and it shielded me against the pitiful sights and sadness I might have felt otherwise. Our job as surgeons was to repair what could be fixed and leave the "social issues" to someone else. When one of us students took a long history from a patient, senior members of the team fidgeted impatiently or cut us off.

"So what are we going to do for him?"

The lesson was relevant: triage, especially with the pressures of managed care, is critical to providing health care.

"Is it a surgical problem?" we learned to ask ourselves. "What else do we need to know before we operate?"

Stalking through the emergency department in the wee hours of the morning, we adopted their skepticism. There had to be a pretty clear sign that a patient required surgical attention for us to give in and admit someone. We had plenty of patients already—most of them gnarled and angry and waiting for our abashed approach with the wound bucket the following morning.

But there are some I remember well. One was a twenty-three-year-old man who had poured gasoline on himself and lit a match in a suicide attempt. The resident called him an "interesting learning case" and bid me to join them in the operating room. There, each of us helped scrub the charred skin from the man's limbs, carefully padding the raw dermis with medicated cream and gauze. His face, I could tell, would be unrecognizable.

The intern knew the patient would not make it. "Nice one a.m. admission, huh?" he grumbled. "Fucking waste of two hours."

When the intern scuttled out of the ICU for the remaining two-and-a-half potential hours of sleep, I stayed to watch the nurses arranging our patient in the glass-enclosed room where he would spend his last hours. Not yet adjusted to staying up most of every third night, I knew I couldn't sleep right away.

While I leaned against the wall, conspicuous in my white coat and surgical scrubs, a small group of visitors was ushered in: his parents and either a sister or girlfriend. They were all crying, but it was his mother I remember, her eyeliner streaked everywhere, eyes red and boggy, a look of desperation on her face. She caught my eye, and startled, I looked down.

"I'm sorry," I might have said. Or touched her arm. At least nodded.

But all I could feel, at 3 a.m. in the face of this young man's imminent death, was my overwhelming inadequacy. I was unable to change any of it—not the intern's lack of compassion, not her son's desperation, not the medical outcome. I slunk back to my call room before the family emerged from his bedside.

Dancing allowed me to feel. Not only allowed me, but also begged me. Convinced me with its mellifluous whispers and sensual fingers. I got so I could let the music fill me up and soothe the worries I brought from the hospital, all the worthlessness and loneliness left at the door as soon as I saw a familiar face, an extended hand, a smile. It inhabited me, and I let it, because there was no reason not to. I became addicted almost as soon as I could follow moves I had not thought up. I loved being asked to dance, held and spun and invited to share in this marvelous orchestration of feeling.

It's not that I didn't feel when I was in the hospital. But all of the emotion went one way; my job was exhausting simply because I took care of patients, but no one took care of me. Perhaps Anne and I gave up on one another too soon. Perhaps our needs were too similar. But when I went home after a day of work, worn out and feeling like a drop of water trying to fight a drought, what I needed more than anything was that candy-sweet connection to another person, the shared adventure of expression, the fantasy of having a whole room full of lovers.

I developed a crush on a man who had seemingly boundless energy and a mysterious emotional inaccessibility. Tall and handsome, he offered me a crooked smile and confident dance cues. He ad-libbed if I missed a step, moving his long limbs in enthusiastic exaggeration, and pulled me into his arms. He loved to dance. With me. Several songs in a row, and almost always the last one. The give-and-take connectedness of couple-dancing, combined with the memory of our physical closeness—his heartbeat against my cheek and the affectionate press of his hand on my back—left me wondering about him long after I went home for my five or six hours of sleep.

I soon filled every available hour with lindy hop. I turned down other plans so I could dance in Golden Gate Park on a Sunday. I scheduled other exercise around the evening events so my legs would not be too sore. I wanted nothing more than to be surrounded by my new acquaintances, moving to familiar strains of Count Basie or the Lincoln Center Jazz Orchestra, skipping or Charleston-ing to more upbeat tunes, sharing the joy of physical language with someone else.

Being on-call two nights a week, I might not have danced for almost a week at a time—if I succumbed to our schedule. Not only did students stay in the hospital overnight on call, but also we were generally wiped out the following night, and it took great determination to wake from a nap and go dancing.

But I lived for those nights. Sleeping in a call room amid unfamiliar surroundings, I would wrap the promise of dancing around myself and drift off. After a nap in the afternoon, I could rise to any occasion, any opportunity to slink, twirl, and slide to that intoxicating music. Somehow, miraculously, this anticipation sustained me. Dancing turned out to be my salvation, though I can't pretend it felt like anything nobler than the rush of a pure, predictable high.

Inherently intrusive, surgery brings doctors into the most physically intimate contact with patients of any medical specialty. Nothing—or very little—remains hidden from the surgeon's eye. The body is stripped of clothing, then stripped of animation under anesthesia, and finally breached by the scalpel. A human is quickly reduced to pulsing blood vessels and diseased organs; he or she is often the playing field on which the surgical pecking order is established and re-established, in the course of treating—hopefully curing—disease. Over and over, I heard attending physicians quiz residents, and residents quiz interns, and all of them quiz medical students: What structure is this? What blood vessel feeds it? What do I need to worry about if I cut through this layer right here?

Being witness to the inner workings of the human organism was an intense privilege; almost daily we saw glimpses of this dark world that most people will never see. At the same time, reverence was demanded in such a way as to kill the simple beauty of life pulsing willfully on. We were given retractors to hold, keeping open the window in which our superiors worked. We were expected not to speak unless spoken to; our questions, if ill-timed, were ignored. If deemed worthy, we might be allowed to close the incision, demonstrating the knot-tying we practiced over and over during scheduled lectures with surgical thread pinned to our scrubs. In all, surgery was ritualized to emphasize the import of being so entitled to another's body. As students, we were at the bottom of a steep hierarchy.

One of the surgeries with which I "assisted" involved removing the thyroid gland from a woman whose history I had taken; she spoke only Spanish, so the residents had been unable to communicate with her. Through me, she had consented to the procedure and murmured that her husband would be in the waiting room, that he was very worried.

All of this became irrelevant once the surgery began. The neck offers a small space to operate on, so only three of us—the chief resident, a second-year resident, and myself—crowded around the operating table. My job, as always, was to retract the skin so they could see. The chief resident placed the instrument and gave me the only instruction he believed I could safely handle: "Pull."

All went well for the first twenty minutes or so. Then the surgery became more technically difficult, as they wished to remove the gland but leave behind the pea-sized parathyroid glands that were hidden by the enlarged thyroid. The chief—a cocky, sarcastic surgeon who was two months shy of becoming an attending physician—put the squeeze on the resident, pushing him to define the anatomy, name the approach they were using, place ties faster. The resident's hand wavered once, and the chief mocked him, "O-ho, looks like we better pour you a stiff one."

When the resident reached the limits of what he felt sure doing, he took over the chief's role as assistant and surrendered his probe. "I think maybe you have a better angle from that side."

Gleefully, the chief moved clamps out of his way and went to work. But he soon encountered a similar difficulty to the resident— the structures of the patient's neck seemed to be placed slightly differently than he expected.

"If I could just see better," the chief muttered. "You gotta pull," he told me.

I increased my efforts, leaning back with the retractor in both hands. I could see nothing of the surgery; my role by this point was purely functional, not educational.

He continued to have trouble, so he re-placed the instrument. "Pull now."

I winced at the thought of placing so much tension on her neck, but I used all my weight. It was clear the chief was becoming flustered. However, he was loathe to request assistance from one of the attending physicians. Nobody spoke while he fished around in the patient's neck, still cautious to avoid critical structures, but apparently having difficulty. I could see bruising on the woman's skin from our retractors. Had she known how callous our hands might be?

"Damn it," he cursed, focusing his frustration on me. "Can't you pull any harder?"

In the sterile seriousness of the operating room, where the only noise came from the bleeping of the anesthesiologists' monitors and no one dared distract a surgeon, I committed the penultimate crime: I laughed. Had he looked before he spoke, he would have noticed that I was hanging from the retractor, bracing my feet against a stool and leaning out at a forty-five degree angle.

"This is all my weight," I said, thinking, *Take it or leave it.*

He cut such a pathetic figure at that moment, lashing out at a medical student because the hierarchy made it okay for him to do so. My resident held his breath.

The chief went back to work. A minute later, he rearranged us, changing the approach he was using.

"I'm sorry, Claire," he said to me. "Thyroid surgeries are a pain because you pull and pull and you can't see anything in such a small space. I promise I'll show you the anatomy as soon as we get through this."

I was so surprised, I almost didn't speak.

"Thanks," I said quietly. Reverently, almost. And as soon as I could get away with it, I moved the retractor off the purplish discoloration on our sleeping patient's neck.

My confidence came from outside the hospital walls, in half-lit rooms where music brought kinship to total strangers. People *liked* to dance with *me*! I ticked off the hours and days in my mind several times a shift, eager to get free. I rushed through morning rounds with haphazard efficiency, stole moments to talk with patients, practiced my knots, tried to learn while I was in the hospital. But had dancing been taken from me, the energy that drove me would have dried up. I would have withered.

On the dance floor, my new friends and I were athletic, playful, life-full, and affectionate when we touched one another. Music elevated and satisfied us. Our bodies were instruments under our own control. We were youth incarnate, in action, and when I joined the dozens of other lindy-hoppers, illness and disability and the discomfort of seeing bodies violated fell away. If asked, I could talk about the wonder of seeing inside people without admitting I had also torn away saturated bandages from five abscesses that morning, or pulled on someone's skin for over an hour while surgeons operated. My contemporaries were impressed that I was a medical student—while that title in the hospital was merely a marker of how little I knew, and what unsavory tasks I was expected to do.

It's not that the evenings of dancing were without turmoil. As in school, I often wondered if I was good enough, and whether I was fun to dance with. I found myself reluctant to dance with some people, either because they had an annoying habit of pressing a thumb into my hand or kept their mouths open while dancing or just didn't look like someone I wanted to brush up against. In the room full of dancers, there were more strangers than acquaintances, and I found myself surprised by my own xenophobia. Had any one of them been presented to me as a patient in my work life, I could not refuse to listen, consider, and touch. But out in the world of ordinary people, I was not bound to reach out to everybody. If I did not want affection *from* someone, I was mercifully not obligated to give it.

Without fail, my crush was there, looming large, dancing exuberantly, grinning sweetly. I took thoughts of him with me everywhere, arming myself against the days. I couched my experiences in terms of what I would tell him, what it would look like to an outsider—not the gloomy outlook I shared with my medical school peers. I could still be worth loving, scrubbing filth and insults from my skin before leaving the hospital for the day and transforming into a woman again. I could still dance, unbeknownst to the surgeons and residents who dominated my daytime life and every third night.

But in the end, perhaps dancing is what separated me most from Anne. I didn't understand the depth of her melancholy, and empathy seemed like a trap-door into the same state. Rather than hug her and share her sadness, I ran to the arms of strangers. Rather than face my own guilt, I pasted on a smile and hugged my new friends, who didn't know me, who didn't ask anything of me.

Dancing reminded me what it was to be joyful, to be appreciated, to be touched, to be alive—and to be someone else. That was my addiction, the buzz that kept me aloof from what I couldn't handle while I was a student of surgery: the ache of loneliness, the responsibilities of friendship, the pain of people who looked to me for care.

I am looking around at all these medical journals, and I want to cry—I feel tiny and trapped and thoroughly squashed by the intangible weight of all there is to know. My own disinterest paralyzes me. Does this mean I shouldn't become a doctor? I have always known I didn't have a passion for science, but I do love medicine sometimes. Challenge me, support me, teach me—it will feel like I can do anything. Belittle me, criticize me, ignore me—this is not what I came here for, nor what I should have to endure.

I have wings under here. I know someday I am going to find my niche by some twist-turn of circumstance and events, and soar. All of this experience and heartsickness is for something—the trick is to close my eyes and balance here, stay strong and poised even in the dark. And then to return to the waking world and bathe in light, stretch wings, fan feathers, glide free...Hopefully.

(END OF THIRD YEAR)

Chapter Nine

LIFEBLOOD
Third-Year Family Practice Rotation

*E*merging like a mole from the hospital microcosm, I was startled to find that nine-to-five medicine actually existed. I spent the entire six weeks of my family practice rotation in a geriatrics clinic, working regular hours. I should have been relieved; instead, I spent the first few weeks trying to figure out why I felt like I had left something behind. I checked and rechecked my backpack, my car, my pockets. I kept reaching for my pager, now cryptically silent. In the sluggish pace of the geriatrics clinic I had been assigned to, I missed the way hours had seemed to pass at a dead run in the hospital. Between appointments, or waiting to present a patient to my preceptor in her small office with the slowly ticking clock, I had more than enough opportunity for my mind to wander.

Which was worse: boredom or sleep deprivation?

Dr. Jackie Callahan emanated patience with her slow-moving, uncertain clientele. Many relied on walkers or canes, or took shuffling steps carefully down the short hall of her old-fashioned clinic. Rushing through traffic and across the bridge, always pressed for time to get where I needed to go, I invariably needed to adjust when I arrived. Dr. Callahan would turn her serene face toward me when I dashed into her office to hurriedly discard my jacket, backpack, and lunch in the corner. Only once I had seated myself on the edge of the chair, inhaling with the self-conscious posture of an eager student and exhaling some of the tension out of my shoulders, would she acknowledge me.

"This patient," she said, handing me a chart one morning, "is seventy-eight years old and lost his wife about six months ago. He is not doing very well, so I have him come and see me every month to make sure his dementia isn't worsening." She paused and asked me, "What do you know about dementia?"

I listed the causes I knew: Alzheimer's, Parkinson's, alcohol, blood vessel disease, Huntington's.

"And grief," Dr. Callahan added, "makes dementia worse."

Then she sent me in to talk to the gray-haired man who sat blinking in the examination room, leaning on his cane. "Mr. Miyoshi?" she called from the doorway.

Slowly he turned toward her, smiling vaguely.

"This is a medical student who is going to talk to you."

He nodded gamely, though it was unclear whether he understood.

"I'll be back in a few minutes," she added.

"Okay, okay," he said with rushed speech, as though the word always had to be said twice. As I entered the room, he struggled to stand to greet me.

My smile mirroring his barely-concealed uncertainty, I entered the room in strides that were still too fast.

"Hello, Mr. Miyoshi," I said, noticing how he wavered on his feet in response to my quick approach. Instinctively, I supported his arm and slowed my speech. "You can sit down."

He looked at me blankly.

"He may not hear you very well," said Dr. Callahan from the doorway.

"You can sit," I tried, louder.

Gratefully he reached his other hand for the table that had been placed right next to the chair. He lowered himself almost to sitting, then dropped into the seat. He gazed at me, nodding.

"Hello, Mr. Miyoshi," I forged into the interview, "How are you today?"

He was still smiling and nodding.

"Do you feel well today?" I asked at higher volume.

"Fine, fine," he sang back at me.

"Dr. Callahan wants us to do some tests," I informed him, in my outside voice.

In the neurology section of my physical exam course, we had been taught how to administer the MMS Exam, or "Mini Mental Status Exam." Meant to provide an indication of our patients' mental capabilities, this list of questions was often administered to our aging patients to convert an assessment of their current faculties into a number.

"Can you tell me the date today?"

He could not. Nor did he know the day of the week. But he was correct about the year and the time of day.

"Where are we right now?"

"Dr. Cal's office."

"That's right," I could not help but coax. "Do you know what city and state we are in?"

He knew we were in Berkeley, California, but not the address or street.

"I'm going to tell you three words to remember," I told him, "and ask you to tell them back to me: book, hammer, and sun."

"Book, hammer, and sun," he replied confidently.

"Perfect. Now remember those words, because I am going to ask you for them later. Dr. Callahan told me you used to be an accountant. Can you count backward from one hundred by sevens?"

I knew he had been administered this test before, but he seemed not to understand my instructions, so I prompted him by explaining that counting backward by fives would start with ninety-five, ninety, eighty-five, and so on. "If you start with seven, what's one hundred minus seven?"

He didn't answer. When the silence seemed to have lasted long enough, I offered an alternative exercise—spelling a word backward—with no more success.

"Can you recall those words I told you?"

"Book!" he said right away. I allowed him time to think of the others, but he shook his head. "Hat?" he asked.

"What's this?" I asked, indicating my wristwatch.

He squinted at me. "Watch."

"How about this?" I indicated my writing implement.

"Pen."

"Yes, now can you repeat a phrase back to me?" I enunciated well to make sure he could understand me. "No ifs, ands, or buts."

"No ifs and buts."

The final element of the test was for him to draw a clock. I offered him my pen and a piece of paper. He seemed unsure what to do.

"Here," I offered, feeling embarrassed that I had forgotten to start the exercise for him. I drew a circle and gave the page back. "This is the clock. Can you put the numbers on it and make the time say eleven o'clock?"

He started with "12" and marched the numbers slowly down the right side of the clock. I found myself quietly cheering for him as "1" through "3" fell roughly into place, and then dismayed when the remaining numbers squished together in the lower half of the clock, with "11" landing approximately where "8" should have been. He did not draw hands on his clock at all.

After I presented the results to Dr. Callahan, who had seen another patient and returned to her office while I had done the assessment with Mr. Miyoshi, she returned to the exam room with me.

Placing her hand warmly on his, she sat down and smiled in silence, waiting for him to speak first. He transformed in her presence. His cheeks spread in appreciation, and he squinted happily toward her, as though he faced the sun.

"Hi, Doctor Cal."

"How is Anna?"

"She's okay. She's busy, busy."

Then he shrugged, a gesture I suspected held frustration and understanding and loneliness all at once. Anna, I knew, was his daughter. She brought him to his appointments and looked after him.

"And the babies?"

"Pshooo," he said, grinning cryptically.

Dr. Callahan waited for him to say more, but he didn't offer any explanation. Gingerly she tiptoed into the reason he was here: his dementia was worsening.

"Is Anna here?"

"Here?"

"Is she in the waiting room?"

As if a cloud had passed over his countenance, he looked momentarily unsure.

"That's okay," Dr. Callahan reassured him. "I'll go check in a minute. How do you feel?"

The truth was, although Mr. Miyoshi hid his declining memory well when he was home, and could follow the same routines to which he had been accustomed—a bedroom he recognized, a floor plan he knew, even his doctor of more than ten years—his lapses in ability to remember what had happened shortly before were becoming dangerous. He could get lost on a walk, or leave the stove on and fill his home with gas. His body would go through the motions still, but his mind was wandering more and more. Outside the bounds of "typical grief," his dementia appeared to be its own separate, and growing, problem.

Looking at his combed-over, thin, gray hair and the tan of his skin, I was reminded unexpectedly of my own widowed grandfather. Unlike Mr. Miyoshi, at ninety-something years old, my jido (pronounced *zhidoo*) had inexplicably started talking incessantly in the three years since my grandmother's passing. It was as though he had stored it up for all sixty-four years of marriage, letting my situ (*sittoo*) have the spotlight. At under five feet tall, she had commanded it effectively. From her I had learned the only Arabic I knew: the names of foods and how to swear.

After Situ died, my mother and her older sister went to Arizona and packed up the house their parents had lived in for almost fifty years, returning with a hesitant old man whose eyes would unexpectedly fill with tears. Within months, though, he started telling stories, all of these bottled-up memories competing for attention and needing to be aired. Every meal stretched over hours as he talked. Finally, my aunt came up with a plan to assuage his constant need for an audience; in the mornings she would drive him to their restaurant, where he would help the morning crew with food preparation. He fit easily into the banter and chatter that was constant during less-busy moments. My mother watched his transformation incredulously, seeing in her father a *joie de vivre* that had never shown itself during her growing-up years.

Mr. Miyoshi might have overcome his sadness, but not the dementia it enabled. He did not react when his daughter entered the exam room with Dr. Callahan. Whatever emotion he felt during the ensuing conversation about his dementia was guarded closely, or perhaps he did not hear. Anna assured us that her father had stopped driving. When she and her husband were not home, there was typically a nanny watching the children. She would ask if the nanny could keep an eye on him as well. Anna placed a gentle hand on his back when it was time to leave, and he seemed to startle as he turned to look at her. She coaxed him to say goodbye, and he turned his glad smile to Dr. Callahan.

"I will see you next month," she promised, and he repeated, "Next month!" before they began a gradual shuffle toward the door.

From Dr. Callahan I learned a new kind of grace. So unlike the bustle and urgency of the hospital-based rotations I had recently finished, her clinic seemed to move at its own quiet pace. She seemed all seriousness at first, from her peppered dark hair cut short to her demeanor and intense focus as she sat scribbling in her office. I was too intimidated by her austerity to interrupt her. By default, I learned to wait for the pause in her charting. She did not waste words, but she did teach me with evident care and thoughtfulness. And she softened entirely with her patients.

Entering an exam room, she stopped in the doorway respectfully, waiting to be noticed and watching the response of the elderly person before her. Moving slowly, she would then take a seat nearby, smiling encouragingly, making eye contact through her thick glasses. She rarely took notes, perhaps realizing how easily a patient's train of thought could pass and refuse to be recalled. She listened longer and more intently than any doctor I had shadowed before.

Geriatrics is not a field of medicine many even realize exists. I had landed in her clinic by chance. Dr. Callahan showed me the nuance of helping people navigate failing health, faltering abilities, and loss of loved ones with extraordinary compassion. I don't think she ever smiled at me, but by her example, she nurtured my battered hopes that practicing medicine and caring deeply could be accomplished together. After the bruising experience I had had with my surgery rotation, once I recovered enough to appreciate her example, the weeks spent under her tutelage nudged me back toward humanity.

Just when I feared that the sameness of the days would be endless, we students were each assigned a home visit. Presented as an opportunity to take a thorough history from a patient, and to get to know them better than we might in the context of a visit to a doctor's office, this was expected to take a few hours. We had all afternoon.

So I found myself in the gracefully decorated living room of an old Victorian house in Berkeley, on a comfortable maroon sofa with tassels on the arms, talking to a straight-backed, elderly white woman named Edith. I had not been a guest in someone's home for years, it seemed, and I found myself unsure of how to behave. Was I to be doctor or friend? Would we talk as neighbors might, or should I ask the more intrusive questions with which we tended to probe patients in the office?

I needn't have worried. Edith eagerly leaned into my interview with questions of her own. "So you want to be doctor? That is so lovely! That wasn't an option when I was your age, so I decided to be a nurse."

Here was a reminder I needed: that I had to succeed in medical school not only for my own satisfaction, but also for the thousands of women before me who had not had that opportunity. Child of the seventies, I had been dressed in androgynous clothes and coached from before I could remember that I could do not just anything, but also everything. I played flag football with the boys in my grade school classes; I now routinely skied or biked with men because few women sought the adrenaline I thrived on; I was used to being one of few women in multiple situations; but I had not spent much time contemplating the barriers that had been moved before I arrived. I now knew I was capable of the work. I had forgotten that not so many years before, ability had not been enough. Unlike Edith, I could absolutely become a doctor.

Her stories enthralled me. Much more than a history of health, medications, and allergies, as we might take down in a clinic office, my afternoon with her offered a glimpse into the rich interior world of a woman who had given up her career after World War II. Married just before the war, she had busied herself becoming a nurse while her husband served in the military. They never were able to have children, so they had traveled instead. Widowed fourteen years before our meeting, she had found creative outlets for her quick mind: she directed and raised funds for a charity; she hosted other seniors over to play bridge and took meals to some who could not cook; she loved crossword puzzles. She was an amateur photographer, and she enjoyed chronicling her experiences every time she went someplace new. A skilled conversationalist, she enchanted me with her tales of discovery: the animals she saw on safari in Kenya, the marketplace in Thailand, an exotic plant in India she caught blooming for the first time in twelve years. I found my eyes tracing the pattern of lace doilies on the table before me, layer after layer of new intricacy budding from the one below it as we talked.

"Have you ever been to Egypt?" she asked me.

I shook my head, trying to imagine her as a younger woman, hair piled on top of her head as it was now. She would be wearing a breezy, white collared shirt and shielding her eyes with her hand, her skin turning pink in the blazing sun.

"Well, those pyramids are not for the faint of heart! My Bill, brave as he was, could not go in them. Such tiny passages! Of course, it probably helped that I am much smaller than he was."

Leafing through her photos from Africa, I barely noticed as the angle of sunlight through her bay windows changed and grew more strident. A few hours had passed while I let myself imagine a life delightfully different from my own regimented, fluorescent-lit existence.

I left filled with a momentary joy, that my career path had brought me to the door of this octogenarian spitfire whose story I was privy to only because of my commitment to doctoring. And also guilty, because in that moment, I did not want to go back to the office and learn about blood pressure medications or anything else. I wanted to know more about this incredible, solitary human who had shared her afternoon with me. At twenty-five, I was acutely aware of her age and, ultimately, her fragility. Edith had no descendants. What would happen to her life experiences when she died? There would be no record of her time as a nurse during the war, of her travels decades before it had been easy to do so, nor how she had turned childlessness into the opportunity to help others. Who but me knew of her generosity of spirit toward a hopeful medical student?

After a short check-in with my preceptor from the geriatrics clinic, I drove back across the Bay Bridge toward the late-day sun, appreciating the way light glinted on the water. The scattered points of brightness on the tips of each wave seemed to offer as many possibilities, each of them fleeting. I wondered what it would be like to chase something different if I had to turn away from medicine at this stage. Where would life lead me?

As the bridge swooped down toward shore, the fog that so often cloaked the city loomed ahead of me, like a down comforter pulled up only halfway. While the near coast sparkled under blue skies, UCSF and my own apartment were hidden from sight.

Arriving home from Edith's house, I pulled out my aging Mac laptop and positioned myself by the narrow window in my bedroom, through which the mist revealed little of the narrow houses around me. Following the template provided by my family practice clerkship director, I dove into writing about Edith—and soon abandoned the structure altogether.

Where in a medical history do you put stories about crawling through tunnels in the Middle East? I was supposed to list "major life challenges," but Edith hadn't focused on those. I could presume losing her husband had been one. Not having children perhaps was another. What about giving up being a nurse? Did she walk away willingly?

Edith had cemented for me the knowledge that I would not quit. The disappointment of generations of women who had made it possible for me to be here would be too heavy to carry. I also knew that leaving medicine would siphon away my lifeblood: the purpose that had carried me through these last several years. I knew I could focus on the shiny apple that had never been extended in Edith's direction. I would graduate beside my classmates in the first cohort of medical students in UCSF's history to include more than 50 percent women. After the war, Edith had had to walk away from her career completely and resume her role as a wife. It felt impossible to consider leaving medicine now, after all I had learned already. But after my experience as a student of surgery, I also worried that the apple might be poisonous. Medical training could change me completely, demanding I surrender the tenderness that had lured me this far. I would have to choose my specialty carefully.

I was already expected to be filing rotation requests for my fourth year and planning what field I wanted to pursue. Somehow, I had managed to keep my head down during third year so effectively that I found myself blinking dumbfoundedly at the openness of the question of what kind of doctor to be.

Turning back to the template, I considered the next prompt for Edith's medical history. *What kind of coping strategies does this patient employ?* I started to list them: charity, selflessness, mental exercise, creativity. I smiled at the memory of her encouragement. "How wonderful!" she had said about my pursuit of practicing medicine. Was kindness a "coping strategy"?

She could have been a hell of a doctor.

A few months after my family practice rotation, Jido suffered a stroke. My aunt found him half-paralyzed on the floor of his apartment. He could not speak.

When I visited him a few weeks later with my sister, driving hours down the western edge of California to San Luis Obispo, he was in a convalescent home getting physical therapy and speech therapy, and making slow progress. We approached his door with careful steps, almost tiptoeing, as if our tentative approach would keep us from being startled to see him. What changes would we see? Would he know us? I prepared myself as I had seen Dr. Callahan do so many times, taking a deep breath in the doorway, entering slowly, ready to give him my most-present self.

He did know us. But he seemed unhappy, greeting us wordlessly, his tongue refusing to obey his will. We filled the silence haphazardly, offering our love and gushing absurdly about how glad we were to see him. An attendant came to wheel him outside, where we would have more room to sit together. In the sunlit courtyard, under garishly clear skies and surrounded by carefully planted small trees and flowers, we tried to entertain him, telling him about family happenings, reminding him we had heard he was making great progress. I brought his water from his room, made sure he was in the shade, fiddled with the blanket when it came untucked from the seat of his wheelchair.

When I came close, he reached for my arm with his left hand, his good hand. Mouth working as if he might be chewing, he gulped and then managed to rasp two words that would haunt me: "Help me." His eyes were rheumy, watery, but knowing.

I felt like a bird that had slammed into a window—instantly grounded, helpless, desperately wishing for wings.

"Oh, Jido, I'm only a medical student," I stammered, my mind careening through the possibilities of what I, what anyone, could do for him—Dr. Callahan with her loving presence; a neurologist with the best of medicines; a speech therapist.

Was he getting enough to eat? Was he sleeping okay? I had been mimicking doctors, but in that moment, it became abundantly clear how far I had to go to think like one.

The sadness on his face told me what I didn't want to hear. Trapped in a crippled body, unable to share the many thoughts banging around in their cage, my grandfather desperately wished to be freed. What good are stories that cannot be told?

By the time my parents visited a week later, he had practiced what he really wanted to say.

"Help me die."

As my family practice rotation ended, I felt more and more adrift. It was time to choose a specialty, but I still resisted launching myself in any particular direction. It was easier to see what I wanted to avoid than to commit myself fully.

More than once over my years of medical studies—whenever I lost confidence in the profession I had chosen—I had turned to writing. Putting words to feelings had long been the way I sorted through my angst, defining what it was my heart was trying to say in the brief fits and starts I allowed it. I pulled out my laptop now, still open to the pages of Edith's stories, and let the words fly.

I concluded that I had come to medical school not just for a degree or a career, but also for wisdom. And almost three years into a four-year program bursting with moments both poignant and devastating, I had a lot to consider.

Quietly, while my classmates were working out their schedules and learning about research opportunities and residencies, I petitioned the registrar for a small stay on my medical education. I still planned to graduate in the same year as my classmates and friends, but a few months behind them. I would start my fourth year of medical school with a universally useful "sub-internship" in adult medicine, in which I would practice for my first year of residency while I worked out the kinks in my career plans.

And I signed up for a writing class.

Jido died three months after his stroke. We never knew his actual age. In with his other tales is the history of a malnourished boy immigrating to the United States, hidden behind the skirts of nuns. After his mother died from small pox, his relatives paid only enough fare to get him as far as Italy from Lebanon—and only enough for a child younger than his age. In order to cross the Atlantic and reunite with his father, he relied on charity and good luck. He was greeted in New York by a father he did not remember and a new stepmother. He helped raise his stepbrothers. He worked his entire life, never questioning the importance of having something to do. He wooed my grandmother with his letters, so he must have been able to write, but I never saw his handwriting—any more than I heard his voice—until after Situ died. Three years of listening to his stories was not enough to make up for decades of knowledge now lost, moments of acute observation that floated away like dust motes, memories appearing and disappearing intangibly in the cloudy skies of aging.

The cruelty of losing his ability to speak has stayed with me, along with the knowledge that he still had so much to say. It was as if, at the very end of his life, the sun shone brightly as ever, but the fog refused to let even a single ray loose.

I did not fall in love with geriatrics, but it turned out to be the necessary counterpoint to my surgery rotation, an enforced deceleration almost incomprehensible months before. I had time to study the creases on aged and leathery cheeks, the wrinkles earned through toil and worry, strain, hardship, love. I realized how unexpected forgetting can be. Beseeching eyes like my grandfather's tried to tell so much more than the body allowed. Paradoxically, as I slowed my gait to match those of my patients, and as I tried to mimic the gentle coaxing of narratives and unhurried pace of practicing medicine my preceptor modeled, my own sense of urgency—and the desire to write—took on a life of its own.

What was happening to me in medical school was a gradual transformation so uncomfortable and unrelenting it would have been easier to just let it happen and get it over with, much like adolescence. But I knew from my geriatric patients, from Mr. Miyoshi and my own grandfather, that there was no guarantee of the opportunity to record these moments later. A shift in perspective, age, or simply losing the sense of novelty could all cripple the telling: these flickers of knowledge would lose meaning when they were no longer new.

The opportunity to create and reflect beckoned me like those sparks of light on the bay, offering a glimmering promise as ephemeral as an impending sunset. I was in no hurry to finish medical school. Here was the silver lining to being romantically unattached: I was the only one whose needs I had to take into account. Amidst all the uncertainty about my career, this one decision—to take time off for writing—I made easily.

My stories would not wait.

Sitting here hugging a book to my chest, I feel the peeling apart of my worlds—like falling in love with someone who has the potential to carry you away from the stability of a warm home. Medicine is my foundation, my credibility, my tool for acting out a desire to love and be loved. Writing is my fantastical lover, visited at the odd hours when I find I can sneak away, kiss the thoughts that permeate my workday. What is love then? That which holds us secure or that which threatens to sweep us away?

(FALL OF THIRD YEAR)

Chapter Ten

BOUNDS OF CARE
Fourth-Year Medicine Sub-Internship

The stench in the emergency department (ED) of San Francisco General Hospital defied description. Thicker than body odor, it was sweeter than vomit and much more pungent than urine. Always, some writhing or passed-out heap of street clothes could be identified as a source, unwashed skin seeped in neglect and buried under layers of dirt, sweat, alcohol, and hopelessness. Parked on gurneys, hidden behind curtains, dozing in hallways, they populated the ED constantly during my month-long sub-internship in hospital medicine.

Most came to us not wanting to be helped. Often paramedics had yanked them from their slumber and wheeled them in for evaluation: "Fifty-one-year-old man found down, A & O to name only, alcohol on breath," the medic might say, handing over a rote assessment. "Found down" is as literal as jargon gets—sometimes "FDIS" or "FDIU" adds the information that a patient has been incontinent, discovered lying in stool or in urine. Their level of consciousness was assessed based on orientation to person, place, and time: "Alert and oriented times one"—scribbled as "A+O x 1"—meant someone knew their name, but not where they were, the day, date, or time of year. Usually drunk, these patients nevertheless had to be evaluated for head injuries, life-threatening drug ingestions, diabetic ketoacidosis, stroke. Some had had four or five head CT scans over the course of less than two years.

The patients who did know where they were had usually been there before.

"Can I get a SAND-WICH, PLEASE?" one nearly toothless woman puffed at me as soon as I walked into the medicine ward of the emergency department on my first night on call.

"I need some Vicodins!" a haggard man next to her demanded. "My back hurts!"

I overheard the resident talking to him in low tones a few minutes later.

"BLOOD DRAW? WHAT THE HELL YOU NEED MY BLOOD FOR?" the patient replied. "I just said my BACK hurts. I need PAIN PILLS. You don't need my blood for that!"

Ultimately, unwilling to undergo evaluation and refusing any other pain medication, he got up and walked out.

Inevitably, someone in the hallway of the ED was lying on a gurney, groaning. When I first started spending time in the ED in my preclinical years, learning to start IVs, do blood draws, and stitch up cuts, I would sidle up to these apparently neglected patients and try to talk to them.

"Hi there," I would start gingerly. "What's going on?"

Moan.

I'd touch a shoulder, call a patient by name. "Mr. Jones?"

Snore.

"Mr. Jones! I want to know how you're doing."

Snort. His eyes would open, he'd see me through what I imagined to be a haze, and breathe alcohol fumes at me. "F-fine. I'm fine."

Then he was snoring again.

Once, a middle-aged man opened his eyes and started jabbering at me incomprehensibly. He struck his forehead in emphasis. Again. Again. I was still trying to decide whether he was speaking a garbled dialect of Spanish when a large nurse bustled over with cloth restraints and tied his hands down to keep him from harming himself. The man kept babbling.

Or a patient might launch into a litany of requests: for pain medicine, for food, for the bathroom, for a ticket to go home, or for admission to the hospital. None of them had been entirely ignored, as I had innocently surmised. Nor, however, had they gotten everything they wanted. One ambulance arriving on the tail of another ensured that a patient with minor needs would have his or her requests postponed for hours at a time. The occasional patient who lost his temper and yelled found himself face to face with a security officer—not a doctor.

One man was walking around with his IV pole, exclaiming louder and louder with each step. Each time he cried out, he looked at the nurses—none of whom paid him any attention. He swore. He hyperventilated. He sighed.

No reaction.

Just then I passed by him on the way to another patient's room. He looked me up and down.

"How you doing today, beautiful?" he asked smoothly. "You jus' keep smiling; that's gold." And he grinned after me until I turned to enter the room. Then he took another step, and moaned.

During my fourth-year medicine sub-internship, a rotation designed to prepare us for being interns the following year, I was called down to the emergency room around 11:30 p.m. to admit a patient "well known to the ED." This expression meant he had been there frequently, for one reason or another, but was not admitted to the hospital on many, if any, of these occasions.

Jacob Thompson lay curled on a gurney in the corner of a room that could hold up to four patients, separated from one another by curtains. I asked a nurse if she knew the whereabouts of his chart.

"Ohhh," she remarked knowingly. "You're admitting ol' Jake, huh? Good luck." And she handed me a chart that was almost blank.

I turned the pages over, looking for information. All I could find out was that he had been witnessed vomiting, and that the emesis contained "coffee grounds"—a sign of bleeding from the stomach or esophagus. Some labs had been sent but weren't yet recorded. "Admit," an attending physician had written and circled at the bottom before signing his name, illegibly, and going off-shift.

As I pored over this meager record and looked up lab results, I noticed that none of the nurses went near my patient. At one point, he raised his head and cursed. The nurses looked at one another and shrugged.

"Are you taking care of Jacob Thompson?" I asked a narrow-faced, older nurse sitting beside me.

"Not tonight, I'm not. Is he back again?"

"Seems that way. What's he usually come here for?"

"Drunk, mostly. Been sick the last few times, throwing up, dehydrated. Anyone warn you about him?" I shook my head. "He can be a bit of a bear sometimes. He doesn't keep up so well on his medications."

The meds listed on his intake form were three: two anti-epileptics and an anti-psychotic.

"Wish me luck," I murmured, walking over to where Jacob lay.

The first encounter with any patient made me nervous—I never knew what to expect, or whether I would be equipped to deal with it. I took a deep breath and steeled myself. A bristly, drunk, schizophrenic patient was about as unpredictable as it got.

I noticed with relief that he was a gaunt older man with white-gray hair matted into odd angles. His back was to me, and I noted the sagging of his stained blue pants, which he still wore under the hospital gown. He also wore ill-fitting sneakers, which were nearly worn through, over mismatched dirty socks. He appeared to be sleeping.

"Mr. Thompson?"

He didn't respond. I tried again, raising my voice.

"Mr. Thompson!"

I felt every nurse in the area turn and stare to wait for his response. I held my breath.

"Get the fuck away from me," he growled, not turning.

I stood still, considering. We couldn't admit a patient to the hospital about whom we knew virtually nothing, and we certainly couldn't claim to be caring for a patient we hadn't examined. As a fourth-year student, I was supposed to act like an intern. This admission was my responsibility.

"I said, 'Get the fuck away from me!'" he hollered, now sitting bolt upright in the bed, inches from my face.

The lines of his face—grayish skin with centimeter-long white stubble—crinkled into a furious scowl, but he couldn't keep his blue eyes trained on me. Only one of them followed his will.

My heart hammered at my chest. I tried to sound calm. "Mr. Thompson, we're going to admit you to the hospital. I just need to ask you a few questions before we—"

"Sure!" he exclaimed loudly. "Just a *few*! Then what are you gonna do to me?" He spat curses through his dark-stained teeth. He reeked of vomit.

"I need to examine you."

"Get the fuck away from me!" He lurched toward me again, one arm clenched and threatening at shoulder level.

I took a step back, ire now creeping up the back of my neck.

"Listen," I said sternly, mustering adrenaline-soaked courage. "We don't have to help you. You are sick, and we want to help, but you have to cooperate with me if you want us to take care of you. If you don't, you don't have to stay here. You can leave."

Had he made one more move to hurt me, I would have walked away. This was a disturbing realization.

His one-eyed gaze wavered, and he leaned back.

"How long have you been vomiting?"

"A week," he spat, shrugging his shoulders like he didn't actually know.

"Has it looked like coffee grounds before?"

"I don't look."

"When was the last time you managed to keep food down?"

"An hour ago."

"And before that?"

He scowled. "I don't know."

"Do you drink alcohol?"

He flopped back to his side, facing away from me, and growled, "Sometimes."

"Just a few more questions, Mr. Thompson. I appreciate your cooperation. About how much alcohol do you drink every day?"

"Enough."

His answers got no more precise, and after a few critical questions, I gave up. He did tell me what medications he took "for seizures," and he could recite the doses—but he frowned when I asked if he was taking the anti-psychotic. My physical exam was similarly limited. When I asked him to stick out his tongue, he flicked it at me. While I listened to his lungs, he cleared his throat repeatedly. He had had a stroke a few years before, I learned from my exam, leaving him weak on one side of his body and rendering his right hand only minimally useful—which is why he had threatened me with his left.

Any patient who has signs of bleeding from the gastrointestinal tract has to have a rectal exam performed. The lore—as residents love to remind medical students—is that there are only two contraindications to a rectal exam: no anus, or no finger. Though I could name dozens of other situations in which it could be skipped, this was not one of them.

To my surprise—perhaps because I promised to leave him alone after this one last thing—Jacob acceded to the rectal exam. I pulled the curtain, rolled him onto his side, and asked him to lower his pants. I gloved both hands to help position him, noticing as I did that his pants were foul-smelling. Then as gingerly as I could, I applied pressure to relax his sphincter. When I inserted a lubricated finger into his rectum, he didn't flinch. I wiped the finger on test-paper and added developer. Blue spots appeared, signifying that he had, indeed, been bleeding.

When I tried to help him raise his pants again, Jacob jerked away from me and buckled them himself.

"Thanks for being so cooperative, Mr. Thompson," I said soothingly, trying to conceal a touch of sarcasm. "The test shows that you have been bleeding like we thought, so we're going to get you upstairs and have the GI doctors take a look at you tomorrow. Okay?"

No answer. I tiptoed away from his bed, relieved.

The fluorescent lights in the emergency department fooled with time. Around 1:30 a.m., I finished telling my supervising resident about Mr. Thompson—minus my offer to let him leave the hospital without getting care. Ken took one look at him after hearing my story and smirked at me.

"I'll wait till morning to talk to him," he suggested.

Just then his pager went off, and I knew before he even picked up the phone that it would be another admission. The interns already had two each. It was my turn again. I readied a pen and paper and hoped against hope that this patient would be easier to deal with than my last one.

My next patient was a Native American man called Luke Stampe. He was heavily intoxicated when he came to the emergency department and announced in a monotonous voice that he was planning to kill himself. Had he not been drunk, the psychiatry service would have admitted him to the hospital. Having been down this road many times before, however, they knew he would soon withdraw from the alcohol. For this reason, he was to be admitted on the medicine service and held on a "5150," or psych hold: a seventy-two-hour mandatory stay conferred on patients who are deemed a danger to themselves, a danger to others, or gravely disabled. After a brief psychiatry interview, Mr. Stampe was deemed suicidal and handed over to me.

Luke Stampe's clothes were already in a bag at the foot of his bed, and his long, thick hair was wet from a Kwell shower. Lice had been visibly jumping off his body when he arrived, so the nurses wasted no time in bathing him and getting rid of his clothes. He was wearing a hospital gown that barely reached mid-thigh when I introduced myself to him. His dull expression didn't change, but he watched me.

"I understand you're not doing so well today," I offered.

"I want to kill myself," he said flatly.

"That's what I heard," I said. "Have you ever felt this way before?"

"She already asked me all the questions," he interrupted, referring to the psychiatry fellow who had just left his bedside.

After I explained that this was a different interview, and that I would ask more medical questions, and that I was admitting him to the hospital, he became no more cooperative. Whereas Mr. Thompson had been outwardly hostile, and even threatening, Mr. Stampe simply didn't respond to many of my questions or requests. He showed no emotion at all, except perhaps wariness of me.

"Can you put your hands out in front of you like you are stopping traffic?" I asked.

Luke stared at my example for a full five seconds, considered for another five or ten, and finally, ever-so-slowly, lifted his arms and extended them in front of him. They wavered a tiny bit, but his hands did not jerk like they would have if he were experiencing withdrawal. Judging by the vodka on his breath, he was decidedly still drunk.

Each step of examining him required twice as long as usual. Sometimes I would wait for him to follow my instructions and realize, half a minute later, that he wasn't about to do what I requested at all. Other times, getting impatient, I would open my mouth to repeat the request just as he would be incrementally starting to move.

All the while he trained his gaze unnervingly on my face.

I slept about one hour that night—from 4:15 to 5:15 a.m.—before my last patient came in. Also intoxicated, this man was brought in by family who had observed his drinking binge over the previous week. He had not eaten much of anything during that time, subsisting primarily on beer with a few pints of whiskey thrown in each night. His sister-in-law told me most of his history while he cried about breaking up with his fiancée. Utterly cooperative and even appreciative, Eduardo Gonzalez needed reassurance and an Alcoholics Anonymous referral more than anything else.

Just as I was about to leave his room, Eduardo started screaming in Spanish, "I can't move my hand! I can't move my hand!"

He held up his right hand, which was bent at the wrist. His fingers splayed forward from his scrunched palm in an unnatural pose. Just then, a lab tech arrived with the news that the level of calcium in his blood was extremely low.

I ran for the nearest physician who could order calcium gluconate. Then Eduardo started squealing, so I ran back to find that his other hand had started to develop contracture as well. He looked terrified, panting and sobbing between wails. I remembered that hyperventilating would change the pH of his blood and make his calcium even lower, but he was too busy panicking to even hear me try to calm him.

"So how much do we give, Claire?" my supervising resident asked, testing my level of knowledge. He had heard the commotion and sensed I might need back-up.

I stumbled over a formula in the back of my mind. This problem was rare; I hadn't ever had to correct calcium before.

"What's his albumin?"

Duh, I thought. *Have to adjust for albumin.*

"I don't know," I admitted. "But he's a binge drinker, not a chronic one, so it shouldn't be very low."

"Let's start with two amps over ten minutes," he told the nurse. "And we need an EKG, stat." He turned to me. "Does he have a Chvostek's sign?"

I shushed Mr. Gonzalez for the moment and explained in Spanish that we were going to tap on his cheek. Classically, this is supposed to elicit contraction of facial muscles. Eduardo was already grimacing, so I couldn't see any difference. It only served to heighten his anxiety.

It was nearly seven o'clock by the time everything was under control. I still needed to check on all of my patients before eight o'clock rounds with the team. As I gathered my things— stethoscope, handbooks, clipboard, index cards—I wondered, *Which of my charming patients should I go see first?* It seemed too soon to see some of their faces again.

Predictably, because we had given him a substantial amount of benzodiazepines, Luke Stampe was sleeping. I visited my two patients who had been there already for four or five days. Both of them were stable; there was little to say or do except check to make sure neither one had had a fever in the past twenty-four hours. One would be going home today, having recovered from a severe asthma attack on top of pneumonia, and I prepared the paperwork for his discharge. I then had fifteen minutes left, and I could no longer avoid my obligation: it was time to check on Jake Thompson.

He was a different man.

I had written an admission note—summarizing what little I had learned about him from the interview and computer records, as well as my physical exam—and orders to admit him, restart his medications, monitor his intake and output of fluids, and recheck labs in the morning. The nurses had also worked their magic and bathed him, shaved him, and deloused him by the time I checked on him. Now groomed and fully dressed in a hospital gown and pants, he was sitting up in bed and smiling when I stopped by.

"Hi, Mr. Thompson. How are you feeling?"

"Pretty good right now."

"Have you managed to eat anything since I saw you last night?"

"Last night? I can't imagine I'd forget a face as pretty as yours if I saw you last night."

I hadn't expected this.

I chuckled. "Yes, we met in the emergency department. And you weren't too happy about it."

"Must've been in one of my moods," he said regretfully, his good eye twinkling.

"Well," I said, "I'm Claire Unis, a fourth-year medical student, and I'm working with the team of doctors that admitted you to the hospital."

I examined him again—minus the rectal exam—and asked questions about his health. All of his answers about the previous week and his current ailments had changed. He hadn't been able to keep food down very well for over a month. His alcohol use was less than I had thought, because it made him feel sick too. And he had taken his seizure medications until a week ago, but he vomited so often, it was hard to guess how much had actually gotten into his system.

"I'll come back and check on you in a little while," I said.

"I'll be looking forward to it," he said. "Don't be long now!"

Flirting. And last night he had almost hit me.

As time went by, I started looking forward to stopping by Jake Thompson's room. He remained charming and pleasant. He had a friend who appeared at his bedside on the second day he was in the hospital and seemed to be there all day, every day, until Mr. Thompson left the hospital. Whenever my patient saw me—in the halls, at the nurse's station, wherever we were—he'd exclaim to his friend, "That's my doctor!" They'd both smile and wave. I couldn't help but appreciate his affection. I returned the greeting and felt pleased that we were getting along so well.

I knew, but ignored, that this had nothing to do with my clinical skills.

"You better check my heart, doctor," he said to me one morning.

"Why?" I asked, instantly concerned. "Are you having chest pain?"

I laid my stethoscope on his chest. He grinned.

"Naw, it just goes real fast—whenever you're around."

I never would have tolerated him before medical school.

Dartmouth College, for all its progress during the years I was there, had still felt like a predominantly male environment twenty years after it had gingerly gone co-ed by admitting fewer than two hundred women to a student body of three thousand men. Even by the time I matriculated two decades later, women's opinions were rarely expressed in the daily paper. *Feminism* was a bad word. Overt harassment was shrugged at.

Largely because a voice for women had been lacking in college, I started writing about gender issues for an off-campus publication, became editor, and then finished out my four years writing op-ed columns in the mainstream daily *Dartmouth*. Largely self- and peer-educated in feminism, I asserted my right to be treated with respect. Had a stranger told me I had an effect on his heart, I would not have dignified the line with a response.

But Jake's winsome comments never bothered me. He was an old homeless guy off the street who was not the least bit attractive to me—and he knew it. Had our sport crossed the line of inappropriateness, it would have ended, and neither of us wanted that. He was never suggestive, did not touch me or harass me. We were playing a game, and it was just easiest to go along with it.

I had already learned my job could be denigrating. I had to take all medical complaints seriously, and there was no excuse (not even being spat at or threatened) to treat a patient badly. A patient was not just another person. A patient's needs and most frustrating qualities were to be approached scientifically, not emotionally—as symptoms, not intentional behavior. Otherwise, the whole roomful of ED patients might never get treated. Whatever feminism would say about me—skating on the approval of my patient, enduring unwanted flirtation to ease my interactions—was completely irrelevant in the context of a county hospital, I decided. Every human being deserved medical care. The goal was not to change others' behavior; it was not letting it affect my own. In Jake's case, he had gone from bitter to amiable overnight. I was not about to send that gift back where it came from.

As a sub-intern, my job lay in negotiating details among patients, nurses, and other health-care workers. Fresh-faced, eager to impress my supervisors, I would reason, plead, barter, and beg my way into getting patients the care they needed. The means didn't matter much if the end result was achieved. I was happy to use Mr. Thompson's flirtatiousness to my advantage.

When Jake almost missed his opportunity to get an MRI of his brain—to see if he had had another stroke—I found him in the TV room with a man who shared his weather-roughened wrinkles and lean slouch. "Mr. Thompson—"

"Hey, look! There's my doctor." He beamed.

"You look chipper today. Listen, I need your help with something."

"Anything for you, doctor."

I couldn't help but smile. "I need you to stay in your room this morning until after they take you to the MRI scanner."

"Can he just go down for a cigarette? We were fixing to go right now," his companion rasped.

"This here is my friend Sammy," Jake explained, as though the fact he had company might change my mind.

I shook my head. "Sorry. You can go after the scan—if you *have* to go."

He already knew I didn't approve of the smoking, and that if this was a new stroke, the cigarettes were partly to blame.

Jacob grinned magnanimously. "For you? Okay."

He gestured for his friend to wheel him back, catching my eye on the way.

It was a guilty sort of pride I felt, talking him into the scan. I know he did it to please me. The end result benefited us both: he got the care he needed during my sub-internship, and I appeared competent to my superiors. But a nagging voice reminded me this small success was a direct result not of my persuasiveness as a physician, but my attractiveness to him as a woman. I should have realized this was an unwieldy tool to employ—and that it would lose its power as soon as he left the hospital grounds.

Luke Stampe also seemed glad to see me each time I went to his room.

Apparently, a friend had told him to say he was suicidal so he would get admitted to the hospital and deloused. Luke figured that after a night's sleep in a comfortable hospital bed, he would return to his favorite neighborhood, the Haight, *sans* bugs. What his friend didn't tell him is that patients who confess to being suicidal—if they are deemed a danger to themselves—are either restrained or supervised closely (or both) for a minimum of three days. Having bought himself that ticket by convincing the psychiatry resident he could follow through with a plan to kill himself, Luke proceeded to exhibit signs of alcohol withdrawal almost immediately, and he had to be sedated to prevent complications.

Then he spiked a fever.

Considering his reticence to answer questions when I admitted him, I had no idea what the source of his illness might be. While he dozed, I took my time examining him. With his heart working harder than usual because of his temperature, I could hear a murmur that had not been evident the night of his admission. His breathing sounded normal. His abdomen seemed a little tender—he winced and moved even in sleep when I pressed on it. I checked his arms and legs for abscesses, having learned that lesson well in my surgery rotation, but there were none—only some faint tracks on his arms. I suspected a history of IV drug use, but he hadn't answered when I asked.

The response to fever in a hospital is almost automatic: I ordered a complete blood count and a blood culture. In less than twenty-four hours, the lab paged me with the news that the culture was growing *strep viridans*, a bacteria that usually comes from our skin, in numbers too high to ignore.

"What do you think is going on?" the resident asked me when I returned to rounds. I had expected this; Jason treated me like I was a medical school graduate already.

"He might have endocarditis," I replied, reporting my findings from his exam. "I can't really get a history from him, but it seems like this grew too quickly to be a contaminant." Thanks to Mr. Long, my patient from the previous winter, I knew to suspect this infection of the heart.

Sure enough, an ultrasound revealed a plaque on his mitral valve. We started antibiotics while he was still too snowed to know what was going on.

Early on, he was also too delirious to mind his restraints. By the third day, he had talked the day nurse into taking them off. But upon being informed that he could not leave the hospital, Mr. Stampe argued, wheedled, and finally got up to go.

His nurse paged me to tell me he had taken out his own IV and was demanding the return of his clothing.

When I arrived to try and defuse the situation—meaning talk him into staying, or call security—Mr. Stampe had been placed back into soft restraints. Just as I walked into his room, he freed his left hand and reached over to untie his right.

"Hi, Mr. Stampe," I called. "I hear you want to leave us."

"That's right," he said, not looking up. The tie was out of his reach with the side bar of the bed up.

"I need to talk to you for a few minutes before we decide if we can let you do that."

"Okay." His voice was very deep, almost morose-sounding, and he spoke slowly and deliberately. I sat in a chair beside his bed, and finally he looked up at me.

"Oh, it's *you*," he said, with a lascivious and nearly toothless grin. "What do you say—want to go get some dinner?"

"Mr. Stampe, we can't let you leave the hospital just yet. When you came here, you said you wanted to kill yourself, and I'm worried that you will do that if we let you leave too soon."

"*You're* worried about me?" Another broad smile.

"We all are, Mr. Stampe."

"But what about *you*? You don't want me to leave, do you?"

"No," I admitted, as non-suggestively as I could, "I don't."

"Are you gonna stay here with me?"

I chuckled nervously. "I can't stay here, Mr. Stampe. I have other patients to take care of. But I'll come back and check on you in the morning."

"So I'm supposed to stare at the wall until you to come back? Are you *sure* you don't want to stay with me?" He patted the bed beside him.

I took a more serious tone. "Yes, I'm sure. Mr. Stampe, there's something else. Do you remember when I told you that you have a heart murmur, and we started giving you antibiotics into your vein?"

He nodded vaguely.

"We think you have a serious infection in your heart. If you stop getting the antibiotics in your veins, you could die."

A long discussion ensued about what antibiotics were and how they worked. He decided they were poison, and he didn't want them. I explained about endocarditis (an infection of the lining of the heart or heart valves, to which intravenous drug users were more susceptible, and which could kill him). As far as I could tell, his thinking was clear—meaning he was no longer intoxicated from alcohol or overly sedated—and he could make his own health-care decisions. That meant that once his seventy-two-hour mandatory stay was over, if he truly had lied about being suicidal, we could not keep him in the hospital.

"If you're sure you want to go," I told him, "I need to call the head doctor on our team to come talk to you. And the psychiatry doctor will need to come too."

"I think you just want to keep me around," he proposed.

I said nothing. He tried different facial expressions to get me to change my own. First his large, round face showed a mischievous smile, then a more suggestive expression, then he was deadpan serious for a brief moment.

"I want you to stay here to get the treatment you need," I said. "I don't want to let you leave and have something bad happen that we could have prevented." According to my reading, he needed six weeks of antibiotics; he'd had one day.

He still wanted to go.

"I'll come back," he promised. "I just have some things I need to tend to."

An hour and a half of discussion followed: Mr. Stampe and me, the psychiatry resident on call and Mr. Stampe, the resident and me, the attending physician and me, and finally the attending physician and Mr. Stampe.

We told Mr. Stampe that he was free to go to the smoking patio— as long as he was back for his next dose of intravenous antibiotics, approximately six hours hence. But to leave the property, he needed to sign out "AMA" (against medical advice). He agreed to stay. Then, pushing the boundary, he left the hospital, didn't sign out, and came back to his bed for his next dose of antibiotics. I found him there in the morning, grinning proudly at his escapade of the night before, an IV still in his arm.

His nurse was furious.

Luke Stampe had learned a few things from getting away with his travels: that he could leave the hospital as long as he was back within eight hours; that he could decide to refuse treatment; and that anytime he raised a fuss of any sort, I would appear at his bedside.

For the first two of these problems, a system was in place to help resolve them: the risk management team. In a conference involving a risk management representative, the head nurse, our attending physician, myself, and Luke Stampe, the hospital's true policies— and liabilities—were laid forth. Although in fact we could not ever deny a patient the care they needed, meaning we could not bar Mr. Stampe from coming back if he left, the hospital could and would give away his bed and any left-behind possessions, and he would have to go back to the ED for readmission.

The last issue—my being on-call for his every prank—continued to vex me. He became more and more overtly lewd in his talk and his behavior. He reached up and touched my hair while I listened to his heart, and then he laughed when I tried to ignore what he had done.

"You like me, don't you?" he teased.

I didn't respond. If this was what it took to be a doctor, I was determined to take it. I steeled myself against his attempts at flirtation, forced myself to touch him—examine him—despite the repulsion I felt when he trained his serious gaze and sour breath on my every move.

Every time I assured him I cared about his welfare, a sickening smile spread across his face. And though my stomach turned, I told myself this bravado was worth it; as long as I kept coming around, Luke Stampe stayed in the hospital, getting the antibiotics that could save his life.

At the end of my rotation, I went to tell him that I would no longer be his doctor. He told me he wanted to take me out sometime, to his favorite restaurant in the Haight district.

"I'm going to build you a house," he suggested.

"Anyway, I hope things go well for you," I said sincerely, ignoring—again—his proposition.

"Give me a kiss before you go."

I smirked incredulously. "I'm not going to kiss you, Mr. Stampe."

"Come on, no one's looking."

"Goodbye, Mr. Stampe," I called, walking toward the door.

He sat there, watching me go.

"Bye!" I heard him call when I was already out of sight, walking quickly away.

I admit I breathed a sigh of relief to be released from responsibility for him. I had done my part to make sure he got the medicine he needed, but now it was someone else's turn.

My triumph was short-lived. The day another intern took my place as Luke Stampe's doctor, he walked out of the hospital for good—three weeks before his life-saving course of antibiotics was finished—and to the best of my knowledge, he never returned.

I read an overly optimistic flyer requesting an ideal live/work situation for a graduate student at the café today. What might that look like for a doctor?

> Female medical graduate seeks meaningful employment in the Bay Area. You provide interesting but manageable clinical problems and patients who appreciate being listened to and treated well. I provide good quality medical care, longer office appointments, and emotional support.

Ha! Even I know that's impossible.

(FALL OF FOURTH YEAR)

Chapter Eleven

WONDERLAND
Fourth-Year Pediatrics Sub-Internship

When I started medical school, I couldn't find my way home. Every day for at least a week, when I walked out of the towering medical sciences building, I turned right instead of left.

"We live toward the ocean," my roommate reminded me.

But I couldn't *see* the ocean from that precise location—there wasn't even much sky available until one walked right or left, off the hill UCSF was perched upon. The gym, too, was disorienting. While exercising, one looked out across the richly green treetops of Golden Gate Park, past city blocks to the forested Presidio area, even to the tips of the Golden Gate Bridge. I couldn't figure out why the northerly view appeared on the side of the building I thought faced south. Every time I walked into the gym, I was reminded of my confusion. A strange feeling of misplacement pervaded every hour I spent there. How did I always end up facing the wrong way?

Three and a half years later, when it came time to decide upon a career, I realized with a flutter of panic that I did not know in which direction I wanted to go. I felt like a small child in a forest that looked vaguely familiar, surrounded by fantastical creatures, and I felt a strange obligation to say *please* and *thank you* even though everyone around me appeared to be mad. I had become Lewis Carroll's Alice in Wonderland.[7] I had been daydreaming; I had followed a neurotic white rabbit into a hole; I had fallen into the strange place where unconscious motivations shook hands with reason, and the only way out had something to do with solving riddles to save my neck. Oh yes, and somehow, I had shrunk to the height of my shoe.

A half-moon smile glowed from the trees, followed by eyes, a head, the pink and purple stripes of the Cheshire Cat. Then a swish of his tail wiped the entire apparition from sight. [8]

"Wait!" I called out. "I was going to ask you which way I ought to go."

"That depends," replied the Cat, now reappeared, "on where you wanted to get to."

A good question, and one I didn't have an answer to. Had I gotten this far in medical school merely by chasing a harried rabbit, whose agitation hinted of great importance? Did I want to keep following the poor fool, or was it time to find my own way?

This much I knew: any residency would make me scurry for the next few years.

I leaned back among the Mome Raths and considered. After sampling most of the fields of medicine—pediatrics, psychiatry, obstetrics and gynecology, family practice, internal medicine, anesthesiology, surgery, radiology, neurology, and a handful of surgical subspecialties—I could come up with only one solid statement: "I'd rather avoid people who are mad."

"But my dear," soothed the Cat, "we're all mad here. I'm mad. You're mad."

And how could I argue?

Coming home from a thirty-six-hour workday in the hospital during my fourth-year sub-internship, I found my new roommate at home, making dinner. Nicole had recently moved out to live with her fiancé. Francine had been an acquaintance from swing dancing, and fortuitously, she also loved to cook.

"How was your night?" she asked.

I laughed. Then I cackled, riding the wave of exhaustion that toppled my sense of the absurd.

"I have the weirdest job," I told her. "How many people have you seen naked in your life?"

A modest woman who worked as a paralegal and spent every possible waking moment swing dancing, always in platonic groups, she demurred.

"Less than ten?" I asked.

"Yes," she agreed.

"I see naked people every day. That's what I do. Do you know how many men flashed me their genitals today? I wasn't even examining them! One needed help into bed. One was just sitting with his legs spread. The other one was wandering the halls and scratching his balls."

Francine laughed at the bewildered expression on my face.

It was something about the white coat. All of a sudden, I was supposed to be comfortable with anatomy I had rarely seen before; I was to pretend to be unfazed, soothe people with my deadpan face and professional demeanor. I had briefly dated a man who wasn't in medicine, who was too uncomfortable with his own body to skinny dip in my presence. *It's okay*, I could have said, *I'm going to be a doctor.* But I was supposed to be two people, and they should never meet. The "doctor" had to forget about shame. The "girlfriend" wasn't sure what other people her age could deal with anymore. Lunacy was creeping up on me.

Still, medicine enticed me. It hadn't been so bad, learning to examine patients, to face the very ill with composure and a maturity I aspired to, but did not quite own. This was the challenge, and I—ever precocious, eager to chase down the potential power to heal—

might endure a little chaos to get there. It might be very important that I did. After all, there was the promise of making a difference, if I could get past the strangeness that surrounded me. I just had to learn new ways to cope.

An instructor had once paused at the front of my medical school class, head cocked to one side in thought. A middle-aged woman dressed in slacks and a sweater, Dr. Hall commanded respect by her very normalcy and informality with us. With her gaze still trained over our heads, she mused aloud.

"Here's something I do that may not work for everybody, but I find it a tremendously useful tool." She wandered a few paces closer to the center of the room and looked at us again. "I find something about each patient to love."

Noticing some disbelief from her audience—which passed around the room as small snorts and chuckles—she continued, "*Even* if all I can find to admire is her earrings. It's a start."

In the third grade, I had tried a similar experiment: I decided to have a crush on every boy in my class, for one week each. It worked! I admired one boy's red hair, another's kindness in kickball, and even the little doodles of the nerdiest kid in class. It was a simple trick of the heart. But sick patients were harder to find attractive. Most didn't wear earrings, or clothing other than a hospital gown. Often, they didn't even open their eyes, and their bodies might be sagging or bloated, distorted or wounded in any number of ways. Sometimes, the pervasive aroma of urine or blood or pus served as a powerful repellant.

Early in my third-year medicine rotation, I had been introduced to Karen, one of the sickest patients I have ever laid eyes upon. The first time I met her, I didn't know what to say. Her skin was a dull yellow, and her short brown hair was thin and falling out. The protuberance of her belly seemed grotesque, larger than even a twin pregnancy, bulging over her thin legs and up under her rib cage. Otherwise, Karen looked and even behaved like a timid child. She complained only about the fluid that filled her abdomen and pushed up on her lungs, making it hard to breathe. Toxins affected her thinking, and conversation with her drifted quickly into incoherence. She was in her thirties, and she was fatally ill with a rare liver disease.

Even though interviewing her was mildly intimidating, examining her terrified me far more. I had no idea how to approach an abdomen this distended. I remember forcing myself to lay my hands on it and press gently. She watched my hands, unconcerned. I thought I could feel the drop-off of the liver edge and skipped ahead to the neurologic part of the exam. Held up in front of her and cocked back at the wrists, her hands flapped forward jerkily—asterixis, a sign of metabolic imbalance. I would learn that her level of consciousness frequently waxed and waned. With enough information to write her admission note, I excused myself, relieved to be away for the moment.

Later that night, with the help of the supervising resident, I drained over a liter of ascites fluid from her abdomen to help her breathe better. I watched how he tapped on her belly to find the fluid level, checking her face for reaction once in a while. Under his hands, the ballooning torso was an object of clinical interest, which he examined with matter-of-fact skill and purpose.

All Karen said was, "Oh, good," when we arrived, and "Thank you," when we left. The rest of the time she stared dully at the wall. She was tired, or confused. Maybe both.

Walking into her room to check on her the next morning, I began to introduce myself again. Her face lit up in one of the loveliest smiles I've ever seen.

"I remember you," she said. "I thought of something I forgot to tell you ...."

She looked radiant.

When I examined her that morning, I found that her body no longer seemed repulsive to me. It was familiar, and it belonged to this angelic-looking being who by some accident had been weighed down with a swollen belly. I laid my hands on her abdomen with more confidence now, thumping gently to check for ascites. She bestowed me with another winning smile, and I wasn't afraid anymore. So much power lay in this trick of appreciation.

Dr. Hall's advice guided me through caring for a grouchy vacationer waylaid by a stomach ulcer; a Filipino woman who tried, on her deathbed, to match me up with her grandson; a stubborn sailor who looked like Santa Claus; a wall-eyed woman who was determined not to stay for treatment of her ovarian cancer. Each time I found compassion through a likeness to family, a grin, a beard, a shared wish, an understanding. Like Alice in Wonderland, I curtsied and showed respect, and I got by.

But did I want to stay in this wonderland forever? Certainly, I met some intriguing characters, and there were lessons to be learned at every turn. But I also felt a constant anxiety at not knowing my way around the daily bustle of practicing medicine. I drank my dose of humility and shrank to the size of a mouse, nibbled on a cookie of success and outgrew myself. One sentence from my superiors—"No, that's not right"—could make me cry in frustration until I drank again of shame and smallness and floated through on my own tears. Was this place I had imagined truly the home I longed for, or was my dream turning into something of a nightmare?

There in the stillness of this dark forest, I felt truly, profoundly lost. How did one get through? Would it be better to turn back? I imagined a glimpse of the purposeful White Rabbit, his coat gleaming as he flashed past on his way to a fantastic party.

"By the way," the Cat mused before he vanished, "if you're looking for the White Rabbit, he went"—and now he gestured right with his left hand, and left with his right—"that-a-way."

There was more than one way to be a doctor.

As I sat in the dusky afternoon light with my new roommate, I felt a wave of nostalgia for the time before medical school, and my childhood home, and the much safer fantasies of picture books read after tea.

Often when I did not know which way to turn, I called my parents. An artist and a radiologist, respectively, my mother and father generally provided a balanced perspective between the two of them. But when it came to anything pertaining to medical school, my mother was more likely to bow out, leaving my father to field my questions.

"What about radiology?" he asked, trying not to sound too coercive. "You can take calls from home, and there is a constant flow of new technology, so it never gets boring. Have you considered that?"

What I loved about radiology was the magic. Invisible beams revealed mysteries no one could see on the surface of a person. Each of us harbors a secret life. This might be a simple quirk of anatomy: a liver lobe that lies a bit askew, a blood vessel many people do without. Or a magic window into our bodies might reveal peculiarities, clues to our lives: old fractures, surgical clips, dental fillings, the absence of an appendix. You can see these things on X-ray images, and it is as astonishing as animals that can talk. You can look at the black shadows on a plastic film and know something of a person's history. You might find the silent first blush of disease and read his fate. All without wielding a scalpel.

Perhaps I also loved the familiarity of these images. I was very young the first time I kneeled on my father's desk chair and tried to copy a skeleton onto a small notepad inscribed with his name. I learned to say "radiologist" when I was no more than five, around the same time I learned the word "physician." Those films were part of the symbols that made up the milieu of my father in my early life: cigars, a Degas print of ballet dancers, his bushy black beard, seafoam-green hospital scrubs, and glowing white ribcages stuck to a lightbox. He looked inside and saw things no one else could see. He spoke long words into a microphone on his desk, in a serious tone of voice, and I always had the sense that something significant was happening.

I expected to be good at radiology the way I inherited my father's big hands and feet, curly hair, and stubbornness. Growing up, whenever I spotted a bird or spied Dad's lost keys in an unlikely place, he complimented my "good eyes" and suggested I "ought to be a radiologist." He did this in an offhanded manner, infrequently, and I had never consciously entertained following in his footsteps. But when my eyes faltered and I needed reading glasses, I felt a twinge of loss: so much for the perfect vision that had linked me to his hopes.

During the introductory radiology course, the winter of my second year of medical school, our teacher placed twenty or so images in a study area for one week at a time. I studied the X-rays eagerly, following the curves of all twelve pairs of ribs, checking the lung fields for haziness and the heart outline for clarity. Each film was a puzzle that relied on having a sense of how things ought to look, and then the vision to discern what was not right. Mixed in with the subtle clouding of pulmonary edema and the blunted angles from pleural effusions, there were many films demonstrating variations of normal. Once, the heart was on the wrong side— situs inversus, a rare enough condition that the aged X-ray was a yellower black than the others. The problem was too obvious; most of us missed it. But the lesson was well-learned: many times in the years that followed, I heard others note, as I did when reading chest X-rays, "Heart size *and position* are normal. ..."

In small group classes with radiology residents, every time I was called upon, I felt expectation from my classmates—as a radiologist's daughter, I should get the cases right. Much of this was probably in my head; only David, Steven, and Nicole even knew this tidbit of my medical ancestry. Nevertheless, I began to search the black-and-white pictures for my own future. I squinted at subtle shades of gray, guessed at diagnoses we had barely studied. I felt an ancient amazement at human anatomy. I could study the lovely symmetry and layering of our insides without cutting greasy, preservative-soaked flesh.

Cross-sectional films particularly piqued my curiosity. In fourth year, I opted to take an elective rotation with a radiologist who specialized in CT scans. Now the challenge to think three-dimensionally intensified—one had to picture that a body had been sliced across and opened so we could see inside. The orientation was important; each cross-section was a view from the feet toward the head. As we looked at a film, our right was the patient's left, and vice versa. But also, it helped to have a sense of direction *around* the body, to know which way the gallbladder would move on successive films, to be able to trace a ureter. Finding my way took practice. I sat watching our attending work at this for hours, letting the shapes blur and reform in my head: pancreas, liver, gallbladder, kidneys. The haze of inflammation. Dark splotches of cancer metastases.

It was my father who had taught me that I had a sense of direction to begin with. In an act of daring, he had once led us on a hike that involved about a half-mile of walking off-trail along a crest to find a different trail back down. The bravado had less to do with the danger of getting lost and more to do with mustering energy to convince my mother that this was a good idea. She had a healthy respect for the dangers of traversing unsanctioned, potentially precarious terrain with two children. We, of course, found it exciting. We tried to match the landscape to the hints he gave us. There would be a field, first, then a sloping traverse, and finally a gentle downhill around a sharp peak. What I learned from this strategy of my father's, more than the desire to set out without compass or map, was simply the assumption that I *could* find my way if I needed to.

Which, as I tried to mentally reconstruct three dimensions from two on the computer monitor, I finally realized might have been a mistake.

By far the hardest area of radiology to understand, ultrasound offers none of the ready topographical landmarks I could sometimes find on CT. A beam of high-frequency sound waves passes easily through fluid and reflects off internal organs and other structures in different ways; the result is a whitish line at the interfaces between areas of varying density. The depth and direction of the beam varies moment to moment, subject to the whim of the examiner. Figuring out what the images represented took all my concentration—and even then, I was often completely wrong.

The most enchanting use of ultrasonography is in pregnancy, when a fetus is small enough to appear as recognizable images. I witnessed several such exams during my obstetrics rotation, sitting alongside the radiologist with bated breath. First the screen was all a blur of grays and black. Then a hint of layers, sketched onto the monitor, swirling and changing direction. A white oval appeared tentatively, faded, and grew. We all watched as a measurement was taken, awaiting the sweep of our window down toward a body, hands, heart, and feet. The beautiful symmetry of the spine came into view: delicate and precisely aligned in these dark waters. We could see the curve of her ribs, watched them separate from each other as the baby practiced breathing.

But we moved on. A flutter marked the beating of her tiny heart, and we focused in, changed angle, saw four chambers flaunting their synchronicity. Her abdomen was measured, then her femur. Feet popped into view, and the doctor adjusted the angle of the beam, catching them both on still-frame, ten toes in mid-womb. Last, we went back to the face, imagined her finer features but knew—could see!—the structures behind them, a nose now, and parting lips. A hand waved into view, aimed for her mouth. Then she moved, and we lost our magical view into her underwater world.

After the beam was taken off, the woman on the examining table and her partner would always remain riveted to the screen. They longed to know more than the doctor could ever tell them, more than anyone could know until time unfurled the baby's tiny fists and her eyes adjusted to the light. When she could balance against gravity on those two perfect feet, when they were much larger than her entire leg was right now.

The doctor once offered me a chance to try to look around with the wand, and I accepted, wide-eyed and hopeful. I asked the tiny tadpole's parents if I might, and they consented, again watching the monitor, barely listening to what the doctor said. And what could I show them? I was in my third year of medical school, my seventh day of obstetrics and gynecology, and I had never held this rectangular instrument in my hand before. But I bravely smeared gel all over the mother's abdomen in the process of trying. In a flash of luck, I saw the head with its thalami and ventricles. Then the fish-child swam away, knowing, I think, that I had little hope of catching her. I glimpsed what might have been a cross-section of her abdomen, part of a femur, the corner of her placenta. She knew her way around the amniotic sea—and I kept missing her, bumping the beam blindly up against the uterine wall. But there! I saw her ribs again, like an otherworldly birdcage, bending with practice-breaths, trying them out.

I kept radiology on the list.

In many ways I had loved obstetrics and gynecology, but the surgeries had scared me away from that field. Not that they were particularly gruesome, but like all operations, they would require me to violate the integrity of human skin and plunge into the dark cavities of the human body that were not meant to see light. Surgery simply didn't suit me. I always shivered at the smell of cauterizing, even when the sight of blood grew routine and I could focus in on the anatomy of a pelvis: the purplish, squat uterus; ovaries like plump beans at the ends of anemone-fingered Fallopian tubes; the deflated bladder tucked deep. Even with the daily miracle of seeing birth, and having the strong female role models I found on that rotation, I could not see myself as even a part-time surgeon. It was a passageway I clearly did not fit into.

Perhaps, like Alice in Wonderland, I could change my height. I could grow, or shrink, by nibbling on bits of toadstool. With a little imagination and a lick of wishful thinking, I might become anyone—but that idea only made my career decision harder.

During my medicine sub-internship, while I had raced around the hospital with all manner of fauna—both patients and doctors—and occasionally took on the near-delirium of weariness, I had also changed my mind repeatedly. Sometimes I could not imagine giving up the satisfaction of seeing a patient through his hospitalization.

Other days—particularly after a string of phone calls between 2 and 4 a.m.—I couldn't fathom staying in medicine my whole life. Radiology residents went home in the morning after being on call. Medicine residents didn't.

"Doctor, the patient lost his IV."

"Doctor, we can't give that medicine."

"Doctor, the patient says he can't sleep."

"Doctor, he vomited. What do you want to give now?"

I wasn't yet a doctor, and I couldn't give the orders they needed. Most of the time, the orders were in the chart—to be followed on an as-needed basis—so I directed the nurses to what was already there. They called me, in a perverted twist of medical hierarchy, as a mark of respect. I was supposed to act like an intern and know everything about my patient.

What had the Caterpillar said? "Keep ... your ... temper."

How had he seen through my smiling veneer? How did he know my days would come to this: driving home post-call; cursing at stoplights and bad drivers; glowering at pedestrians; feeling myself chased by the hours of botched blood draws, late-night requests, protocol, medication issues, and trying to pretend I knew what was going on? I looked up one morning and the thin spread of clouds looked like pulmonary edema on a chest X-ray. I couldn't even laugh at myself. The world outside the hospital had ceased to exist. I was still running on the adrenaline that had gotten me through a call night. Strangers were all potential patients to me, and I was too tired to be a doctor anymore—not today.

What else did the Caterpillar know? Could he see, for example, that I sat through conferences like an uninvited child at a tea party, bored by the academic discussions that buzzed like nonsense between an old man and a hare? Did he see that I longed to be treated like a grown-up, and grew weary with the constant demand to "recite, recite!"? Worse, perhaps he could tell how it taxed me sometimes to try so hard to be polite, and likable, and diligent, so that even when I was complimented for my rapport with patients, I doubted whether I could keep it up forever.

Radiology would excuse me from some of these aspects of patient care. And I wouldn't be required to endure the smells of self-neglect, the weeping skin infections, the tongue-lashings of patients who mistook me for a personal servant. I wouldn't have the satisfaction of laying hands on a patient in the process of trying to heal, but I would also escape the heartache of not succeeding. Radiology was about making the diagnosis, seeing inside, and calling on powers of observation and intuition to tell others how to proceed with a patient. It was a life of pictures—with room for imagination. I could envision the patients to be any sort of person I wanted.

But then I wouldn't have those precious surprises like Jacob Thompson's transformation into a gentleman; like Edith with her wonderful stories; like Karen and her endearing smile. I would be excused from doing the work to care about people, but I might start to forget how unstereotypical individuals turned out to be. The world would seem quite flat if I allowed that to happen. But if I chose medicine, there was also the chance that I would burn out.

When I had first come upon the Caterpillar, hoping to ask for advice, he had asked me, quite wearily, "Who are *you*?"

That was when it occurred to me: I didn't know. With each rotation, I had squeezed myself into a slightly different costume, until I couldn't remember what I was wearing when I first arrived.

All I could say was, "I'm not myself."

I was disconcerted, I explained, by being so many different sizes all in a day. I could feel elated and a mile high, when things went well—or tiny and very nearly trodden upon, when they did not.

"What *size* do you want to be?" the Caterpillar asked.

Just a bit bigger, I explained, because I felt about three inches tall—his height, exactly, it turned out—and felt "wretched."

The Caterpillar was offended.

"You'll get used to it in time," he announced.

That was what I was afraid of.

If I had a compass in medical school, it was my Healer's Art group. Halfway through my fourth year, as I sat considering which way to go, and trying to remember who I was, their faces came to mind. As first-year students, fresh out of the elective course designed to protect us from burnout by preempting it, eight of us had pledged to reunite every month. We agreed on a code of confidentiality, an inclination toward introspection, and a commitment to be present for all meetings. We were all afraid of losing ourselves in medical school. Each one of us would serve as a reminder for the others, like a trail marker high on the trunk of a tree, helping us back to the path on which we believed we had embarked. One that led toward compassionate humanism, not callousness. And not burnout.

Our meetings had been easier to plan in our preclinical years than later on when rotations got in the way; call schedules had to be worked around, significant others appeased, travel plans taken into account. Sometimes, when the appointed hour arrived, I didn't much feel like taking out my feelings and examining them. It would have been easier to just keep getting by, and not to look.

But whatever our individual moods were when we arrived, we found safety in one another's commitment to listen. The influence of a ring of people concerned for our collective survival worked like a magnet, drawing us back toward the true north of empathy, integrity, courage, life. It never failed to amaze me how we gravitated toward the same goal.

At the end of each meeting, we joined hands in a circle, creating a short series of links. Then the chain broke to the left of whomever most needed reassurance, and that person stood still. The rest of us walked around him or her again and again until we were all wound up in a sandwiching hug: a human jelly roll. We never knew where the hug would place each one of us, embracing whose elbow or with nose buried in whose hair, but somehow even being the last person on the outside, arms stretched around our whole group of eight, then six, then five, felt like an enormous, affectionate squeeze.

That was the mark of a Healer's Art meeting come to a close, another month come and gone in our medical school careers. We always parted with magnanimous goodwill, having been reminded that we were not the only ones struggling with large decisions, or our own inner conflicts. Even at our most isolated, most bitter moments, we were not alone.

Just now, however, I felt quite lonely. No one but me could make the decision about what sort of doctor I should be.

One evening, shortly after I had finished my psychiatry rotation, the members of our group gave ourselves an assignment: draw the floor plan of a house, filling it with whatever was on our minds. Symbols of doctoring appeared alongside broken cars, pianos, images of home, mountains, hourglasses, people. A serpent appeared in one; a dying patient in another. An alarm clock, and music. Mine was a Dr. Seuss house, each floor tilted and precariously balanced on top of the others, windows askew, the whole six stories leaning toward a schoolgirl's rendition of the sun. I envisioned myself running from room to room in a fun house, laughing to scare away my fears. I had begun swing dancing; I still went rock climbing several times a week; I coveted the interest of a few different men but didn't date any of them with serious intent. I didn't feel fully in possession of myself. I had the sensation my house was growing of its own accord while I leaned out fuchsia windows from my topsy-turvy mind. Meanwhile, I was giggling and dancing and swinging through my so-called life.

I was the only one of our Healer's Art group who had not shown the house's interior in my drawing. When it was my turn to speak, I admitted that I worried about what the picture really meant: progressing toward the unknown, uncertainty about the doctoring role. Solitude masked by a flurry of activity.

I don't remember who pointed out that my colorful rendition revealed something else.

"There's a wonderful spirit to it though."

"This *is* a crazy life, and that makes playfulness really important."

"I think your creative side needs an outlet," someone said.

And then this: "I think pediatrics really had an effect on you."

What *about* pediatrics?

There had been a time, before I even started medical school, when a well-intentioned family friend had exclaimed over my acceptance: "Wow, a doctor! That's great. Are you going to be a pediatrician?"

I had blinked at his white hair, his presumption that a woman would surely choose the most nurturing of medical fields, and stammered, "N-No, I don't think so. I don't know what I want to do." And silently, to myself, I vowed, *Not pediatrics*.

Although I had loved my clinical rotation as a third-year student, I could explain away my assessment: I had been away from home, in Fresno, and untried as a doctor-to-be. I was so relieved, at the time, to discover that I could be of any help to anyone, that I had no idea whether this had to do with the field of medicine or physical location or just plain dumb luck (as I feared).

I had a friend two years ahead of me in medical school, Greg, who had become a resident in pediatrics. I had laughed when he told me what kind of doctor he was going to be. On the surface, he wasn't anything like my expectation of a pediatrician, unless you count immature. I knew him from the climbing gym, where he brought his angst to throw at the walls. He was hyper and impatient. He shouted from his car at other drivers; he liked loud, screaming music; he hated waiting for people. Pediatrics?

"I'm not that way with kids," he said.

End of discussion.

Eventually I knew him long enough to realize something: he was actually quite patient with *me*. I was a far inferior climber, with a tendency to let go of the plastic hand- and footholds and dangle from the rope, just as I reached the most intimidating section of a route.

Greg never yelled.

He never said a word—except in encouragement.

"Ni-i-i-ce!" he would shout, when I finally mustered enough courage to try. Or, if I looked down at him helplessly, he'd explain how to get through the section that stumped me.

He stumped me. Nice, nurturing, schoolmarmish or mommy-like women (and a few men) were supposed to become pediatricians. Innocence suited them to a young patient population. They were quick to coo in sympathy, and tolerant to a fault. Maybe even a little naïve. Not, like Greg, fiercely aggressive athletes with a tendency to break hearts and cut short any conversations that threatened to linger over feelings. I couldn't picture him kissing boo-boos. But as I spent more time with him, I grew to suspect that he understood children like few adults do. That he cared about them as ardently as he professed his obsession with Pearl Jam, baseball, and *South Park* cartoons.

"Pediatrics is like being a veterinarian," someone once told me. "You have to guess what's wrong, because the children can't tell you." Or there was the stereotypical criticism of a pediatrics practice: "All you do is look in kids' ears all day." And yet another: "You have to deal with *parents*." But there was also Greg, who simply gushed, "Pediatrics is *awesome!*" and whose enthusiasm always finished the statement with a poignant exclamation point.

"I think it's perfect," my sister said, giggling, when I tried out the idea on her. "You're just an overgrown kid yourself!"

That was the first *ah-ha!* The *ah-ha!*, a professor once explained, is the moment at which a student's face lights up because a concept makes sense. That flash of understanding was his entire reason for teaching.

Play! I could picture myself blinking up at the imposing figure of the Queen of Hearts and reminding her, "I'm a little girl!" Not, as she seemed to assume, one of the playing cards who were her subjects. I did not want to be like everyone else, didn't savor the thought of following protocols and doing everything "the Queen's way." The only way to wriggle out of such obligation was to play the trump that children hold—creativity. Caring for children would require the very traits I so desperately fought to keep in medical school: flexibility, ingenuity, a willingness to laugh and reach out and ... play. Let go of the expectation of maturity. Revel in the surprise of children's imaginations.

Looking for a climbing partner, I paged Greg one evening. He was on call, wandering the hospital ward wearing a baby slung against his chest.

"It's the only way he'll stop screaming," said Greg. The same Greg who hated carrying around too much "stuff" when going climbing outdoors. Eventually he stopped climbing and only bouldered, staying closer to the ground in order to reduce the necessary supplies to a pair of climbing shoes and chalk, leaving out the rope, quick draws, harness, belay device, and other assorted equipment.

"He's cute when he's sleeping," Greg explained.

The better part of a year would pass before I found out what it felt like to hold a baby myself—when I finally decided to try pediatrics on for size.

In a chapter of Lewis Carroll's *Alice's Adventures in Wonderland*, Alice comes upon a small house, about four feet high. She chews a bit of mushroom to shrink to the appropriate height before she approaches and finds it to be the home of the Duchess, a baby, and a cook. The cook intermittently throws pots and pans at the Duchess. The Duchess sings of beating her baby and gives him a few rough shakes. And all of them sneeze repeatedly from the excess of pepper that fills the air.

"Here! You may nurse it a bit, if you like!" says the Duchess unexpectedly, throwing her baby at Alice before disappearing to prepare for a croquet match.

And that's precisely how it felt when I started my second sub-internship, this one in the newborn nursery and intensive care unit at San Francisco General Hospital. I hadn't even learned how to examine a baby yet, and there we had babies whose mothers had been crack addicts, and who needed special care. For the first few days I just tried to figure out what was normal in an infant, and what I was supposed to do.

Premature babies, when wrapped tightly in warm blankets, amount to a bundle no bigger than a football. With hats propped on nearly-bald, birth-bruised scalps, they submit to being ferried around the room with a limited range of personality: outrage, somnolence, wonder. The ones who are in withdrawal, especially from heroin, may become inconsolable. The rest, wrapped up too tightly to move, stare passively wherever their gaze is put and, eventually, drowse.

I took to carrying babies around on my first night on call in the hospital. Waiting for new deliveries to happen, or after they did, I spent my time doing paperwork or studying, both of which could be done while holding an infant. It was quiet there on the top floor, with only the squeak of nurses' shoes and the occasional squalling of a newborn from somewhere in the dark. Most of the babies stayed with their mothers overnight; only a few remained in the nursery for close watch, or by happenstance.

Baby Lorren was one of these "boarders." He was my first patient on that rotation, passed to me from an intern who had rotated on to another service. I scoured the chart for information about him when I started, dismayed to learn that his mother had a history of drinking alcohol and using cocaine, and it sounded as though she no longer had custody of any of her five other children. By the time I began caring for her youngest son, she had been discharged from the hospital. She promised to return for him. She agreed to meet with the doctors and then didn't show up. To us, she said she wanted him; to her friends, she said he died in the hospital, cord around the neck.

On those late nights, kept company by the blip and blare of monitors and baby warmers, drifting around the nursery in the half-light to keep moving and stay awake, I often paused by Baby Lorren's bed. He was scrawny; born early at thirty-three weeks, he had been remarkably healthy, but he was to stay in the nursery, getting extra calories and being monitored for apneas, until he was big enough to leave—and when he had somewhere to go.

I picked him up because he was crying. Newborns sound like sirens, or mechanical animals, mewing each time they exhale and pausing only for more breath. They can cry endlessly, it seems—piteously, instinctively, reflexively. They do not know the source of their wailing. Once started, they go until some sense of comfort envelopes them and the impulse flickers, softens, fades.

In the crook of my arm, he felt like a doll. Heavier, though. And warm. I wrapped both arms around him and carried him with me on my night prowl, bouncing as I strolled from cradle to cradle. I found myself murmuring. I sat and rocked when I had nothing else to do, and I stared at the tiny features that soon became familiar to me. As he gained weight, over the weeks that I knew him, his face became rounder and more human. Even his eyes, sunken and haggard in the premature baby, seemed softer and more animated as time passed. He started to look more and more like a real baby.

I began to look for excuses to hold him. After all, he had no mother to visit him, and babies need the warmth of another body. No medical studies told me this; I just felt it, knew it somewhere down where the soul recognizes touch and knows all is well. Before long, I felt certain he recognized me. He quieted when I held him. He slept.

And then the day came that Baby Lorren was too big and too healthy to stay in the nursery any longer. His mother had defaulted on one meeting too many. Once we could say with certainty that he could maintain his body temperature and had no signs of withdrawal, Child Protective Services scheduled a day to pick him up and deliver him to a temporary foster home. I almost cried when they carried him away; he was a creature swaddled and still blind, cozy in his blankets, unaware of the change in his world. I hoped someone would love him. I hoped someone would hold him and rock him and chatter about the strangeness and gloss of the world around him, and stare at the gentle lift of his nose and curl of his lashes, and watch his fingers close in his sleep. All I could do was steal a few moments to hug him to my chest before they took him away, and then busy myself with other chores.

Later that month I called my parents to ask what they thought about the idea of me adopting a baby. I had given it a lot of consideration, I told them, and I would make a better parent than a lot of the people infants were born to.

"At least I care," I said. "And to these little guys, that's a lot."

I had fallen in love with the wrinkled creases of newborns' skin, their fingernails, their warmth.

"What about residency?" Mom asked pragmatically. Having stayed home to raise my sister and me while my father finished his training, she knew what each of these endeavors entailed. "It isn't really fair to try to raise a child when you're gone all the time."

"I know," I sniffed, the ridiculousness of my proposition suddenly showing through. How had I fooled myself into thinking my affection would be enough? "That's why I never got a dog."

But I was hooked. The babies fed off my innate desire to nurture—and thrived on it. Perhaps this kind of pediatrics *was* like being a veterinarian. Instinct guided my actions as much as intellect or my few weeks of experience, and that was perfect. My hope for my patients' well-being was as genuine as the impulse that had brought me to medical school to begin with.

There were other reasons to choose pediatrics, I reasoned. Children haven't yet lost their instinctive responses to others, the intuition that becomes more difficult to honor in adulthood. Trusting or wary, affectionate or screaming, their honesty seemed refreshing to me. Plus, children were different creatures as newborns than they were at one year old, four years, adolescence—it was like having a whole range of life in one field of medicine. Teenagers were notoriously the hardest patients to handle, but also the most rewarding—they'd call me out if I didn't listen, didn't dish out the same respect I wanted in return. I liked the idea of having someone hold me to being my best self for no more convoluted reason than because it was purely the right thing to do.

"You had a happy childhood, didn't you?" a friend asked, when I told him I was thinking about pediatrics.

I smiled. Well, yes. I mean, I'd had a good education, nice clothes, parents who cared, a home. But, no—I also had the usual childhood angst over learning to share, being called names, not fitting in, growing up, doing petty things I was ashamed of. They were big issues at the time. Many children deal with very adult problems that I had not even dreamed of when I was eight or twelve or even sixteen. But although I never bore bruises from protecting my mother, never had to forage or steal for food, never knew what it was to hate a bottle of alcohol or endure molestation so my family members wouldn't be killed, I remembered being uncertain about adults who didn't relate to children. I remembered lashing out in self-protection, and feeling much too small. I never forgot how it felt to be a child. Or to wish someone would understand.

One summer during medical school, I worked with incarcerated teenagers at a detention center in the forested hills south of San Francisco. Each Saturday I sat outside with about twenty male teenagers and four "grown-ups" and helped guide the boys through outdoor exercises intended to help them problem-solve in the real world. As part of an awareness exercise, I told them about an expert rock climber who was a friend of mine. He had fallen more than six stories and broken twenty-some bones in his body, and after showing the teens how to wear a harness and use a climbing rope, I asked them why they thought he fell.

"His friend dropped him," one said.

"The rock broke off."

"There was an earthquake."

I waited for them to figure it out. Finally, Mateo suggested quietly, "Maybe he didn't tie his rope right."

"Exactly," I told him. "My friend fell because he didn't finish tying his knot—something he had done so many times, he didn't think about it anymore."

The teens brainstormed a list of things they did without thinking, and the potential dangers of going through life unaware of what was around them. I left having learned more from them than I had taught.

After this experience, I helped plan a medical school elective course for first- and second-year students that would bring to light some of the obstacles and needs of "high-risk" adolescents—boys and girls who had already been to jail. Specialists from the prison system, health clinics, and grassroots activist organizations shared their knowledge with the thirty medical students who took the course. The highlight was the day some of the youth who had graduated from the detention center came to offer advice to the students gathered in a small lecture hall at UCSF.

One first-year raised her hand and asked how she, a white girl with a privileged upbringing and no real understanding of street slang, could really be a good doctor to a Black teenager who was in and out of jail, with a totally different life experience from her own.

"Be real," one of the teens said, and shrugged. "The most important thing is that you care."

I spent a lot of time with those young men in my one summer at the detention center. Many of them were larger than me, bulked up with young muscles and beard stubble that made them look older than their ages. But there was something puppyish in the way they mimicked the terse speech of tough guys, something vulnerable in the scowls that were occasionally passed around. Most importantly, there was the power of their own wistfulness to dream a better life for themselves, to make our meetings a safe place to try out their plans.

"Keep it real," they admonished one another. And in the earnestness in their eyes, and the language of their hopes—in the simple beseeching to "Keep it real"—I found my own home, my new teachers, my *ah-ha!*

My future profession.

Twilight had already arrived when I found my path out of the woods of indecision. In the murky darkness, I had to pick my way carefully. A few times, I thought about turning around, and once or twice I knelt to squint down low passageways through the thistly underbrush. I had yet to meet the Queen—would that be residency?—but I felt I had spent quite enough time in Wonderland, and I would just as soon go home for tea and return later on for more madness. I didn't regret the roads I had *not* taken—medicine, radiology, OB/GYN, family practice. I paused when someone asked what I intended to *do* once I got to pediatrics, but since I hadn't known what I would do when I ran *into* the woods, it didn't much bother me, not knowing what I would do once I got out. There was still the White Rabbit, that beacon of high achievement, to think about. He seemed much less important when I returned to my normal size.

In my second-to-last month of medical school rotations, just after I had submitted my residency applications and before I interviewed anywhere, I received a message from one of my professors that I should stop by to see him in his office regarding something "personal." Though he denied it had anything to do with my application, I hurried to his office that afternoon, filled with apprehension that something had gone wrong.

He smiled indulgently and shook his head. "I told you it had nothing to do with that!" He reached down to remove a packet from his briefcase. "Do you recognize this kid?" he asked me.

It was a photograph of a six-month-old, smiling and delighted in his blue pants and sailor shirt. I once had seen a photographer specializing in taking portraits of children; there must have been a toy waving in the air just up and right from the camera to have made the baby so responsive.

I shook my head.

"What if I tell you his name is James?"

Again, I slowly denied having seen him.

"You took care of him at SFGH," he said.

I lifted my head from the photos and waited for him to continue. "Here."

He handed me the photocopied medical records, which bore my signature. It took only a moment to recall: this was Baby Lorren. My Baby Lorren. The one that prompted me to call my parents and propose that I would adopt a baby whether I ever married because I couldn't think of a damn thing in this world more important than raising a child. I almost cried before I even heard his next words.

"My wife and I are adopting him."

The magic in that forest was thicker than I ever imagined.

I wanted to know too much that no doctor could tell me, the what-about-my-body and why-does-it-do inquiries that grow in the fertile imagination of a girl half-educated, half-creative, with the luxury of time to think about her body's whims and worries. Dr. S talked as though I should know I asked too much—that really my mind ought to be confined to the known, not wandering off in a dark wood where tree stumps and gnomes mistake one another.

(FALL OF FOURTH YEAR)

Chapter Twelve

ADOLESCENCE
FOURTH-YEAR PEDIATRICS ELECTIVE

Cocooned in my sleeping bag beneath jagged black treetops, and beyond them a panoply of stars in the charcoal sky, I felt content.

I realized this with surprise: I wanted nothing. Children slept open-mouthed around me, and the silence rolled in and out with my own breath. My eyes drooped. In a little over an hour, my alarm would wake me. I would rise with the other camp counselors and one by precious one, we'd wake the ten- and eleven-year-olds to prick their fingers, squeeze out a drop of blood, and test it for glucose.

It's okay, someone had told me the first night, *they won't even remember it in the morning.*

And they wouldn't. Not even after those nights when they'd had to sit up enough to drink a cup of juice or swallow graham crackers to raise their blood sugar levels. We tiptoed among them anyway. This was no hospital; there were no machines bleeping and flashing impertinently all night long. No one laughed in the hall, or cleaned the floor, or turned on lights at 3 a.m. We were surrounded by a living, breathing forest, and around the wooden deck on which our sleeping pads were laid out, the wilderness continued its peaceful lullaby. We interrupted it as little as we could.

For a week and a half, as part of an elective medical school course for fourth-year students, I worked at a summer camp for children with diabetes. The kids were beautiful, running around and laughing in the high Sierra air, forming new friendships, watching each other give themselves injections, and envying the children who had insulin pumps attached to their bellies. It was the first time in all of medical school that I spent days with healthy children. Diabetes, in that setting, was a culture—not a disease.

Out on a backpacking trip with one of the boys' cabin groups, I encountered an elderly man who had made the three-and-a-half-mile hike with the aid of his family. Infused with wonder and well-deserved pride, the man stopped to offer advice at the lake where the boys were swimming.

"If you just stay away from drinking and smoking and a few other things, you can stay this healthy when you get to be my age," he told Zack, one of my campers. "And don't eat sugar and fat. Kids eat too much junk food."

Little did he know that these boys counted every carbohydrate they ate. They could tell him how many wheat crackers or vanilla wafers make up a "carb," which foods are free of sugars, or how even a single candy bar would push their blood sugar out of target range. Most of them had needed extra carbs—delivered in the form of horse-sized, square sugar pills—to get up the hill without their blood glucose going too low.

Zack smirked as he went to get his towel. Above his swim trunks, the catheter port for his insulin pump was taped blatantly to his skin. "When you have diabetes, it's kind of hard to forget that," he remarked wryly.

The man didn't hear him. I cleared my throat. "Well, these kids are here with a camp for children with diabetes," I told him. "So they are pretty good at keeping track of what they eat."

He looked stunned. "You mean they are at risk for diabetes? Or they have it already? I hear there are more and more kids getting diabetes from their diets these days."

"It's another kind of diabetes, but that's true too. That kind is associated with being overweight. These boys have type 1 diabetes, which is different. They definitely are careful about what they eat."

He watched the children quietly for a few minutes. Four of the twelve-year-olds were splashing each other and squealing about the slime on the bottom of the lake. They looked like any other group of junior high school kids, hyper and active and just starting to show underarm hair and the gangly look of growing adolescents.

What he didn't see was how casually they milked blood from their fingertips before every meal, or how bravely they pushed needles into their skin to give themselves insulin. Long before most people first began to think about preventing heart disease or eating right, my boys were in constant touch with their state of health.

The first night we were in the woods, tucked into sleeping bags and long past bedtime, the boys sang songs they had learned at camp. Giddy as they were with mingled exhaustion and excitement, the chorus of voices soon dissolved into giggles and their version of pop rock.

"Sing to us!" they called.

Their camp counselor had done this every night, in a lovely, tuned, and practiced voice. But he was not with us that night. And my singing was generally confined to the shower or car—nowhere anyone could hear it.

A clownish towhead named Jon made a farting noise, and another boy rolled off the ground tarp to get away—kicking Zack in the head as he went. Zack's complaint mixed with the laughter of the others, and Jon filled his cheeks for a repeat performance.

"Shhhhhh." I tried softly.

Jon's next "fart" was cut short, and his neighbor wiggled back to the tarp. Zack had lain back down. A stifled giggle failed to catch on, and rolled away.

"Shhhhh."

For a moment, there was only the distant sound of the creek, the rustle of sleeping bags, a faint breeze adding to the nighttime chill.

And then I sang. It felt like the right thing to do. I sang to calm them, though my voice wavered. I sang to ward off the strangeness of this new place. I sang an old John Denver song, and I had to change the high notes a little bit, and the verses went out of order, but it was a heartfelt lullaby, and no one laughed. No one corrected me.

They slept.

I dreamed only once while I was at camp—that I could remember.

Back in my apartment, my dreams had played out like movies while I slept, stuffing my mind with images and thoughts I had no time for during the day. I would wake every morning and lie still for a few minutes, letting the flurry of ideas settle. Otherwise, a cloud followed me out of bed, down the hall, into the shower, and maybe partway through the day. Some of my imaginings had morals; most were just the product of my revved up, overactive mind.

At camp, my sleep became rapturously deep and undisturbed. I would wake thinking only of the day that was just spilling forth through cracks in the forest canopy. And then, on the fourth or fifth night at camp, I dreamed about a woman who had been an intern on the medicine service when I was a third-year student. Julie was one of my greatest role models that year—cheery, good-humored, utterly on the ball, and earnest in her kindness toward patients. Her smile and the sunny inflection in her voice would flash into my mind many times over the year and a half that followed our month together. By envisioning how Julie would handle situations that arose, I survived them with something akin to her magnanimous grace. She cared for some of the most difficult patients I could imagine. One vain patient whose masculine features and Adam's apple stood in sharp contrast to her heavily made-up face and teased blond hair had end-stage AIDS and would let no other doctor get near her. She finally turned against Julie too, calling her a snake and wagging her tongue deliriously. Even as Julie dealt with insults and manipulation and angry people, she surfaced each time with a smirk and a giggle.

In my dream, Julie had finished her residency and decided not to practice medicine. An inside-outsider myself, with my dual pursuit of medicine and writing, I lent her my ear. Some part of me wanted her to offer me a way out of medicine, even as the rest of me reckoned with the long path still ahead. Why, I asked, had she decided to quit?

Julie looked at me with tired eyes. I noticed that she was wearing makeup (she never did in real life), and she remained lying down on a single bed in what appeared to be a transformed call room. With the cheap-looking eyeliner, she resembled a prostitute, battered and worn out, the bitterness of experience caked on her cheeks.

"I think we just see too much at too young an age," she told me. Residency had ground her down. Julie was throwing in the towel.

I awoke into whitish dawn. The girls in my cabin group were all still asleep around me, naïve to the arrival of a new day. I yearned for their usual exuberance, the way sleepiness rolled off of them like beads of water once they remembered where they were. In contrast to my surroundings—the chirrup of birds and emerging green of the branches above me; incredible, far-reaching quiet; and the occasional whoosh of small limbs inside sleeping bags—the Julie of my dream seemed nothing more than a specter of my former life, melting with the morning mist as the wake-up bell began to sound.

I have tried to imagine that first week after finding out one's child has diabetes. The paraphernalia alone must overwhelm a family: glucose meter and test strips, lancets, needles, syringes, insulin. This is how to give an injection, and when, and where. These are two kinds of insulin—there are more, but let's start here, just two kinds, two shots, two times. Two hundred is too high. Below sixty is dangerous.

One counselor described taking responsibility for his own testing and insulin dosage in his early teens as living with the knowledge that he could die in the night—that if his blood sugar got too low, he might not wake up.

The thought caught my heart.

I had first realized I might die when I was twelve years old. It was my mother's birthday, and the four of us—Mom, Dad, my sister, and I—were vacationing in Mammoth Lakes, many years before I moved there after college. Mammoth was our family's safe haven, a mountain town surrounded by pines and peaks that always inspired reverence for nature's majesty. From our condo we looked out over the flat valley we had come through, admiring the clarity of the view and the cornflower blue of the sky. My father called it his church.

That day, the sun poured through the windows into our condo's living room, and the ancient bristlecone outside our patio creaked in the wind—as it had for as long as I could remember, and would for another decade afterward. Danielle and I were playing Sorry. It was midmorning, and we planned to go hiking in a little while. There was no hurry, nowhere we had to go.

Someone knocked on the door. I don't remember who. A manager. A man who worked there, who asked, in a gruff, low voice, to speak to my father.

Then Dad called Mom into the foyer, and I heard her gasp.

I don't think I had ever heard her gasp before, not that way, with the timbre of awe and tragedy mingling and competing.

Danielle and I stopped what we were doing and looked at each other. Should we run to her? Pretend we didn't hear? Mom started crying then. She asked Dad questions he couldn't answer; his voice sounded hurt and flustered. Danielle looked as concerned as I did. Our eyes asked the questions we couldn't get out; something was unfolding that would change us, freeze us in that moment, on that patch of carpet, with the glowing stillness of eleven o'clock on a summer day in the most beautiful and peaceful place we had ever known.

There had been a car accident, Dad explained. On the way to Mammoth that morning, a car flipped, and the son of my parents' closest friends had been killed. Paul, a skinny towheaded thirteen-year-old boy with whom we often played—swimming, computer games, listening to music—was dead.

Dead.

Dead? We met the survivors when they arrived—we brought them food, watched TV with the other kid who had been in the car. He had a broken leg and a somber face. One time I thought I heard him sob, but when I turned around and asked if he was okay, he shrugged and wouldn't look at me. His best friend had just been killed. They had flipped a coin for the front seat. Paul had won.

A memory kept intruding while we sat in front of the glowing television: I had been impatient for Paul to leave the last time he was at our house. I had been bored. I *wanted* him to go. Guilt was starting to settle in around me. I should have appreciated him more, thought about him more. Then he might still be here. Might walk in and brighten up the whole kitchen where the adults huddled under a dull lamp. Night was gathering all around us, and I got the feeling we weren't leaving any time soon. We just sat there full of sadness, sharing it and breathing it and not really doing anything to make it go away.

The gloom followed me. That thick gray fog of melancholy filled my lungs and continued to haunt me. I watched the clouds all the way home to Southern California, looking for answers. I watched everything, everyone, for signs of impending mortality; had I known he was going to die and just not noticed? Is there a certain way people say goodbye, or don't, that means they won't be back? If I died, would any of my schoolmates cry?

The incredible thing about kids, Greg told me once, is they just keep right on being kids, even when they're dying. He meant children on the cancer ward who had lost their hair from chemotherapy, children whose odds of survival might be tiny, who just kept wanting to play. One of his patients, a little girl in an isolation room, used the intercom to giggle with nurses, squeezing her talking doll into the intercom and laughing and laughing.

None of the children at diabetes camp were dying. But some of them had relatives who were, from complications of diabetes, while the children ran around at camp and learned to feel comfortable with insulin injections as part of normal life. Rosy-cheeked, bright-eyed, they could not have looked healthier. For many years the standard of medical care had been not to worry much about tight control of glucose in children, because complications like kidney failure, eye problems, foot ulcers, and infections only happened later in life. These kids looked like any others: tall or small or skinny or obese. They were pale-skinned, Black, Asian, Latino. They acted indestructible.

It was hard to believe the first microscopic damage to their blood vessels could be taking place here at camp, or that important cells might be suffering from lack of glucose. But medical science had surpassed physical diagnosis. With something like faith, we treated the number that came up on a glucose meter, checked it again if someone felt low or irritable, and introduced the children to self-injection that became as second nature as brushing their teeth. With enough conviction, it was almost possible to believe these daily rituals kept them safe.

But we shared a secret, the children and I. For me, the danger of disappearance had swelled every time my family drove the long desert highway toward the mountains, right through Paul's memory, aimed for the other side of dying. I knew the curve where he had died. The skid marks were still there the first time we passed by, and I held my breath until we couldn't see them anymore. Each time we arrived in Mammoth, the air was sweeter for having survived; we plunged into the forest with confidence, a new lease, profound relief. And then there would be another drive.

For the kids I treated at camp, that precarious road was the path to sleeping, and the bend might come up out of nowhere in the dark.

When we sent them home at the end of the session, the campers chattered excitedly about hikes and dances, told jokes, promised to write to new friends. They had felt the pulse of the forest, slept and risen to its rhythm, experienced a sprinkling of Mother Nature's spell. They had learned about themselves in relationship to her: how to adjust their insulin to a strenuous hike or a day of splashing in a stream. But more importantly—most importantly—they had found one another, travelers of kin through the mysterious shadows of mortality.

Cleaning out my bedroom in my parents' home when I was twenty-seven years old, about to graduate from medical school, I came across a framed photograph in the bottom of my sock drawer. I knew without turning it over what it was. I had kept this memento for fifteen years already, and I still could not imagine where else to put it.

In the black-and-white picture, Paul's face is pensive. He is sitting outside, wearing a windbreaker, squinting a little bit in the desert light. This was a copy of the last photo ever taken of him, and I knew it by heart—the slightly opened mouth, part of his chin covered by the jacket, the furrow of his brow and reflection in his eyes. He was thirteen, but he is forever a year older than me. I still wanted to protect him when I saw the image, wanted to reach back and change the way things happened, as though I could be there when the picture was taken and undo history. I was twelve when he died. I had almost believed it possible.

I had a small box of the things I was keeping, and into it I placed the picture of this boy I used to know. What else could I do with it? I could not throw away what had become a part of me, the slight child I vowed to love, who taught me not to take life for granted, whose picture I kept tucked away and carried with me.

I will care for thousands of children in my lifetime.

I have not forgotten.

Steven said it became white noise, the metro running past his window while he slept. If such a monstrous, loud train can sneak past, what of the little clues that would direct our lives, if only we would listen?

(FALL OF THIRD YEAR)

Chapter Thirteen

UNSURE FOOTING
UNCERTAINTY IN MEDICINE

*I*t was an ominously beautiful day in my last few months of medical school. September squatted back on its haunches before surrendering to the progression of time, sitting expectantly, waiting for something to happen before it was forced to slink away.

We arrived in that moment of anticipation. I could feel it in the softness of the sky, blue and uninterrupted. A breeze massaged the pine trees near the top of the hill, but down lower the air was still, a perfect seventy-five degrees, clear and quiet and utterly unobtrusive. Nothing distracted us from our goal: climbing a solid dome of granite rising twelve hundred feet above the carefree forest.

Getting to the base of Castle Dome in Castle Crags State Park presented a few unexpected challenges. Starting from high on the west side, where my boyfriend of three weeks and I had camped overnight just beneath a ridge, we waded downhill through manzanita bushes, the branches clawing at our legs and the straps of our backpacks, as we circumnavigated the mountain. Then Kyle and I stepped out onto crumbly rock that dipped us into a ravine of strewn boulders, weeds, and moss. All at once the passageway dropped off, and we used our rope to rappel over the side and continue our scramble. It happened a second time; the water-worn granite that surrounded us on three sides ended abruptly at an overlook to a rock garden far below. This time we could not see where the rope would leave us.

We tiptoed along small ledges to either side, leaning out just enough to get the lay of the land. We had almost achieved the tree-littered bottom, the starting point of our all-day adventure. Slinging the rope around a root, Kyle threaded it through his own belay device and leaned out.

With a wink, he was gone, leaving me on the side of a mountain with my harness not yet fastened, on the most insidiously lovely September afternoon I could have imagined.

As soon as he hollered he was safely down, I shouldered my backpack and prepared to follow. I didn't know which one of us disaster was going to strike, but I knew I'd rather not be alone when it happened.

We had one more rope-aided descent and then a short hike up to the east face of the dome, which rolled like the nose of a sleeping giant up to the sky.

In the morning light, which was quickly taking on the pallor of midmorning approaching noon, the granite wall shone, breathtaking and intriguing. My eyes wandered up over its features—marble veins, cracks in the rock, bulges and small roofs where some part of the rock had sloughed off in the distant or not-so-distant past—and tried to predict our route.

We didn't have a guidebook. This bothered me more than it bothered Kyle. He had been here before, ten years prior, but was forced to give up climbing all the way up due to a hailstorm. He was excited to finish the route. I was worried that it might be too difficult, or even impassable. Who could tell what had happened in ten years? What if Mother Nature had been trying to tell him something?

Today she was silent. Too silent.

Kyle's confidence had sparkled in the swing-dancing scene where we met. When he was serious or downhearted, I noticed his slightly receding hairline and the asymmetry of his face, but when he smiled, his hazel eyes lit up, and his toothy smile was dazzling. His sister had highlighted his hair with streaks of fruit punch red, but his slightly auburn sideburns still lent him a debonair look. He was an incredible dancer, charming as well as capable, and the combination just dissolved my common sense. Unfortunately, I reflected, realizing why I had agreed to this climb.

He would lead the first rope-length. We checked each other's harnesses before he started to climb; both were fastened correctly. His knot was tight, my belay was good, and we each had the appropriate climbing gear to use or carry until we met up again, nearly 180 feet above. Once we had assured ourselves that we were as safe as any land animals trying to scale rock could be, he started the ascent.

Much of the time Kyle was climbing, I faced out over the wooded valley and hills that lay inland from Castle Crags. The sun graced my cheeks and arms. I was momentarily soothed by the stillness, until I remembered that no one was likely to happen by here. What if we needed help? I checked Kyle's progress frequently, willing him up the rock safely. I indulged myself in a quick review of what I would do if he were injured: get him off the rock, check ABCs (airway, breathing, circulation), assess any injuries, then decide whether it would be safer to go for help or yell for any passersby. I had left the medicine kit in the car, along with his cell phone. Right now that felt like a grave error in judgment. With less than three months left of medical school, what kind of almost-doctor was I? The tension built in my chest and hands. I turned back to squinting at the lulling ocean of sky. *Worry gets you nowhere*, I reminded myself. *Just deal with what happens.*

As I climbed up to join Kyle on the first ledge, I shouldn't have been frightened. Tied into the rope he was controlling, I was reasonably safe—and that's about as safe as it gets in rock climbing. Still, I swore I could hear a faint hiss of the rock beneath my shoes, like the crunch of gravel sliding loose. The previous day, when we had climbed the other side of the dome, a flake of rock the size of a serving platter had come off in my hands. My grip tightened with the memory.

The higher we went, the more haunted I became by the sibilance of rock shifting under my weight. I placed my hands as gently as I could on each feature, hoping it would return the consideration and let me stay balanced there long enough to pass through, just a small human flying in the face of nature—and trying to prove what? All I felt was my own insignificance. I could fall and die, and the moment would fold into history, but even that was too large an idea for my fear-wearied mind to consider. All I could do was focus on one hand at a time. One good foothold and a place to attach the rope for a short time. Moment after moment, we were allowed to survive.

This time, whispered the rock.

This time.

I had taken up rock climbing about a year before medical school. Resting on the deck of a coffee bar in Mammoth after a mountain bike ride, I had struck up a conversation with a woman who lived in town. Fiona spoke with the earnest sincerity of a serious athlete. Blond and blue-eyed, lean from years of outdoor activity, she was attractive but unselfconscious, and I liked her immediately. When she heard the wistfulness in my voice—that I longed to learn to climb—she offered to take me. I didn't hesitate to accept.

On our first day of climbing, she placed her life in my hands. Nothing could have impressed me more. She explained the gear, how to manage the rope, safety, and the commands we should use to communicate, and then she climbed fifty feet up the rock, leaving me holding the other end of her lifeline. I watched her from the ground, diligently feeding rope when she needed it and taking up slack when she didn't. At the top she called, "Take!" and I hurried to tighten up the pull in the rope. Slowly, watching it feed through the belay device, I lowered her back down.

"Nice job!" she remarked.

I smiled, but the real compliment belonged to her.

Over time, Fiona and I became friends as well as frequent climbing partners. My relative lack of experience did not bother her. Her faith in my abilities was the nourishment that allowed my attachment to the sport to take root; that she felt safe with me belaying was a compliment of the highest order. She seemed invincible to me. When she said I could do something, I believed her. Even the risks I took early on were cushioned by this voice of experience.

Later, learning to lead climb for the first time, I would feel fear more keenly than I ever had following Fiona. On lead, a climber ventures up the crag with a rope trailing, and she must attach protection to the rock (in the form of quick draws—two carabiners linked by nylon webbing—if the rock has bolts in it, or by placing metal pieces or devices in its features, if not) and then clip the rope through this protection. If she falls, she relies on that piece to hold, and she will fall twice the distance between herself and the device below her. With top-rope climbing, by contrast, the rope is already through the anchors above and usually pulled tight enough that the climber will not fall freely away from the rock. Now leading my own routes, I had Fiona as my model, her voice in my head: *Relax. Conserve strength. Climb fast. Keep going. You are strong.*

When I left Mammoth for medical school, I took up climbing in a gym. Lost was the spiritual dance with nature that is part of climbing outdoors, but I still felt addicted to the flow of movement, the improbability of ascending walls. Two days a week I stretched myself across the sandpaper surface, leaning from one side to the other as I extended and grasped the designated handholds, toeing odd-shaped pieces of polyurethane long enough to balance and rise and reach out again. For the first year, it seemed that I made no progress in ability at all. Then, gradually, something changed—a shift in mentality perhaps, a relaxation of my fears.

Medical school was just that way too. At first hindered by my own insecurities and feeling overwhelmed, I wasted almost as much energy worrying about exams as I did preparing for them. But as each quarter passed, and as I developed a systematic approach to studying, I could maintain my balance. Focus was an instrument I could turn on and off. In climbing I could lose myself, lose hours, and come home relaxed and calmed. I learned to approach studying the same way.

Much to my surprise, during my third and fourth years when I went to the climbing gym after a night on call and was mentally exhausted, I climbed best of all. Too tired to be afraid, I focused moment to moment on the task at hand: balance, movement, fluidity, strength. With my fears dampened, I developed an intuitive sense of my body's capabilities. I began to take risks. I pushed myself and leaped for holds I previously considered far out of reach; more than once I amazed myself by reaching farther than I thought I could. Hanging on with a few fingers, I could get my feet under me, shift my bodyweight, and scale routes I had never attempted before.

Still, there were times I encouraged myself out loud, talking down the anxieties that threatened to drain all of my strength while I tried to stick to rock (real or fake) that was a little too slick, or crumbly, or steep. With climbing, I never knew what kind of experience I was in for.

But as my confidence bloomed, my trepidation became manageable. Not insignificant, but manageable.

The first time I felt personally responsible for a patient was in my third year of medical school, during my required clerkship in internal medicine. Rumors circulated about this rotation: supposedly students sabotaged each other to look smarter; residents made students run around doing menial tasks; attendings "pimped" students (pumping them with questions to assess their level of knowledge) and ridiculed them for their deficiencies; students didn't sleep for eight weeks because even when they weren't on call, they were expected to be studying and preparing presentations.

As far as I could tell, most of this lore was exaggerated. The classmate I worked with was a mildly nervous, kind young man I knew from a small group class that had spanned my previous two years of medical school. He was diligent about reading up on relevant topics and likely to understand what was going on with his patients, and often mine. No sabotage in that—he was thorough, and I aspired to be too. My residents—or one resident, Tim, and two interns—seemed more interested in teaching than giving us work to do, and were encouraging. Tim's only flaw was a touch of overexuberance, manifested as a tendency to cut off student presentations with his own assessment of a patient. And our attending, a baby-faced oncologist with a Southern accent and an incredible memory for minutiae, had yet to show any teeth. He needn't; his very title and knowledge were enough to intimidate us. As for sleep—well, I hadn't figured that part out yet. So far, as was true throughout medical school, I had gotten seven hours, except on call nights, when I got two or three.

My new patient was a forty-year-old woman who had a number of medical problems, which is not unusual in a large, academic medical center. The night she became my patient, she was confused and difficult to interview, so the resident directed me to her chart for most of the background information. As I started to write down her past medical history, I felt increasingly intimidated: she had liver disease, deteriorating kidneys, a failing heart, high blood pressure, arthritis, gallbladder blockage, leg ulcers, neuropathy, ascites fluid in her abdomen and lower chest, and a history of a severe, untreatable urinary tract infection. The longer the list became, the tinier I felt beside it. It took me hours just to write her admission note—sixty minutes to interview and examine her, another sixty to stare at the list of diagnoses that lay like runes before me, at least fifteen to figure out where to start, and another hour to do the basic research to continue. When I finally wormed my hand into a solid grip on her history, I started with the present: what did she need *today*?

She had had a seizure. With that information in place, I could go in several directions; the list of possible causes was enormous. But the clue likely lay within the list of troubles she already had. I tried to focus my eyes and concentrate, scanning for a clear foothold. What had happened recently?

Almost too many factors, unfortunately: medication changes, transfer to a skilled nursing facility, institution of dialysis to help her kidneys filter her blood. But what caught my eye was the most exotic of her problem list. She had chronic active hepatitis C with cryoglobulinemia—a rare complication in which one's body makes antibodies against the antibodies that normally fight infections (as I learned from a textbook), forming cryoglobulins. Cryoglobulins could precipitate out of the bloodstream at low temperatures, causing kidney disease as well as irritation of small blood vessels and a wide range of symptoms from muscle aches, rash, and ulcers, to loss of sensation in fingers or toes and swelling of lymph nodes. From there, it wasn't a large leap to the conclusion that cryoglobulins could induce seizure as well. It topped my list.

Using my handbook of medicine, with its catalogue of possible seizure causes, I came up with six more possibilities. But the more I read, checking each candidate against her lab values and radiological studies, the more likely cryoglobulins seemed. If they were the culprit, what, besides treating her with anti-seizure medication, should we do for her?

Textbooks weren't current enough to advise a treatment plan, so I went to the library the day after we admitted her to the hospital and printed the most recent journal articles I could find. There I found the information that very nearly got me in over my head.

That day in rounds—a meeting of the attending with resident, interns, and medical students—after I dutifully reported my patient's vital signs and current condition, the question of her treatment arose.

"Well, that's not entirely clear—" I began.

Tim interjected, "We'll definitely continue her interferon therapy while we have her in the hospital." My patient had been receiving interferon-alpha therapy, the only treatment approved for hepatitis C, for thirteen weeks already.

"Is that what her primary doctor planned for her, or what we want to do?" Dr. Clark asked, his attention diverted to Tim.

"Both," he said. I could tell from Tim's hasty reply that he didn't know this with much confidence.

"Actually," I spoke up just loudly enough to be heard, "I did some reading on cryoglobulinemia, and I'm not sure that would be the best thing for her."

No one spoke, so I continued, apologetically at first but with increasing confidence as the others listened. "It sounds like interferon-alpha can improve symptoms associated with cryoglobulinemia, but it can also worsen them. A number of other autoimmune complications of hep C are aggravated, not improved, by therapy. And there is a rebound effect after stopping the treatment. If her seizure was caused by cryoglobulins, we might be putting her more at risk by continuing interferon. Or the seizure could even be a side effect of the alpha-interferon—that's been described in some cases too." It was amazing how knowledgeable I could sound with the information fresh on my mind.

Tim hastened to say we should talk to the other doctors before deciding.

Dr. Clark looked bemused. "Fine," he said. Then, speaking slowly, he turned to me and added, "But I want Claire to manage this patient. This is *your* patient," he told me. "You've done the research on her, you admitted her, and as far as I am concerned, you are the expert on this condition. Tell me tomorrow what you want to do."

I barely nodded, sitting stock-still and tensed as long as his attention remained on me. *My* patient? What *I* decided? No one gave that sort of power to a third-year medical student. Surely, I had fooled him into thinking me more competent than I felt—all because I looked up a few articles? His trust astounded me.

Once I had recovered from the moment, and rounds concluded, the new responsibility spurred me to action.

Someone had to call her primary physician. Usually, the job fell to an intern or resident, someone more experienced than a student in her first month on the wards. But this time Tim dodged it.

"You should call," he insisted. "You know what to say."

I didn't, actually. But I knew what I wanted to ask.

After a brief introduction, and a reminder of who the patient was and why we had admitted her, I made my pitch. "The journal articles I was able to find suggest that if no response occurs by twelve weeks in, that there isn't a benefit to continuing the interferon-alpha. And if it could be doing some harm, since she just had a first-time seizure two nights ago, I guess my question is whether we ought to consider stopping the therapy."

On the other end of the line, Dr. Prause asked me for some lab data to back up what I was saying. He asked what I proposed to do for her, what studies we had planned, and how long we expected to keep her in the hospital. I shuffled my notes and tried to quiet the thudding of my heart in my throat as I answered his questions to the best of my ability. I was waiting for him to tell me the piece I didn't know, the missing link that would explain why the therapy wasn't as questionable as I thought.

But the ax never fell. Instead, he praised my thoroughness. He asked my name again. He said he agreed with my assessment, and he would confer with her other doctors but expected they would stop the treatment.

"There are risks on either side of it," he pointed out, "but it sounds to me like you're right. The risk of continuing therapy probably outweighs the benefit."

Even on the most clear-headed of her ten days in the hospital, my patient was not able to understand the decision we ultimately made for her. Interferon-alpha had been her only hope as a medication for hepatitis C. By stopping it, she would be spared the problems and chance of seizures the medicine had probably conferred on her. From her lab studies, it seemed that the interferon was not working, anyway. But without any treatment, the hepatitis was more likely to progress unchecked.

When I told him the interferon would be stopped, my attending pointed out that the forty-ish woman I had yet to get to know would most likely live less than six months, regardless of therapy. He praised me for being thorough, adding that her last months would be more bearable because of my research.

Then he turned to the business of the next patient, leaving me contemplating the relative worth of good days, compared to more days, when someone is dying.

Who can know whether ours was the right decision? All we have sometimes is one leg to stand on, a choice between two shaky alternatives, and the pledge to be more safe than not. I know my intentions were in the right place. I know I researched the problem as well as I could.

Years later I looked my patient up on the hospital computer, wondering if she might still be alive. She was never admitted to the wards after the time I cared for her, or even seen in the emergency room. She had no more lab studies recorded. Nor was there an end-date to her life. My patient had simply vanished from the system, whether to die or thrive I will never know.

I went on to care for dozens of other patients, ever mindful that treatment could be helpful—*or* could do more harm than good. Each decision required reading, consulting, reasoning—and ultimately, faith.

"Big wall" climbing involves more gear and more uncertainty than shorter rock faces demand. When Kyle and I climbed Castle Dome, we expected to get about six rope-lengths (called "pitches") off the ground by the time we reached the top. This meant that he or I—whoever was leading—would ascend almost as far as our 200-foot rope would allow, create an anchor by fixing at least three pieces of equipment in cracks in the rock, and then latch ourself onto the temporary mooring site. The leader then belayed the other climber up—pausing as the follower removed nuts, hexes, and cams from the rock on the way—and attached that second person to the rock face as well. The gear was reorganized, the next leader was designated, and on we went.

In this case, because neither of us had climbed the whole face before, nor did we have a guidebook to show us where to go, the stakes got higher as we rose farther off the ground. We might, as we hoped, have made progress. If we reached the top, we could scramble down an easy couple hundred feet to the ridge, near our campsite. On the other hand, if we deviated from the normal route, the necessity of retreat became an ever-looming possibility, and we might only be prolonging the time it would take to get back down to the bottom if we came to an impasse.

The first and second pitches, though they meandered slightly on the way up, were each marked with one bolt permanently fixed in the rock. Rusted slightly, square-edged in the style of a generation that had climbed in heavy-soled boots and jeans, these did not impress me as having been used in recent history. Nevertheless, we thought they must have been placed on the original route, and we expected we were on-course.

The second pitch ended on a large ledge. Here, for the first time since leaving the ground, we could stand comfortably side by side. We shared water and snacks, luxuriating in the sun on our skin and the bird's-eye view stretching all the way across tree-covered skeins to Mount Shasta. All was still, except for a gently circling hawk hovering in midair near the forest edge below us.

"Ready to lead the next pitch?" Kyle asked me, treating me to an encouraging smile.

I considered the granite path that lay ahead. If I climbed directly perpendicular to gravity, I would make little progress before coming up against a featureless bulge of rock. To the left, the face was completely sheer. Off to the right, a decent-sized slit promised handholds, slicing a slightly off-centered but consistent course beyond where I could see. To start this last line, though, I would have to climb out over a roof, leaning almost parallel to the ground, and then hoist myself up to a standing position. There was no way to protect myself while I tried it; if I fell, I would either land on the ledge we were now standing on, or tumble below it, trusting our anchor to hold me.

I ran my fingers over the handholds I could reach from the ledge, testing each one with my body twisted to maximize my reach. There was a hold big enough for all four fingers of my right hand just at the lip of the roof. The left hand must make do with a half-centimeter crack just above it. I couldn't see what I might find immediately past that point; I would have to climb up and take a look. For my feet, there were few features to speak of. I would have to trust a small defect in the rock with all my body weight at first, and then try to push off an apple-sized fist of rock far to the right, if I could get to it. My heart thundered its misgivings.

"I'll give it a shot," I told Kyle optimistically.

He nodded and passed the gear sling to me.

When all was arranged—the rope knotted through my harness and passing through Kyle's belay device, a loop of nylon bearing wire-strung pieces of metal strapped over my shoulder, and my fingers chalked for better grip—I stepped gingerly out to the corner of the ledge and took a deep breath. There was still a slam dance taking place in my chest, but I contorted myself as planned and curled my fingers over the one good handhold. The hollow comforted me: it was a gift that promised a way forward, a starting-place for progress. This much, I knew, was true. Exhaling a quick puff of air, I pulled with my right arm and flung my left hand up to where I knew the second handhold should be. At first, I felt only smooth rock, and my fingers fanned out like search parties at sunrise, but I found nothing. I was nearly horizontal, my ponytail whipping at my cheeks as I swung there, my head more than 300 feet off the now-distant, boulder-strewn ground. I caught a glimpse of the handhold, but I knew I would be too tired to continue once I reached it. I retreated.

I tried again, this time stretching my feet apart to use both available footholds. The extra lift was just enough: I could hover with both hands on the rock, my nose barely above the ledge, and see where to go next. Another pocket angled to the right, then a patch of rough surface to the far left. Otherwise, I could pick out only a few pushpin-sized nubbins—not enough to hold onto while swinging my feet out and onto the upslope of rock.

As it was, I would have to let go of my precious right handhold to move forward. The left was too thin to hold me, unless I did it quickly and the next handhold was good enough to keep me from tumbling back down. Or if I could find another foothold? While I tried to decide, my hands started sweating from the sensation of exposure. I knew it would hurt to fall backward just then. Once again, I retreated, rested, and planned my next attack.

I made three more attempts. Each time I grew both more determined and more discouraged. The bottom of the next pit for my hand was sloped downward and fairly slick, and the only other place I could get purchase on the rock was a finger-sized hole with a sharp edge. I could get my whole body just under the lip, but not over it. There was too much distance between handholds, and fear had created a ceiling above me; the harder I pressed into it, the more oppressive the resistance it gave back.

I looked at Kyle, who had been patiently belaying me all this time. I knew his heart was set on finishing this climb today. I didn't want to say what I did.

"I don't think I can do this. I'm at my limit."

Much to my surprise, he smiled ruefully and shrugged. "Then you shouldn't. You've got to respect your limits—that's the only way to be safe."

I looked out over the forested hills below us, rolling languidly beneath the midday sun, and breathed in a little bit of the clear sky. Retreating wasn't what either of us had had in mind. But maybe it was the better decision after all.

Half in jest, I was advised on my surgery rotation, "It doesn't matter if you're right or wrong, as long as you form an opinion."

In other words, "decisiveness can avert catastrophe"—as my father told me when teaching me to drive. I was sixteen years old and had stomped on the accelerator to pull the car out in front of an oncoming truck. Surgery is a field of doers, so do-something almost always trumps do-nothing. When do-nothing seems like the right thing, uncertainty holds doctors back. Decisiveness doesn't come so easy anymore.

My team once had a patient in the ICU who was dying. He had had two cardiac surgeries in the past, suffered a massive heart attack, and had blood pressure almost too low to keep him alive. It was likely that his neurological function was already damaged beyond repair. He had various lines and catheters, was intubated on a respirator, and had multiple monitors evaluating his situation. His heart wavered in and out of arrhythmia. Infusions of various medicines kept him teetering on the crumbling brink of life, but it was clear he could not hold on much longer.

The resident spoke with the family about our patient, warning them that their father/husband/uncle's time was most likely just about up. He suggested they sign a DNR—Do Not Resuscitate. This order would allow him to die without being shocked, having chest compressions performed, or other "heroic" measures. It would be more peaceful, the resident assured them, than the alternative. The chances of successfully resuscitating him, should his heart stop, were extremely low.

Through tears, the family refused. They said they wanted everything done for him, that they would feel too responsible if they allowed him to die.

But "everything" had already been done for him. The resident called our attending, and the two murmured about the patient's vital statistics from the monitors and blood studies. They agreed he was dying, and that efforts at resuscitation would be traumatic and futile. But to write an order to do nothing—to allow a patient to die—two attendings must sign a DNR if the family will not.

Another attending physician was called, and a small conference ensued. The two attendings tested one another. Was there any chance of neurological recovery? No, the second attending agreed, the patient was not waking up and had signs of severe mental impairment. How bad was his heart function? Dismal, and worsening. How old was he? Could he withstand a code (resuscitation)? What other medical problems did he have? Was there anything more they could possibly do to turn him around?

Only then, reassured by one another that nothing had been missed, did the two men sign the DNR. I had never seen them question their own confidence before. Either could be called upon at a moment's notice to suggest various therapies for the sickest of patients in the ICU. But giving up on a life was harder than trying to save one; neither doctor would take that risk alone.

Despite the extra six inches of height and "ape index" (equivalent to wingspan for a bird) that Kyle had over me, he could not get past the roof that had thwarted me. We stood together silently on the ledge for a few minutes, scanning the rock and the horizon for our best course of action. Both of us settled our gaze on a crack in the rock that we had ignored at first—thin, leading up to a blank bulge only twenty feet above us, it had seemed unimportant only moments before. Suddenly it represented the difference between moving forward and retreating to the base of the dome: progress, or giving up.

What Kyle hoped for, as he prepared to try this avenue, was a way to move around the bulge when he got there. We had metal "stoppers"—trapezoidal pieces for wedging into cracks—small enough to place into a slit where even a pinky finger wouldn't fit, so he was reasonably sure he could protect a fall on the way there. But whether he could get around the hump, leaving the safety of the crack and the fingerholds it offered, neither of us was sure.

Kyle was more of a risk-taker than I was. This had always been true, but at a time like this—faced with a last resort—the fact rang with a note of bravado, a chime of hope. A few minutes later, Kyle was just beneath the point where the protuberance of rock erupted outward like an enormous pimple, slick and waxen-sided and insurmountable. Kyle's long legs trembled noticeably as he extended himself rightward, pinching the unmarked rock to get a thumb hold, to balance before moving on. He was a spider, pulling filament behind him as he inched away from security.

All at once, he scuttled back. When he was close to the last stopper he had left in the rock, he asked me to take in the slack in the rope, and he gently trusted the piece with his weight. This lasted only a moment; then he moved out, right and upward, with swift determination, and found his way to a clean line up the rock.

I exhaled as I fed him rope to clip through another piece of gear. We were past the impasse. Our dance with the rock continued.

Working in the newborn nursery as a fourth-year medical student, I frequently attended deliveries. My job, as a member of the team of pediatricians that rushed into the labor and delivery rooms on a moment's notice, was to prepare for anything: don a clean gown and gloves, check the warmer, turn on oxygen and have a newborn-sized mask ready, test the suction tubing, lay out warm blankets, and have hands out to receive the tiny new being the moment he or she arrived.

And as soon as that slick little body was placed onto the two-by-three-foot table under a radiant heater, we followed a well-defined resuscitation algorithm. First, we dried the baby. If the obstetrician had noticed greenish-colored fluid coming from the birth canal, a sign that the baby had been stressed, we took care not to stimulate the baby too much until a nurse could use suction tubing to clear its nose and mouth. Then we rubbed the newborn with dry blankets more vigorously. Most babies, if they had not yet cried, would do so at this point, gulping air by the mysterious, deep-seated reflex that converts them from aqueous beings to land animals. A pink, vigorous infant could be examined with some leisure at this point. But if the baby didn't open its lungs, if the skin was bluish or mottled, the intensity of our attention thickened. We would then give breath by applying a face mask and squeezing oxygen through an inflatable bag. One of us was assigned to check heart rate. The other might tap those tiny, thumb-sized feet, or prepare for the next stage of resuscitation if there was no response to our efforts—get ready to intubate, to take blood, to give medicines. I knew what to give, how much, and in what order. Over and over, I had reviewed the algorithm, asking our attending to test me on the resuscitation doll in the corner of the nursery.

A well-groomed man with white hair and a carefully shaped beard, Dr. Hammett carried himself with the relaxed air of someone who has seen too much to be easily surprised. He smirked at my enthusiasm to be tested and humored me, twisting the circumstances of each make-believe scenario to find out just how much I really knew. Each time, I followed him pace for pace as long as he followed branch points I could recognize.

"Bomp ... bomp ... bomp ..." He mimicked heart rate for me while I held a stethoscope to the plastic doll.

"So the heart rate is still less than sixty, and I want to give epinephrine again, same amount."

"What else do you want to do?"

"It's time to check a blood gas. And I'm going to intubate."

Taking the metal instrument in my left hand, I scooped the doll's make-believe tongue up away from the trachea with the curved blade, then followed it with a piece of plastic tubing and withdrew the blade.

"I think I'm in, but I need to check," I commented smoothly, listening over both sides of the infant's chest and its stomach with my stethoscope while squeezing oxygen-rich air into the tube. "Equal lung sounds, so it's right. Now I resume giving O2 and check heart rate again."

"The baby starts shaking."

"Shaking?"

"And his eyes roll back."

"So he's seizing?"

I paused and reviewed what I knew. This was definitely not part of the resuscitation tree I had studied.

Finally, Dr. Hammett stepped back and waited for me to look up. When I did, he grinned.

"Perfection is the enemy of good," he said. "You are a very good student. Keep it up. But beware the trap of perfectionism, because it only causes problems."

That was all he said, letting the mystery of his words twist and linger in his wake.

Not everything we encounter can be managed by algorithm.

When the end of our ascent of Castle Dome was almost in sight, and the cant of the rock face had started to soften near the top, the sun was already dwindling out of sight behind the mountain. We estimated that there was an hour or so of daylight remaining, and one pitch—maybe one and a half—left to go.

"You've got this one," Kyle told me.

"Yep," I agreed.

Once we passed the bulge, I had gotten my "lead head." Being the one in front always took away some of the room for fear. Even though following was more protected, it allowed time for the mind to wander, a laziness of focus that made obstacles seem greater. Honing in on the basics of climbing—positioning, balance, gear placement, rope—I had mustered courage to traverse a featureless area and curl myself over a roof, successfully this time. As I led, I grew more comfortable on the granite, and I was surprised when I had only twenty feet of rope left before it was time to pass on the lead to Kyle. My body tingled with exhilaration. This, I realized, was why we climbed.

Now it was my turn again, and I examined the most likely route eagerly. We were almost there. The lateness of the day worried me a little; climbing in the dark would be extremely difficult—and dangerous. I chalked my hands and prepared to climb, unhooking myself from our anchor. I glanced back just in time to realize Kyle was unaware of my preparations and was looking down at the rope.

"Ready?" I asked.

He grabbed for the rope, checked his belay device, and nodded. "Climb on."

His smile—encouraging, proud, confident—squeezed warmth into my chest. Nothing like a flutter of affection to distract you when you're 950 feet off the ground.

I regained composure as soon as I started to climb, channeling the flush of energy into paying extra attention to safety. I couldn't help thinking of Fiona's husband, a climber with twenty-five years' experience who forgot to finish tying his knot and plummeted one hundred and five feet to the ground. *It doesn't take much*, I reminded myself. Gary survived, miraculously enough. He had twenty-three broken bones requiring multiple surgeries, but against all odds, he made it through. And climbed again.

I fitted a perfect-sized hex into a V-shaped crevice and clipped on a quick draw, then the rope. I glanced down to make sure Kyle was watching me. I turned back to the wall and hoisted myself up to the next good foothold.

I knew couples who bickered all the way up the rock; vulnerability and fear manifest as shortness of tongue, anxieties let loose to whip one another into furor and frustration. I felt thankful for Kyle's clearheadedness. Like the attendings whose examples I followed in the hospital, Kyle was not flustered by the challenge of proceeding without a map. I longed to follow that example.

A two-inch-wide crack swerved within reach of my right hand, and I balanced on an extended foot while I reached for the one Camelot in our rack. Spring-loaded, the device exerts enough outward force to catch a Volkswagen Beetle—or so I was once told by a climbing partner with a mind for such details. I secured it in the crevice, attached the rope, shifted my weight right, and continued up the wide rift for another ten feet.

Even better than great doctors to mimic—and rarer—were those who, ever watching my back, encouraged me to lead. There's no substitute for the feeling of responsibility, knowing someone else's confidence was in my hands. Every muscle and fiber of concentration devoted itself to proving myself worthy of the challenge.

But I would not do it alone. Someone must be at the other end of the rope, looking out for that splinter of misfortune that could be my downfall, or someone else's. Fate is stronger than we are; if she whispers that the time has come, no safeguard can prevent catastrophe. But if I could be mindful enough, balancing vulnerability with confidence, pushing myself to greater heights one cautious step at a time, ever aware of the risk at hand and not overstepping the bounds of what I know, I might survive to do the same for someone else.

We summited just after sunset. The western sky was still blushing orange and pink, and a wind ushered in a star-sprinkled night. Carefully we minced our way down the gentler slope of the backside of the dome, and just as darkness dropped its curtain over the last glow of light, we reached the backpacks we had left there. We hiked out in silence, triumphant but exhausted by the day's gradual, suspenseful unfolding.

A few hours later, safely in the car, tires whirring on the highway as we drove home, we started planning the next climb.

Some mornings during my rotations, light beckoned me before my alarm. More often, I rose into darkness, confused and heavy-headed as I stumbled down the hall to the shower. Dawn often spread across the sky as I drove to the hospital, the sun's bright appendages poking above and below a cloud layer on the horizon directly in front of me, or brightening the fog-cloaked sky.

Once, when I was not quite thirteen years old, my father woke us at 3:30 a.m. to see Halley's Comet. My sister and I climbed obediently out of bed, put on sweat pants and jackets, and slumped against one another in the bench seat of our Dodge van. There was no sign of impending sunrise. The night was as blue-black and dark as it ever got in Southern California. It felt timeless.

We drove like escapees, away from the half-lit streets of our small town to the base of Mount Baldy, quietly and all-too-slowly rolling through stop signs and then speeding on the open road to the first turnout partway up the mountain. No one spoke until we had almost reached our destination, and then my father reminded us: "Girls, you will probably only see this once in your life. They say Halley's Comet is only visible once every seventy-six years or so."

Just then he pulled off the main road and turned off the headlights. Around us were four or five other cars and small clusters of people stargazing. I felt privy to a fantastic ritual as we, too, positioned ourselves and waited.

Below us to the west, scattered lights marked upper Claremont, which had only recently been developed at all. Beyond that, streetlights marched in patterned rows, and farther still, neon shop-signs and freeway lights glowed vaguely. But above the milkiness of the horizon, where the stars were too muted to see, the sky turned indigo and then black. We could see a panoply of stars, but no moon. As we waited, a cold breeze, no stronger than a collective sigh, passed around and between us. I watched with blunted expectation, not entirely believing we would witness anything at all on this strange morning. Our own existence, barely visible to one another in the blackness, seemed to hinge on the appearance of a streak of light across the sky.

It emerged gradually. The swath of fire in the comet's wake arched into view around the twilight of dawn, hovering there while we passed around binoculars and took second and third looks. An hour passed while we marveled at its semi-permanence: there had been only a bright dot, and now this smudge, floating motionless above us. As the sun's approach grew more imminent, the apparition withered. Tail first, it faded and was gone. A lifetime's journey had just ended. And begun.

The predawn hours since then have always been pregnant with expectation. I watch fellow travelers blink as new light arrives. We pass easily through streets that will soon be crowded; we are privileged to a great secret. In the minutes before I arrive at the hospital, I am blessed with incredible perspective. I can never know what challenge awaits me, what life will end or begin under my watch, or what I might learn if I pay attention. Uncertainty is medicine's greatest gift. The day, when the sun has found its way free, is already gilded.

Elated today. Working hard but loving it. Not minding staying late after getting to the hospital early. Not minding being interrupted to go to a delivery. What more important task is there than to help bring new life into the world?

It occurs to me now that this is the feeling—the adrenaline buzz—that draws people into medicine and creates from them people who barely exist outside of the medicine realm. ... In short, the "doctor-type" I have been so fearful of becoming. And yet, for now, it is perfect. I can't believe how happy I am there.

(SPRING OF FOURTH YEAR)

Chapter Fourteen
LOST GLASSES
FOURTH YEAR AND BEYOND

Three weeks before officially graduating from medical school, I lost my glasses.

The error was simple enough: an object misplaced, left in inanimate silence, stripped of value somewhere in a dark, forgotten location. How many items fall into the creases of a sofa, or are unwittingly nudged under furniture, to resurface years after their utility has expired?

But my grievance felt greater than that. The spectacles symbolized something larger, a deep and insidious process of losing my balance that had begun to wind itself around my ankles and gradually pull me to its hoary, bestial self. Until then, by struggling just enough, I had managed to stay above ground. Until then, if I looked at it out of the corner of my eye and squinted just right, I could believe that this loss of equilibrium was merely an ominous shadow, a nightshade of the imagination that only became threatening to those who believed it existed. *I* could escape. I could stand on my toes and sidestep its slithering advances. But the evidence had become clear: I was caught. And the only way to break free would be to let go of one of the acts I was juggling and hang on to something solid for a change.

I retraced my steps. Because this was Sunday, I'd had no predictable pattern to my day. Before the glasses slinked away to some very logical place where I had put them, and then forgot, I had used them two days before at work to read patients' medical charts and handwrite my own additions. They almost certainly adorned my face when I sat down to sift through emails and schedule residency interviews, analyze my calendar and respond to offers. I had made flight arrangements on the computer, contacted acquaintances for places to stay, and coordinated my holiday plans. Sitting down to homework for a literature course just a day before, I had read essays and written responses. I pontificated in my journal. I had been writing thank-you notes for graduation gifts at a rate of about four per week—slow, but making progress. Because all of this was easier when I could see without straining, I assumed my specs had been with me.

By this point in my education, I had become used to balancing disparate activities and negotiating a path that allowed me to keep them all. My days were scheduled but full in a robust, almost healthy way. I woke before sunrise, showered as I blinked at the bathroom light, and bicycled to the hospital, where I was enveloped in the artificiality of fluorescent lighting and quickly forgot the warm, dark bedroom I had left. Then the bustle started: seeing patients, checking data, talking with my superiors, answering pages, trying to learn and appear competent at the same time. By four o'clock I was always anxious to leave, knowing the daylight was already waning in the lull of late afternoon. Whenever I was dismissed—often closer to seven than five—I hurried home and on to a quick dinner or writing classes or the climbing gym. Whenever daylight permitted, I jumped at the opportunity to be outside. Often I had homework to do, friends to see. I existed in an ever-changing, organic equilibrium: some stubborn reluctance to do things I ought to do, a little bit of satisfaction when I got tasks done, glee when I got away with going dancing and then sleeping less than I ought in the name of pleasure and relaxation. I slept well, just never enough.

I didn't usually lose things.

If I did, it was something like a pen, and I knew where I left it, I was just not willing to go back and retrieve it. I tracked five patients' lab values, knew their histories by rote, kept my calendar in my mind, called my parents once a week, and always remembered to feed the neighbor's cat. I knew more phone numbers by heart than I ever had time to use, and important birthdays rarely escaped me. It was a phenomenon of conditioning: with enough adrenaline, miraculous tasks of memory became both necessary and possible. It was the things that didn't require thought that slipped away, unnoticed, until their absence became a problem. Like reading glasses. Door keys.

I'd only once been locked out of my house. During final exams in my second year of medical school, I wandered out the door with crib sheets in hand, cramming last-minute facts on the way to school. I couldn't even remember whether I had closed the door—but evidently I did, letting the lock click on my way out. Not until I returned did I realize my error. I sat on the doorstep, forced into a half-hour of doing nothing until my roommate arrived home. I noticed the red geraniums our neighbor tended, the freshly painted gold trim on the Victorian home across the street. I smiled at a woman jiggling a baby stroller as she passed slowly by, and I thought about a friend I had neglected to call. It was exactly what I needed.

What did I need this time?

An almost-superstitious watcher of signs, I reviewed my situation. I was twenty-seven years old, and I prioritized largely by intuition and chance. I had less than a month of medical school left. I was taking graduate school classes at the same time, and I was dating Kyle, a swing dancer/rock climber whose presence always distracted me. Residency loomed ahead of me, and with it, decisions much larger than I felt prepared to make: whether and where to move, whether my boyfriend could make the transition with me, how to survive with so little time to myself that I would have to choose which outside interest to honor, not which *ones*.

Such a future flew in the face of the way I had lived my life—respectful of real boundaries, shifting those that could be moved. Indulging my mind and heart and body in equal parts. Maintaining enough presence of mind to call friends and check up on them, or sneak in an hour-long walk in the park at twilight to catch up with my sister. My vision, usually farsighted, had become more and more blurry as the future got closer.

Other things were lost at times like this, when I was too busy to consider my exact actions on a given Friday afternoon. The glasses were only the most tangible. Dozens of opportunities fluttered away each time I turned my back to put out one fire, and then the next. I didn't always have time to learn about myocarditis or aminoglycoside antibiotics. I couldn't take hours to sit at my desk and write until my pupils withered in the computer light, dreaming up the moments I meant to record. Good friends were occasionally neglected in favor of a chance to exercise.

Why did I try to do so much?

For many years, I did because I *could*. Holding on to my many pastimes was a way of hanging on to my mountain self, my whimsical self. It kept me from suffocating.

Thriving had seemed impossible when I started medical school. I would not have wanted my dying thought to be about cell nuclei or biochemical pathways. I evaded my homework valiantly, whether to go for a bike ride or cook dinner or take off for a weekend, back to Mammoth. I resisted scheduling my time with the desperation of a prisoner who sees the end coming. I craved freedom until, as school assignments amassed, I could not escape, except for an afternoon in Golden Gate Park, or a day or two in the mountains. I was soon in danger of failing for the first time ever in my lengthy school career.

And then something shifted. An idea grew, no more forceful at first than the trickle of snowmelt on spring's first sunny day. If I figured out when to eat, and where to study, and made plans I could stick to, I could also schedule free time. The realization was like a breath of sky. I didn't have to live small to succeed in medical school. I just had to be selective about when to run away, and enjoy those moments all the more.

So that's what I did. The habit grew, and soon I found myself bouncing from one pastime to another, filling my days to overflowing. I did it because I could. I did it because it was fun. And because everything I made time for—breathing, listening, creating—had meaning.

The most sustaining of my pastimes has always been exercise. I still find it hard to define the importance of action; I might as soon explain the value of water. I know what it is made of, how it looks and acts and tastes, but I cannot find words to explain my need for it. For me, movement has been as necessary and instinctive as quenching a thirst. Out on a trail with Nicole, pedaling with David, climbing with Greg or on my own, I found clarity of thought that was hard to achieve amidst a to-do list hours long. I fought battles wordlessly, pummeling frustrations into the dirt beneath me, growing stronger with every step or pedal stroke or foothold. In motion, I was confident and capable. Outdoors, I imagined a freedom of will and thought I could only find on my own—certainly not within the confines of my job as a medical student. I made tangible progress in the span of a half-hour, an hour: something was achieved, climbed, finished before I returned home, even if it was only the summit of the small hill in Golden Gate Park. From there I could see all the way out to the horizon. Without these escapes, I would feel myself settling into stagnation, too lethargic to make a difference to anyone, even myself.

But something else had changed in the four years since I started medical school: I became a physician. It sounded as ludicrous to my ear as the words "medical student" had sounded when I first tried them on my mountain friends. Somewhere during the years of juggling my hiking boots, notebooks, eyeglasses, and stethoscope, the study of medicine had transformed from a wormy obligation to cram information into my weary mind, to the winged possibility of making a difference in people's lives.

I had changed too. When I first started seeing patients, I would pause outside each door, stricken momentarily by fear. Not only was I new to the doctor role I was mimicking, and consequently insecure about what I could offer, I was also afraid I might not like the person I was to meet. I knew he or she might show me something about myself, something I would just as soon leave behind the laundered curtain in the room full of sick people where I believed I did not belong.

Even more disturbing was the realization that I *did* belong: I had been a patient too.

My last patient in medical school was Shelly. At ten, she was a skinny, blond haired little girl with braces that made her lips stick out. Even as sick as she was when I met her, I could see that she was a combination of wiry tenacity and sweet childishness. She had been articulate, a straight-A student. She had played soccer. Like many kids her age, she had asked questions incessantly.

The first time I saw her, she was drooling on a starched hospital pillow, and her eyes fluttered shut after less than three seconds of looking around for her mother. She thrashed once or twice when I examined her. She pointed to her teddy bear, but couldn't say its name.

I must have spent several hours in her hospital room over the handful of days that she was my patient. As a student on a consulting service—infectious disease—my task was primarily to consider what sort of organism could have caused this bright preadolescent to become dazed, feverish, and nearly wordless in a two-day span of time. I interviewed her father once, her mother twice. I asked questions like, "What is the source of water in your house?" "Has she had any contact with bats?" "Could an animal have bitten her?"

Much of the time I simply listened to her parents trying to sort through clues of the past month. I answered what questions I could, and I looked up answers to others. Shelly had encephalitis, a viral infection of the brain that might go away and leave her mostly the way she had been beforehand. More likely, she wouldn't ever fully recuperate. The tests we sent would take weeks to come back, and were not expected to change anything.

I said goodbye to Shelly the day my four weeks on the infectious disease service were up. She raised her head from the pillow briefly, then a hand. Both slumped back, and she seemed asleep again.

My attending explained to the family about the change of service—the fellow would stay, while the attending and students would swap places with others. Dr. Klein had just talked to us, privately, about Shelly's unlikely recovery. The doctor had warned us about the importance of professional distance, that we should not take tragedies like this one home with us. She spoke impassively and then reapplied her lipstick as we headed out to see them. She was right, of course. We cannot accept everyone's burdens as our own.

But as soon as Shelly's mother heard that I would not be coming back, she frowned and stepped forward with her arms outstretched to hug me.

"You've been so great," she told me. "Thank you for everything you've done—all the time you spent with us. Good luck. I know you'll be a wonderful doctor."

And as I hugged her back, while my attending stood watching impatiently, I realized that I would not forget them. I had not been afraid when I met Shelly and her mom, not scared of what I might see or of impotence to help. Their grief did not frighten me. Somehow, after years of searching for a wellspring of meaning in everything from paragliding in Switzerland to skiing Cornice to climbing Castle Dome, I had found it—in the very endeavor I had been trying to avoid.

But could I be so supportive if there were ten Shellys? Or if I didn't have time on my own?

The too-obvious question at the heart of my daily, half-blind existence was how I would endure the all-consuming next step in my medical training.

"You could be a medical writer for a magazine instead," one friend suggested.

"Have you thought about going back to the dot-com you worked for last summer?"

And the residency interviewers themselves: "How will writing contribute to your career in medicine? Why do you want to be a pediatrician?"

Even Kyle, just starting to understand what a residency entailed, questioned my plans morosely. "Sounds like you are going to have to stop dancing."

Residents work six days a week, staying in the hospital and often not sleeping every fourth night—for three years. In my entire life, I had not had to commit so wholeheartedly to anything except final exams and a few other short-lived academic projects. My longest relationship had lasted only eleven months, four of them maintained by telephone across a distance of five hundred miles, then three thousand. I had held a full-time job for five months. I had written a thesis. For a month at a time, I had thrown myself into acting as an intern in the hospital. Twice.

Now I heard a rustling underfoot, the slithering of a career that had threatened to swallow me all along. It slid across my feet, wound sinuously around my ankles, and I didn't resist. In its sickly breath I smelled the intoxication of learning, growing, caring. I looked forward to not minding what time I would go home, not fussing over a bulging schedule or a way out. Maybe it was time to give in.

"Thank you, doctor." Words of appreciation from a mother whose child still teetered on the brink of recovery.

"I know they explained it to me, but I didn't understand, and I thought you could explain it better." The family of my four-year-old leukemia patient had written down what I said and told it back to me, relieved to know what a bone marrow biopsy would entail.

"Can we come back and see you?"

"No, it will be a long time before I can really be her doctor," I replied.

"We won't forget you."

I felt the pull of laughter—children giggling, their joy bubbling forth, as stubborn a celebration of living as anything that could ever be said. I was afraid of the responsibility of making medical decisions, haunted by the lurking shades of burnout. But I was also seduced by my own hopes of making a difference. Despite my fears, I was not ready to walk away.

I would keep going.

Five months before I officially graduated, my sister and I signed up to do an endurance mountain bike ride in Moab, Utah. Neither of us had strong technical skills or the requisite stamina at the time; we signed on with the Leukemia and Lymphoma Society's Team in Training Program, which pledged to get us through the ride in exchange for our fundraising efforts. Suddenly, I was required to get on my bike and ride. I was supposed to keep track of how far I went, and for how many hours.

Within the first month of training, trying to adjust to pedals that locked my feet in place, I fell and bore a deep gash and some road rash on my elbow, a bruise on my thigh. I had no choice but to finish the ride. We kept practicing. By the end of a few months, Danielle and I pushed ourselves and biked seventeen miles on a hilly dirt trail. We limped back to the car, exhausted. We needed to be able to do forty.

I learned to jump curbs. I biked faster, but I also fell down more than I had in the previous four years combined. I went farther. Each week we learned something new: we should put our weight back on the downhill, we should look exactly where we wanted our bikes to go, the cadence of our pedaling ought to hover at about 80 to 100 rpm. Our coaches also warned us that taking care of ourselves was critical: wearing tights if the temperature was less than seventy degrees, eating carbohydrates every twenty minutes or so, drinking water throughout the ride.

Ever so gradually, our bimonthly team rides stretched to twenty miles, twenty-four, twenty-nine. Having company fueled us. The cheers of fellow bikers stroked our fledgling egos, and conversations swallowed up miles of plodding progress. We saw our teammates develop confidence, mirroring our own individual growth. Some doggedly pushed ahead, others were easily intimidated. Some of us fell over in sand pits or on rocks and roots every time. But everyone kept going.

All this time, I debated whether I ought to buy an odometer for my bicycle. I contemplated having the register on my handlebars, ticking off tenths of a mile as I went. Progress would be quantifiable; I could congratulate myself at the halfway point, three-quarters, almost there! I could write down the numbers at the end of the day, know totals for the week and month, mark my cadence and push harder when I got lazy. I would know, before the endurance ride, whether forty miles would even be a remote possibility, based reliably on the maximum number of off-road miles logged in my three months of training.

But would this distract me from the pleasure of just going for a ride? I couldn't decide how much I wanted to know.

We were fifty bicyclists, spread out over whole courses of sandy dirt and rock-littered paths, but when it came to getting through hill climbs or bouncing descents, each of us relied on our own determination and skill. We trained on our own during the week, and biking gradually replaced other pastimes and swallowed whole afternoons. The key to training, it seemed, was to lock into a sustainable rhythm, hit that cadence, and hover there. Miles folded up and disappeared that way. My mind rested. When the labor was peaceful, I didn't need to know how far I'd gone, or what lay ahead. Obstacles could be jumped or avoided. I maintained my momentum. But when I felt anxious, my mind raced ahead. Impatient for the end, aching and anticipating more pain, I wanted to know: How much farther did I have to go? Was I on the right trail? What had I accomplished, and what lay ahead? If I had an odometer, no doubt I would have counted down the exact distance to each junction along the way.

The long-anticipated day of the endurance ride bloomed startlingly clear. In the new morning light, in stark contrast to the rusty red and ochre of Utah's canyonland crags, the sky arched in a never-ending dome of cobalt blue. I stuffed my one-hundred-ounce hydration pack with a bike pump, snack bars, lip balm, sunscreen, water, an

inhaler, and a tank top, opting to leave out the bike tights, long
sleeves, and full-fingered gloves. As an afterthought, I tucked in a
thin, hand-me-down windbreaker that had once belonged to my
father. It seemed obvious that desert heat and sun exposure would be
our major handicaps on a day like this one. I decided to pack light.

Two hours later, fed and changed and geared up with bike shorts,
team jerseys, water, and our five- and six-year-old mountain bikes,
Danielle and I fell into line with the others. As we snapped visors
onto our helmets and adjusted sunglasses to block the glare, we
were too nervous and excited to look up. Moab, Utah, is a mecca
for hard-core mountain bikers looking for a thrill. And although
the notorious "slickrock" is forgiving, making it possible to climb
steeper trails than on any other surface, we knew that some of the
trails teetered on the edges of small and large cliffs, then plunged
from the rock to deep sand and then up series of ledges to do it all
again. My confidence was not particularly high as we struck out in
a large pack for our butt-bruising and potentially dangerous ride.

The night before, a woman who had survived leukemia and was
now riding alongside us, had stood up to address the assembled
group of us.

"No matter how bad this ride gets," she said, "it is going to be
a hell of a lot better than chemotherapy."

Three miles into the ride, I felt the heat on my back wane.
Through my sunglasses, the desert colors faded noticeably, and the
slightest cool breeze stood my arm hairs on end. I looked up to see
a few wisps of cotton clouds veiling the sun. Beyond them, on the
eastern horizon, rows of white fingers lined up to slide forward.
Just then, I realized it was going to rain. And with at least four
hours of biking ahead of us, we were sure to be caught in the storm.

Suddenly our plans to take things slowly and enjoy the day
crumpled. Each mile passed was one less to tackle in the rain, and
we charged ahead.

Just as we left the twenty-mile sag spot—a point where a vehicle
could make its way in to cross our path, and bundled volunteers
in rain ponchos passed out cookies and fruit and sandwiches—the

first drops of rain plunked onto our cheeks and thighs. It might have been merciful, because the next section of the ride involved nearly ten miles of sandy, gradually climbing road. Sand on a mountain bike feels like walking through knee-high water. We shifted into easy gears and pedaled for an hour, and we had gone less than five miles. But as rust-colored mud caked itself in our gears and streaked our bare arms and legs with chilly rivulets of rain and dirt, at least the incline kept us warm.

Thirty miles into the ride, we had gained a couple thousand feet in elevation and had no significant downhill—and the thrill of leaping over rocks and pounding rutted trails on the way down was really the only reason for going up. Finally, the road ahead of us dipped and turned, and our long-awaited descent lay before us. Then, on a prolonged straightaway before the first section, I hit an unexpectedly deep bar of sand and keeled over, landing with a soft *whump!* on the soggy earth.

Specks of red paste on the lenses of my sunglasses obscured my vision. In our persistent pedaling to keep warm, Danielle and I had caught up to the fastest riders that were part of our Leukemia Society group; now as I removed the dirty lenses from my eyes, I could see them continuing steadily on ahead of me through a rainy haze, unaware of my confrontation with the gritty sand that stretched in all directions around us.

I disentangled my legs from the pedals and staggered to my feet. Standing still, I felt much wetter than I had while moving. My jacket, socks, and gloves dripped with moisture. The whispers of rain emphasized the dangers of being alone out there, and a momentary fear seized me. Danielle was the last biker in the single-file progression that had gone on without me; I couldn't yet muster enough lung-power to shout to her to wait.

I shivered as I climbed back onto the triangular seat and tried to cycle onward, still clutching the mud-blotched glasses in my hand. A few minutes later, I had to stop; my breaths were coming in labored gasps that felt like the sobs of a dying fish. I focused on the effort: inhale slowly, ribs out and up, and exhale, calm, calm,

calm. Danielle noticed my absence and came back, urging me to dig for the inhaler I had not expected to need, and temporarily forgot I had. Still gasping, but fearing that hypothermia would set in if we did not move, I followed her, pedaling slowly, generating just enough body heat to keep from shaking.

I squinted as drops of water batted at my eyes. I had not realized how much the streaked lenses had impeded my ability to see textures in the ground we traversed. The consistent terrain had required little depth perception; now as we tilted into a canyon and the light faltered slightly, I blinked away the sky's tears and strained to see what the trail had in store. Danielle removed her sunglasses too. Eye protection was less important, for the moment, than being able to see.

On the downhill, we followed the path of the others, bouncing and picking up speed as the slope became steeper, then slowing as two women ahead of us got off their bikes and walked a rocky section. Past that, the sand deepened again, and we passed a car mired in the soft mush. Miraculously, I stayed on my bike. My fingers were almost too numb to brake, but I pushed my weight as far back as I could and hoped for the best. The trail pitched us back the direction we had come from and then switched back again.

By this time the wind chill had penetrated my soaked windbreaker and uncovered legs, and my teeth were chattering. I couldn't tell if the bumpy road or my core temperature was at fault, but by the time we caught up to the first members of our band, my whole body was trembling. In a desperate effort to warm up, I pulled off my jacket and team jersey and layered my tank top underneath them. It was a dry layer, at least. Then one of the coaches urged us on; we were close to the thirty-five-mile sag, our last support before the end. Cold as I was, my coordination was poor. More than once, I almost toppled over. We passed another stuck car. Then the sand eased into hardpack, and the road flattened like a sigh of relief.

At the bottom of the canyon, the air seemed warmer. We paused for a quick sandwich—low on peanut butter, high on jelly (which has more carbohydrates)—and a few cookies before we were urged to keep moving. Hypothermia was our biggest threat, and we remembered that eating and staying hydrated were important defenses against it. I had drunk less than half of the water on my back.

Just as we started to ride away, one of the volunteers remarked that we had "more like ten or twelve" miles left. The distance didn't matter anymore, Danielle and I decided; it was not raining at this lower elevation, and we would be on pavement most of the way back. All we had to do was ride.

That last hour or so seemed suspended in time. Danielle and I let the others go ahead, opting instead to move at our own pace and enjoy the last of our ride as much as we could. Our legs were comfortably numb by this point, but they still worked. The road sloped ever so slightly as we traveled upriver, and the warmth generated by the exercise was comforting.

When we hit forty miles, we actually felt pretty good. We chatted along the way, craning our necks to take in the spectacular rock formations on either side of the Colorado River. We fantasized about hot showers and the warm clothes waiting in our suitcases. We thought we were almost there.

We guessed when forty miles had fallen behind us, and then forty-five. Somewhere close to mile fifty we reached the highway, and Moab was still four miles ahead. Stopping was out of the question; we had tried once and immediately felt our muscles throbbing and tightening up. Three miles more, and we ran out of things to say. Two miles never took so long. At the end we were moving slowly, but by this point our progress was mechanical. I'm convinced that if I had fallen asleep, my legs would have kept going.

If I'd had an odometer, I might not have enjoyed the end of our ride. More than an objective measure of our progress, I needed water, fuel, courage. The route we ultimately completed was nothing like the one we had envisioned over our four months of training—and it was fourteen miles longer. What got us through were the skills we had developed, and one another. We had to keep perspective. We had to lose ourselves in pedaling and go on faith.

Back in the hotel room, we draped wet clothing over chairs and dug through our backpacks. I couldn't remember what I had done with my sunglasses. Had I left them when I put my tank top on? I pulled out my pump and the uneaten food. There was my sunscreen, a banana, an uneaten protein bar. The front pouch yielded smaller items: lip balm, room key. I pinched a soaked twenty-dollar bill. One side pouch was empty. The other contained my inhaler and a useless bandage. And then, buried behind a strap, I found the sunglasses—right where I must have left them, with me the entire way.

With residency approaching, I liked to envision what I felt with biking: muscles growing toned and confident, a positive outlook guiding me through long hours that might otherwise feel grueling.

My next travels would take me into the wilderness of human health and illness, not the mountains. But I could taste that thin Sierra air and the thrill of risk, right there in my apartment's living room. I knew the allure of momentum, the gritty flavor of determination, and the tangy, metallic smell of fear. I'd held hands with the sensation of escape, wandered shadowy woods of self-doubt, and shivered in the wan, first-morning light of realization.

What mattered, I knew, wasn't how often I would get outside, nor how many songs I would dance to in a night or a year. It was how much of the wonder I could carry inside me to share with other people. It was listening with an open heart, risking sadness to care, being present enough to make someone else's life better.

What mattered was appreciating the fragile miracles of everyday humanity.

When the sun dipped closer to the Pacific Ocean, spilling its golden hue into my small window, I gave up searching and followed the light outside. Maybe losing my reading glasses wasn't a portent of things to come. Maybe it was a reminder to slow down, to breathe. I sat down on the porch, temporarily blinded by the rays of light that reached between buildings to my front stoop, and I noticed the moment: too many yearnings competing for the hours of a day, transforming into the shining hope of doing one thing right.

Epilogue

A WORLD ON FIRE

This morning, like so many since the COVID-19 pandemic began, I am up early, sitting in front of my computer, looking out the window at a redwood tree that now reaches up above my house. I hope the evergreen will survive the current drought. Today the air is hazy, evidence of wildfires that have plagued the western United States every summer of late, and I squint to see any blueness in the sky.

My younger son is awake already, buried in a book just outside my office door. The older one will sleep in a bit longer, having entered that same adolescent growing phase I wrote about so many years ago when I was a camp counselor. Still, after staying up late last night, my husband may out-sleep him.

This morning, I've just received a concerning lab result, so instead of letting creative musings find their way onto the page, I keep checking the clock, weighing when to call my young patient's family. As a colleague once said, "I may not always be in the office, but I am always a doctor."

I realize that I still attempt to do too many things. Here in this little room, I try to parse the right words for my experiences, writing a short blog that teeters between finding wonder and trying to understand human nature. Soon I will go feed my horse, who is my excuse to be outside at least twice a day, no matter the weather. Then my husband and I will take our kids to ride bikes, before it gets too hot or too smoky.

Neither of my children seems inclined toward medicine anymore, and I have to admit I am relieved. My father recently expressed that he felt guilty for not steering me away from it—a sentiment I found as laughable today, over twenty years after graduating, as I did when I started. Now, as then, it felt like medicine chose me.

The smoky air feels apropos when I reflect on the changes of the last two decades. Truly, as this nearly-vanquished pandemic surges back for a second time, it feels like life as we knew it is on fire. All the knowledge gleaned from study and experience is worthless in the face of stories on social media that undermine confidence in doctors, in medicine, in vaccines. My profession has not been perfect; some skepticism makes sense. But disinformation is as rampant and unruly as flames across sun-scorched hillsides in August. How has collective trust in expertise eroded so completely? How can I fight an inferno with a garden hose?

I worry about the world we are leaving for our children. In the face of COVID-19, a virus that has killed millions of people, the lack of willingness to come together seems painfully selfish. So, too, the lost opportunity to slow climate change, preferring instead the dazzling declarations that environmental scientists are wrong, and that buying gas-guzzling SUVs is patriotic. All of us end up suffering. Despite everything I have tried to teach my own children about selfless decision-making and social responsibility, my chest aches with the knowledge that their lives will be hard enough without adding practicing medicine into the mix. We humans have the capacity to work together for common good—but goodwill currently seems as combustible as the wilderness that has given me solace all these years.

My work is not done. For all that I have chafed at the growing imbalance between responsibility and reward in my profession, I can be grateful that my life has always had purpose. I have had to grow and keep adapting, to keep up with medical advances. I also own my share of humility, realizing both the limitations of knowledge and my own fallibility. Finding equilibrium requires intention. Not surprisingly, that quest has driven me back to the regenerative wellspring of writing: a bright poppy growing in the dry grasses of the California landscape.

Children tend to absorb much from their parents, and mine have born witness to the joys of a doctoring life as much as the difficulties. While the enormous challenges of the last few years have brought many opportunities for anger, anxiety, and disillusionment, altruism offers its own kind of transcendence.

A beloved icon of my childhood, Mister Rogers, famously said, "When I was a boy and I would see scary things in the news, my mother would say to me, 'Look for the helpers. You will always find people who are helping.'"[9]

I would add this: be one of those helpers. No matter where their lives take them, I hope my sons will remember what truly matters: caring about other people, listening with compassion, and feeling the lift of offering oneself up in times of need.

If I manage nothing else, may I leave them a legacy of acting with kindness.

Glossary

- **Attending** — the fully licensed, experienced physician who supervises a team of residents, interns, and medical students.

- **Clerkship** — a period of weeks during which a third- or fourth-year student participates in caring for patients within a certain area of medicine.

- **Clinical** — involving direct patient care; in the last two years of medical school, students take on increasing responsibility for patient care.

- **Fellow** — an upper-level trainee who has already completed residency and is being trained in a particular specialty.

- **Intern** — a first-year resident trainee, straight out of medical school.

- **On Call** — a designation indicating that one was expected to stay in the hospital late into the night or overnight to continue admitting patients and caring for those already in the hospital.

- **Post-Call** — a designation indicating that one had spent the previous night on call.

- **Preclinical** — in the first two years of medical school, when students' education is primarily textbook-based and takes place in classes and laboratories.

- **Resident** — a trainee who has already completed medical school and internship. The first year of residency is called internship.

- **Rotation** — see "Clerkship" above.

- **Rounds** — a meeting of the attending with the resident, interns, and students.

- **Sub-Intern, or Sub-I** — a fourth-year medical student who acts as an intern in a field of medicine he or she is considering pursuing.

Acknowledgments

When I started writing *Balance, Pedal, Breathe*, the only person whose schedule it affected was my own. Decades later, when this book again demanded my full attention, it stole time from my husband and sons, my parents, my career, and my friends. It is not easy to support someone else's creative endeavor, but my inner circle held me up in a plethora of ways large and small. "Thank you" hardly seems sufficient.

My husband, Leo, has been a more wonderful partner than I could have dreamed up in my medical school years. Not only does he tolerate my dizzying list of passions, he encouraged me when I decided to both pursue my writing and develop a literature in medicine program for my medical group—in addition to my work as a pediatrician. While I close myself in the office to write, he corrals our kids into helping around the house to keep things running, making space for my dreams to come to fruition.

My sister, Danielle, has been my most important beta reader, and so much more: my traveling companion, my ski buddy, my mountain biking sidekick, my reality check, and my best friend. Thank you for simultaneously keeping me grounded and encouraging me to fly.

My parents, the doctor and the artist, facilitated many of my pastimes and cheered me on throughout my life. Their support has enabled my dual pursuits of medicine and writing, along with skiing, mountain biking, traveling, and so much more. Some debts can never be repaid.

One of the hardest things about writing a memoir for me has been facing my own shortcomings. Reviewing past events with one of my medical school friends, I had to ask, "Did I really do that?" In prioritizing time away from school, I had behaved selfishly. For saying, "I love you anyway," I am forever beholden to Kristen and all of my medical school friends who helped me through and helped me grow, especially Lisa, Katherine, Leslie, Michelle, Saam, Ivan, Brian, and Brig.

In truth, a memoir is indebted to every person who appears in it. Melanie held the mirror early in my life. Margo taught me courage I didn't know I had. Kevin brought adventure back into my life. Claudine kept me dancing. Warren made me laugh when I needed it most.

Although they appear here under pseudonyms and with identifying details changed, the patients who loaned me their stories left a deep impression on my life and my work in medicine. So too the attendings, residents, and professors who showed me the way through medical school—I am eternally grateful to UCSF for my education.

For getting me writing narrative nonfiction, I credit Terry Osborne, my advisor and mentor at Dartmouth College. Paul Linde at UCSF believed in this project and made me feel like it was possible before it was even started. My classmates and teachers in the master's program at University of San Francisco offered encouragement I have held onto all these years, especially Cathy Miller, who almost got me to complete this book years ago.

More recently, my writing workshop group at Sutter Health and Kat Terrey's workshop both helped me get back into the groove. Debra Blaine put me in touch with Mindy Kuhn at Warren

Publishing, and Amy Ashby helped hone this manuscript into its final, complete form. It has taken a village.

P.T. Koenig deserves mention for giving me the nudge I needed to start a literature in medicine program, along with Suzanne Koven for offering the mentorship to continue. Writing and doctoring have finally come together in my life, decades after I first dreamed they might.

Finally, I am deeply grateful to all the doctors and other clinicians who have taken literature and writing classes with me— for reminding me on a regular basis that our stories need to be told.

Publication Credits

Five chapters of this memoir have been excerpted for publication previously. They have been reprinted with permission.

"Medical Experience." In *Bicycle Love: Stories of Passion, Joy, and Sweat,* edited by Garth Battista. Halcottsville, New York: Breakaway Books, 2004.

"POOF: The Psychiatrist." *The Awakenings Review* 2, no. 1 (2002), ed. Robert Lundin, The Awakenings Project, Glen Ellyn, Illinois.

"Touch: A Surgery Rotation," *Intima: A Journal of Narrative Medicine* (April 2001), ed. Donna Bulseco.

"Twelve." In *Reflections on a Life with Diabetes: A Memoir in Many Voices,* edited by Diane Parker and Ruth Mark. College Station, Texas: Virtualbookworm.com Publishing, 2004.

"Unsure Footing." *Sport Literate* 4, no. 2 (2002), ed. William Meiners, Pint-Size Publications, Inc., Chicago, Illinois.

Endnotes

1 Oriah "Mountain Dreamer" House, *The Invitation*, (San Francisco: HarperONE, 1999).

2 Sara Berg, MS., "Half of health workers report burnout amid COVID-19," Physician Health, American Medical Association, July 20, 2021, https://www.ama-assn.org/practice-management/physician-health/half-health-workers-report-burnout-amid-covid-19.

3 Cami Rosso, "New Survey Shows Significant Increase in Physician Burnout," *The Future Brain* (blog), *Psychology Today*, Sussex Publishers, LLC, August 19, 2021, https://www.psychologytoday.com/us/blog/the-future-brain/202108/new-survey-shows-significant-increase-in-physician-burnout.

4 The Physicians Foundation, "2021 Survey of America's Physicians COVID-19 Impact Edition: A Year Later," June 2021, https://physiciansfoundation.org/wp-content/uploads/2021/08/2021-Survey-Of-Americas-Physicians-Covid-19-Impact-Edition-A-Year-Later.pdf.

5 Jeffrey M. Jones, "COVID-19 Vaccine-Reluctant in U.S. Likely to Stay That Way," Gallup, June 7, 2021, https://news.gallup.com/poll/350720/covid-vaccine-reluctant-likely-stay.aspx.

6 The John Hopkins Hospital, *The Harriet Lane Handbook: A Manual for Pediatric House Officers*, 14th ed., ed. Michael A. Barone, (St. Louis: Mosby, Inc., 1996).

7 Lewis Carroll, *Alice's Adventures in Wonderland*, illustrated by Malcom Ashman, rev. ed. (London: MacMillan and Co., 1865; London: Dragon's World Ltd., 1990). Citations refer to Dragon's World edition.

8 *Alice in Wonderland*, directed by Clyde Geronimi, Wilfred Jackson, and Hamilton Luske, (The Walt Disney Company, 1951).

9 Fred Rogers, "Look for the Helpers PSA," (PBS, 2001), https://www.misterrogers.org/videos/look-for-the-helpers/.

Bibliography

Berg, MS., Sara. "Half of health workers report burnout amid COVID-19." Physician Health. American Medical Association. July 20, 2021. https://www.ama-assn.org/practice-management/physician-health/half-health-workers-report-burnout-amid-covid-19.

Carroll, Lewis. *Alice's Adventures in Wonderland*. Illustrated by Malcom Ashman. London: Dragon's World Ltd., 1990. First published 1865 by MacMillan and Co., (London).

Geronimi, Clyde, Wilfred Jackson, and Hamilton Luske, dir. *Alice in Wonderland*. The Walt Disney Company, 1951.

House, Oriah "Mountain Dreamer." *The Invitation*. San Francisco: HarperONE, 1999.

The John Hopkins Hospital. *The Harriet Lane Handbook: A Manual for Pediatric House Officers*, 14th ed. Edited by Michael A. Barone. St. Louis: Mosby, Inc., 1996.

Jones, Jeffrey M. "COVID-19 Vaccine-Reluctant in U.S. Likely to Stay That Way." Gallup. June 7, 2021. https://news.gallup.com/poll/350720/covid-vaccine-reluctant-likely-stay.aspx.

The Physicians Foundation. "2021 Survey of America's Physicians COVID-19 Impact Edition: A Year Later." June 2021. https://physiciansfoundation.org/wp-content/uploads/2021/08/2021-Survey-Of-Americas-Physicians-Covid-19-Impact-Edition-A-Year-Later.pdf

Rogers, Fred. "Look for the Helpers PSA." PBS, 2001. "http://www.misterrogers.org/videos/look-for-the-helpers/" www.misterrogers.org/videos/look-for-the-helpers/.

Rosso, Cami. "New Survey Shows Significant Increase in Physician Burnout." *The Future Brain* (blog). *Psychology Today*, August 19, 2021. https://www.psychologytoday.com/us/blog/the-future-brain/202108/new-survey-shows-significantincrease-in-physician-burnout.

CPSIA information can be obtained
at www.ICGtesting.com
Printed in the USA
BVHW040839010522
635492BV00002B/158